Minotaur Press, a Top Cow Productions company, presents...

Published by
Top Cow Productions, Inc.
Los Angeles, CA

Minotaur Press, a Top Cow Productions company, presents...

written by: **John Mahoney and Filip Sablik**

art by: **Thomas Nachlik**

letters by: **Troy Peteri**

Created by: **John Mahoney, Filip Sablik and Thomas Nachlik**

For this edition, cover art by: **Thomas Nachlik**   Original editions edited by: **Rob Levin & Phil Smith**

For this edition, book design and layout by: **Jana Cook**

IMAGE COMICS, INC.
Robert Kirkman - chief operating officer
Erik Larsen - chief financial officer
Todd McFarlane - president
Marc Silvestri - chief executive officer
Jim Valentino - vice-president

Eric Stephenson - publisher
Todd Martinez - sales & licensing coordinator
Sarah deLaine - pr & marketing coordinator
Branwyn Bigglestone - accounts manager
Emily Miller - administrative assistant
Jamie Parreno - marketing assistant
Kevin Yuen - digital rights coordinator
Tyler Shainline - production manager
Drew Gill - art director
Jonathan Chan - senior production artist
Monica Garcia - production artist
Vincent Kukua - production artist
Jana Cook - production artist
www.imagecomics.com

TOP COW PRODUCTIONS, INC.
Marc Silvestri - CEO
Matt Hawkins - President & COO
Filip Sablik - Publisher
Bryan Rountree - Assistant to the Publisher
Elena Salcedo - Sales Assistant
Jessi Reid - Intern

To find the comic shop nearest you, call:
1-888-COMICBOOK

LAST MORTAL HARDCOVER. JANUARY 2012.
FIRST PRINTING.
ISBN: 978-1-60706-456-5 • $19.99

Want more info? Check out: **www.topcow.com**
for news & exclusive Top Cow merchandise!

Table of Contents:

Introduction by **VICTOR GISCHLER**

I've heard so many definitions of noir in my professional lifetime that the very idea of trying to pin down an abstract concept that contains such a long history of bleak human misery seems like a loser's game to me. Almost every definition is ultimately unsatisfactory to somebody. Ask an academic and expect to be pummeled with ten dollar words. Ask my wife and she'll say, "old black and white films."

I think the best, most accurate and satisfying definition I've ever heard is "Noir is when you start out fucked, and it's all down hill from there." I want to say noir aficionado and author Eddie Muller said that. I could be wrong, and probably I'm paraphrasing. But more or less that's the definition I like and use.

John Mahoney and Filip Sablik's LAST MORTAL is the perfect example of the above definition. Alec King's life starts out fucked, and it's all down hill from there. If you've read any of my novels (shame on you if you haven't) then you'll know I'm not a fan of squeaky clean protagonists. I like them dirty and bruised and cynical. In the world of noir, the notion of "good guys" and "bad guys" is nearly always boils down to perspective. Alec King isn't anyone's idea of a hero. He's not supposed to be, man. This is noir. At some point during Alec's story, he asks, "How the hell did I get here?" He answers his own question: "A long line of bad choices and losing compromises." Indeed, this is the case. It is the hallmark of the best noir tales that the protagonist is the chief architect of his own demise, and Alec's long line bad choices began years ago when he chose Brian for a friend, the king of all bad influences.

Alec has a few opportunities here and there to turn onto a different path, but these opportunities rapidly fade out of reach as Alec goes further and further down a path toward an inevitable destination.

Death and doom awaits most protagonists at the end of many noir tales. In LAST MORTAL, Mahoney and Sablik have offered a wonderful twist to this tried and true theme. Alec King can't die. Shoot him and he springs up later for another helping of abuse. This twist is simultaneously Alec's doom and also his salvation. He can't be killed and can literally live to fight another day... and yet... really this means there is no end in sight to his hellish predicament. Alec's misery will go on... and on...

And on.

Thomas Nachlik's simple, clean pencils are the perfect compliment to this noir tale, and the entire layout and package works incredibly well.

LAST MORTAL takes noir and does with it only what comics can. Making the best use of familiar tropes and themes while introducing just enough of a novel element to lift it above the ranks of the derivative. The book feels complete while still leaving the door open for more.

Ultimately, Alec's curse is what offers hope – the idea of a second (and third? fourth?) chance. How many chances Alec might waste before he finally gets it right is anybody's guess.

But it'll be fun to watch.

Victor Gischler
December 2011

Victor Gischler is a critically acclaimed, award nominated crime fiction novelist and comic book writer. He is the author seven novels including, *Gun Monkeys*, which nominated for the Edgar Award in 2003 and the Anthony-nominated *Shotgun Opera*. Gischler has written some of Marvel Comics' most popular titles including *Punisher Max, Deadpool: Merc with a Mouth*, and *X-Men*. He lives in Baton Rouge, Louisiana with his wife and son.

LAST MORTAL

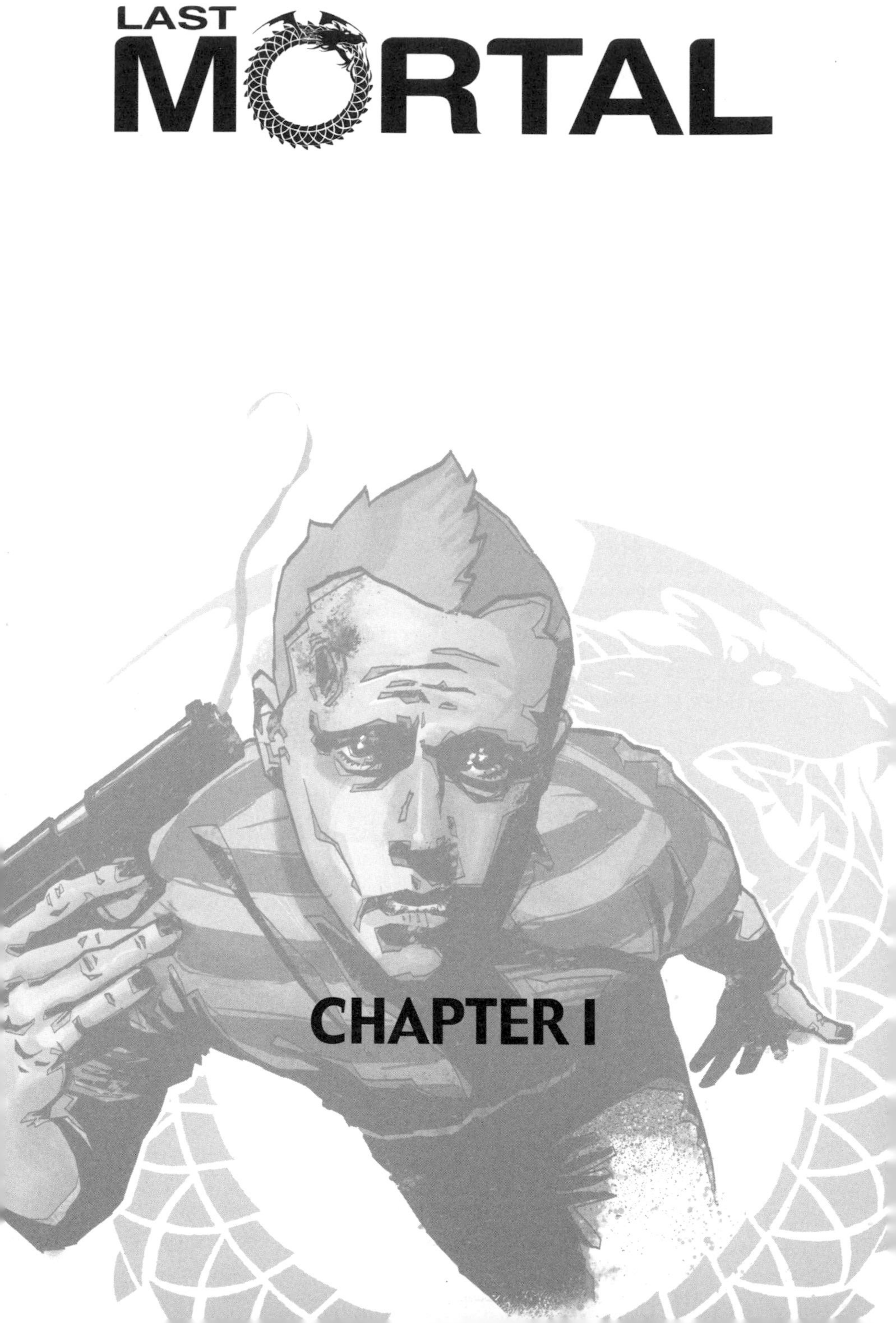

CHAPTER I

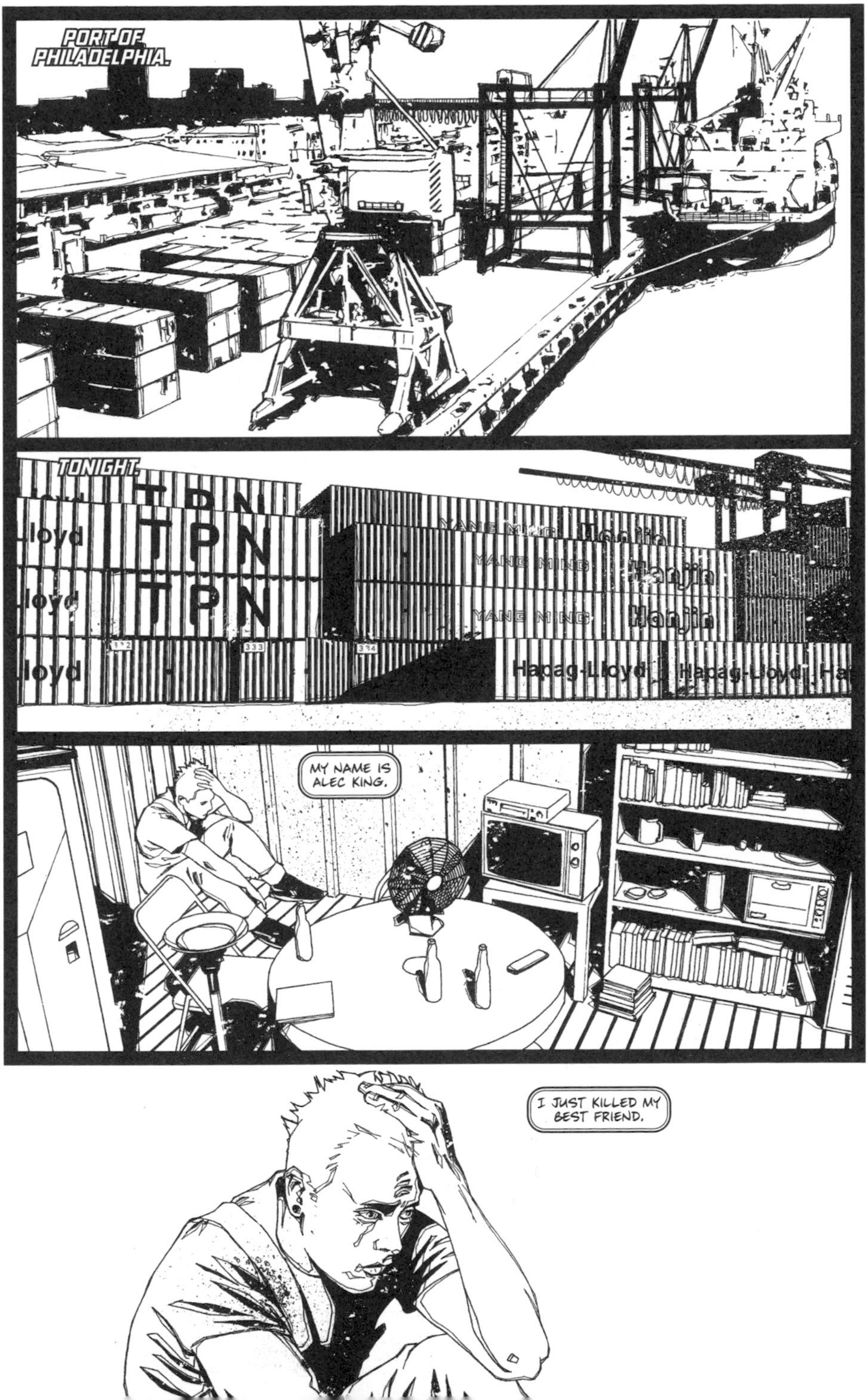
PORT OF PHILADELPHIA.
TONIGHT.
TPN
TPN
TPN
Lloyd
Lloyd
Lloyd
Lloyd
YANG MING
Hanjin
Hapag-Lloyd
MY NAME IS ALEC KING.
I JUST KILLED MY BEST FRIEND.

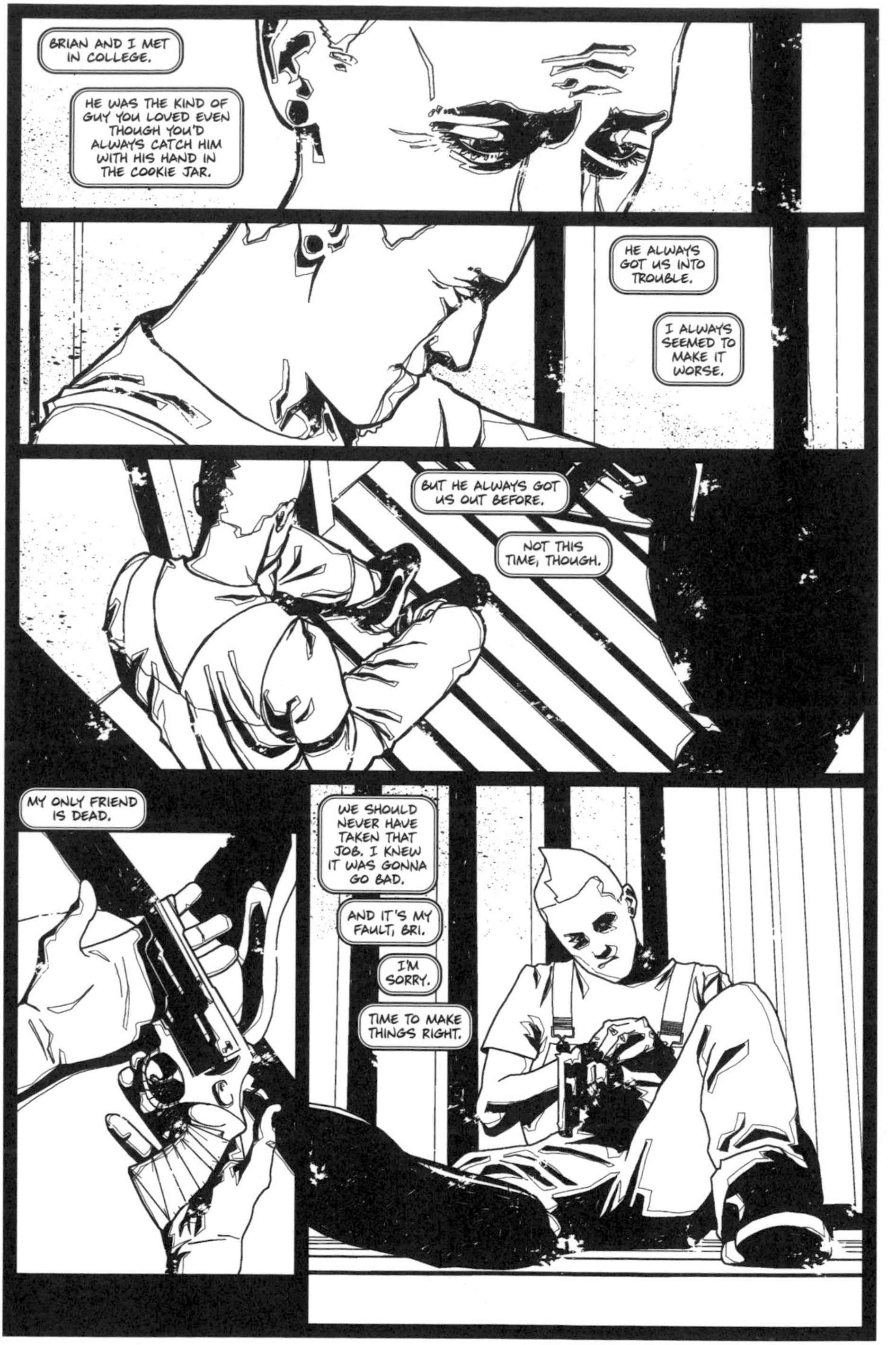
BRIAN AND I MET IN COLLEGE.
HE WAS THE KIND OF GUY YOU LOVED EVEN THOUGH YOU'D ALWAYS CATCH HIM WITH HIS HAND IN THE COOKIE JAR.
HE ALWAYS GOT US INTO TROUBLE.
I ALWAYS SEEMED TO MAKE IT WORSE.
BUT HE ALWAYS GOT US OUT BEFORE.
NOT THIS TIME, THOUGH.
MY ONLY FRIEND IS DEAD.
WE SHOULD NEVER HAVE TAKEN THAT JOB. I KNEW IT WAS GONNA GO BAD.
AND IT'S MY FAULT, BRI.
I'M SORRY.
TIME TO MAKE THINGS RIGHT.

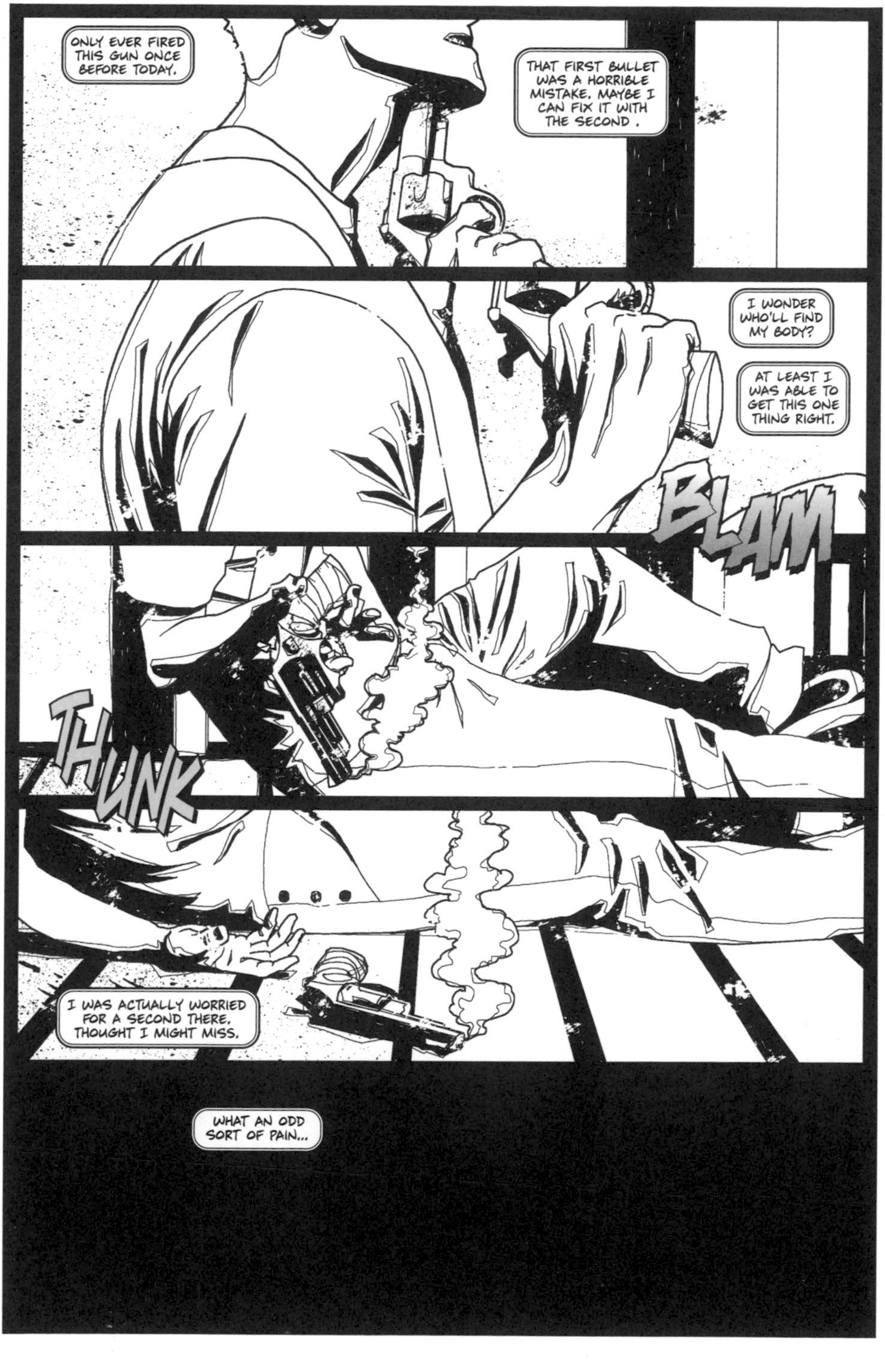

ONLY EVER FIRED THIS GUN ONCE BEFORE TODAY.
THAT FIRST BULLET WAS A HORRIBLE MISTAKE. MAYBE I CAN FIX IT WITH THE SECOND .
I WONDER WHO'LL FIND MY BODY?
AT LEAST I WAS ABLE TO GET THIS ONE THING RIGHT.
BLAM
THUNK
I WAS ACTUALLY WORRIED FOR A SECOND THERE. THOUGHT I MIGHT MISS.
WHAT AN ODD SORT OF PAIN...

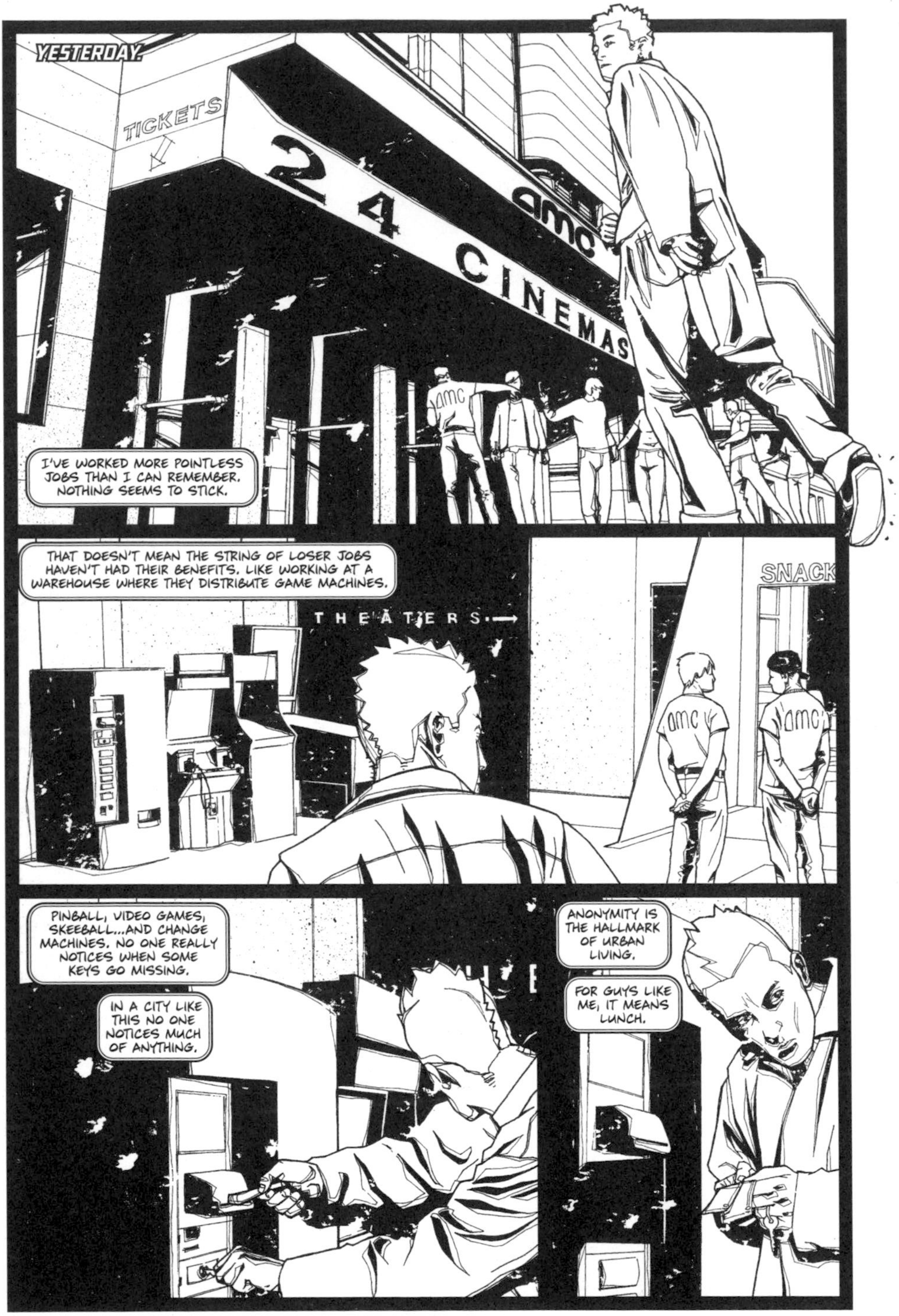
YESTERDAY.
TICKETS
24 CINEMAS
amc
I'VE WORKED MORE POINTLESS JOBS THAN I CAN REMEMBER. NOTHING SEEMS TO STICK.
THAT DOESN'T MEAN THE STRING OF LOSER JOBS HAVEN'T HAD THEIR BENEFITS. LIKE WORKING AT A WAREHOUSE WHERE THEY DISTRIBUTE GAME MACHINES.
THEATERS
SNACK
PINBALL, VIDEO GAMES, SKEEBALL...AND CHANGE MACHINES. NO ONE REALLY NOTICES WHEN SOME KEYS GO MISSING.
IN A CITY LIKE THIS NO ONE NOTICES MUCH OF ANYTHING.
ANONYMITY IS THE HALLMARK OF URBAN LIVING.
FOR GUYS LIKE ME, IT MEANS LUNCH.

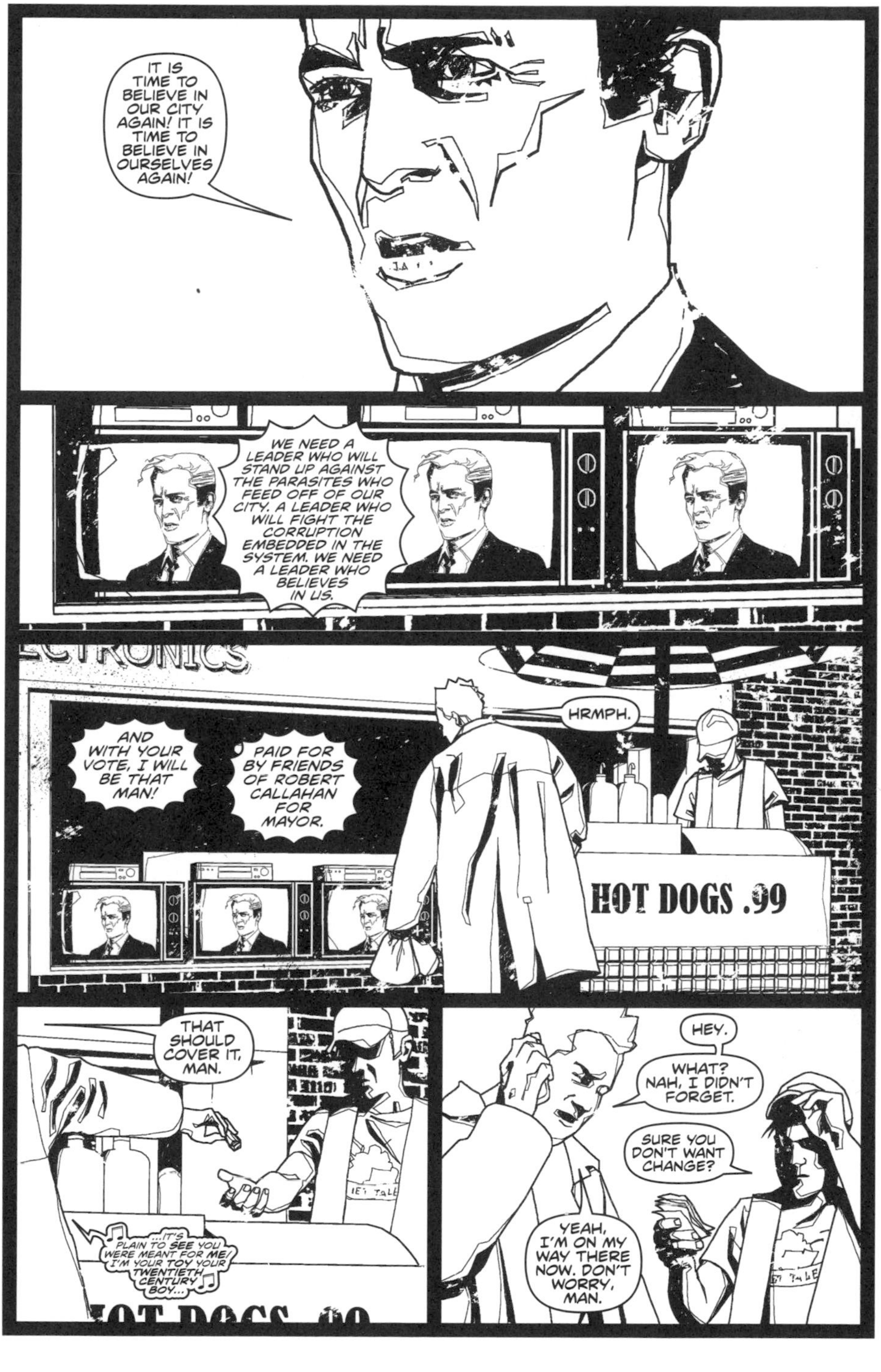
IT IS TIME TO BELIEVE IN OUR CITY AGAIN! IT IS TIME TO BELIEVE IN OURSELVES AGAIN!
WE NEED A LEADER WHO WILL STAND UP AGAINST THE PARASITES WHO FEED OFF OF OUR CITY. A LEADER WHO WILL FIGHT THE CORRUPTION EMBEDDED IN THE SYSTEM. WE NEED A LEADER WHO BELIEVES IN US.
LECTRONICS
AND WITH YOUR VOTE, I WILL BE THAT MAN!
PAID FOR BY FRIENDS OF ROBERT CALLAHAN FOR MAYOR.
HRMPH.
HOT DOGS .99
THAT SHOULD COVER IT, MAN.
...IT'S PLAIN TO SEE YOU WERE MEANT FOR ME/ I'M YOUR TOY YOUR TWENTIETH CENTURY BOY...
HEY.
WHAT? NAH, I DIDN'T FORGET.
SURE YOU DON'T WANT CHANGE?
YEAH, I'M ON MY WAY THERE NOW. DON'T WORRY, MAN.

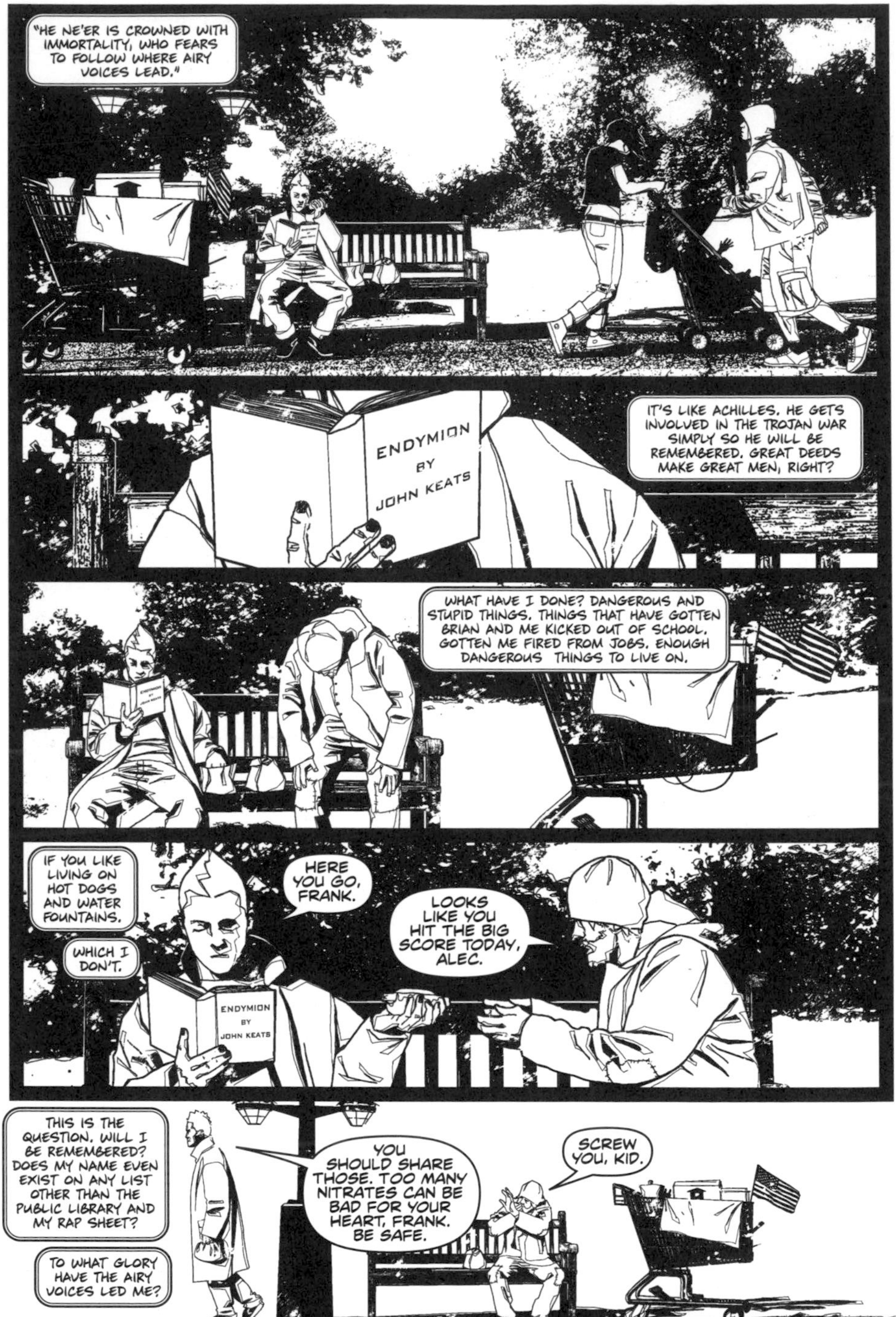
"HE NE'ER IS CROWNED WITH IMMORTALITY, WHO FEARS TO FOLLOW WHERE AIRY VOICES LEAD."
ENDYMION BY JOHN KEATS
IT'S LIKE ACHILLES. HE GETS INVOLVED IN THE TROJAN WAR SIMPLY SO HE WILL BE REMEMBERED. GREAT DEEDS MAKE GREAT MEN, RIGHT?
WHAT HAVE I DONE? DANGEROUS AND STUPID THINGS. THINGS THAT HAVE GOTTEN BRIAN AND ME KICKED OUT OF SCHOOL. GOTTEN ME FIRED FROM JOBS. ENOUGH DANGEROUS THINGS TO LIVE ON.
IF YOU LIKE LIVING ON HOT DOGS AND WATER FOUNTAINS.
WHICH I DON'T.
HERE YOU GO, FRANK.
LOOKS LIKE YOU HIT THE BIG SCORE TODAY, ALEC.
ENDYMION BY JOHN KEATS
THIS IS THE QUESTION. WILL I BE REMEMBERED? DOES MY NAME EVEN EXIST ON ANY LIST OTHER THAN THE PUBLIC LIBRARY AND MY RAP SHEET?
TO WHAT GLORY HAVE THE AIRY VOICES LED ME?
YOU SHOULD SHARE THOSE. TOO MANY NITRATES CAN BE BAD FOR YOUR HEART, FRANK. BE SAFE.
SCREW YOU, KID.

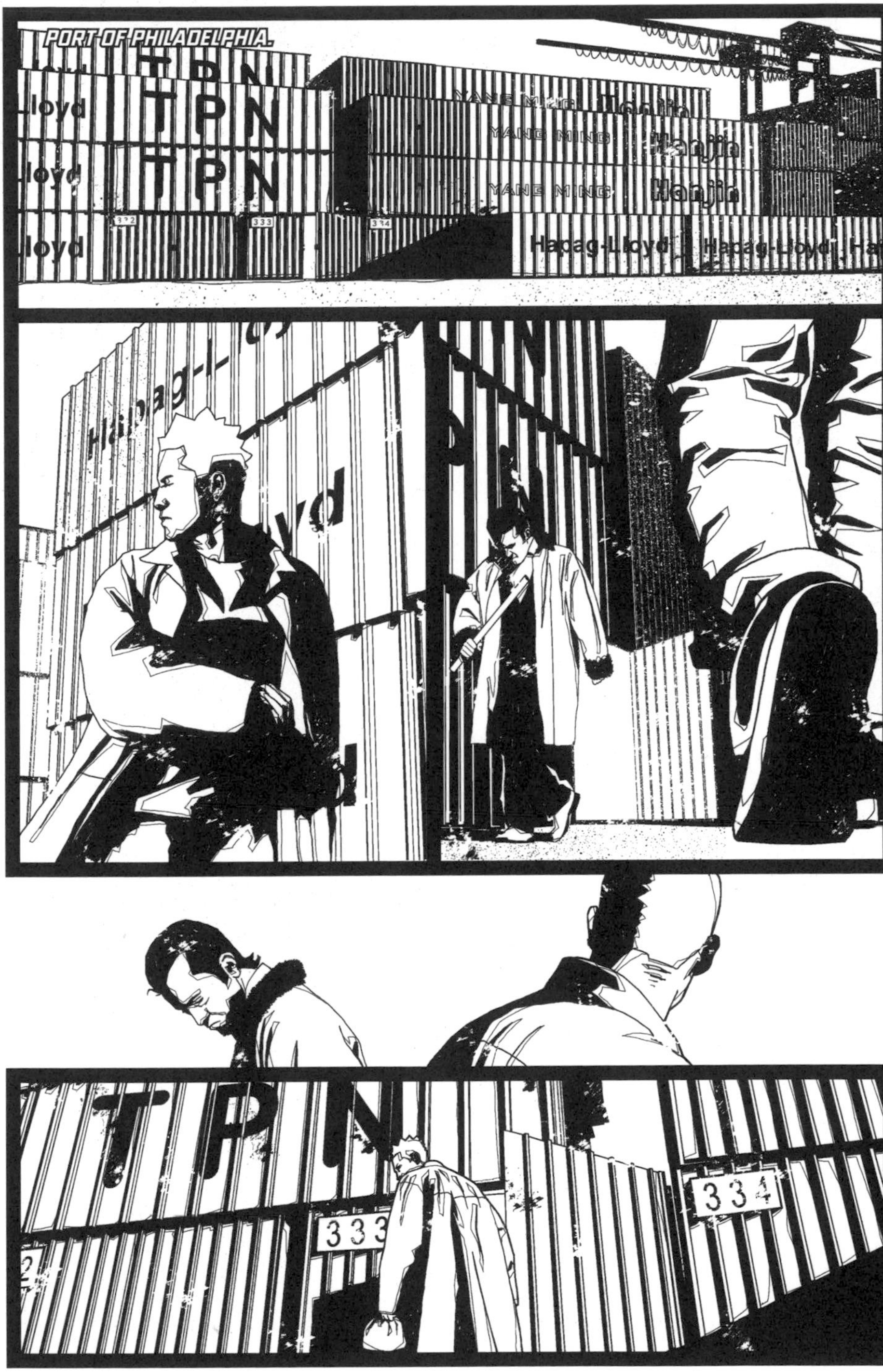
PORT OF PHILADELPHIA.
TPN
TPN
Lloyd
YANG MING
Hanjin
Hapag-Lloyd
333
334
333
334

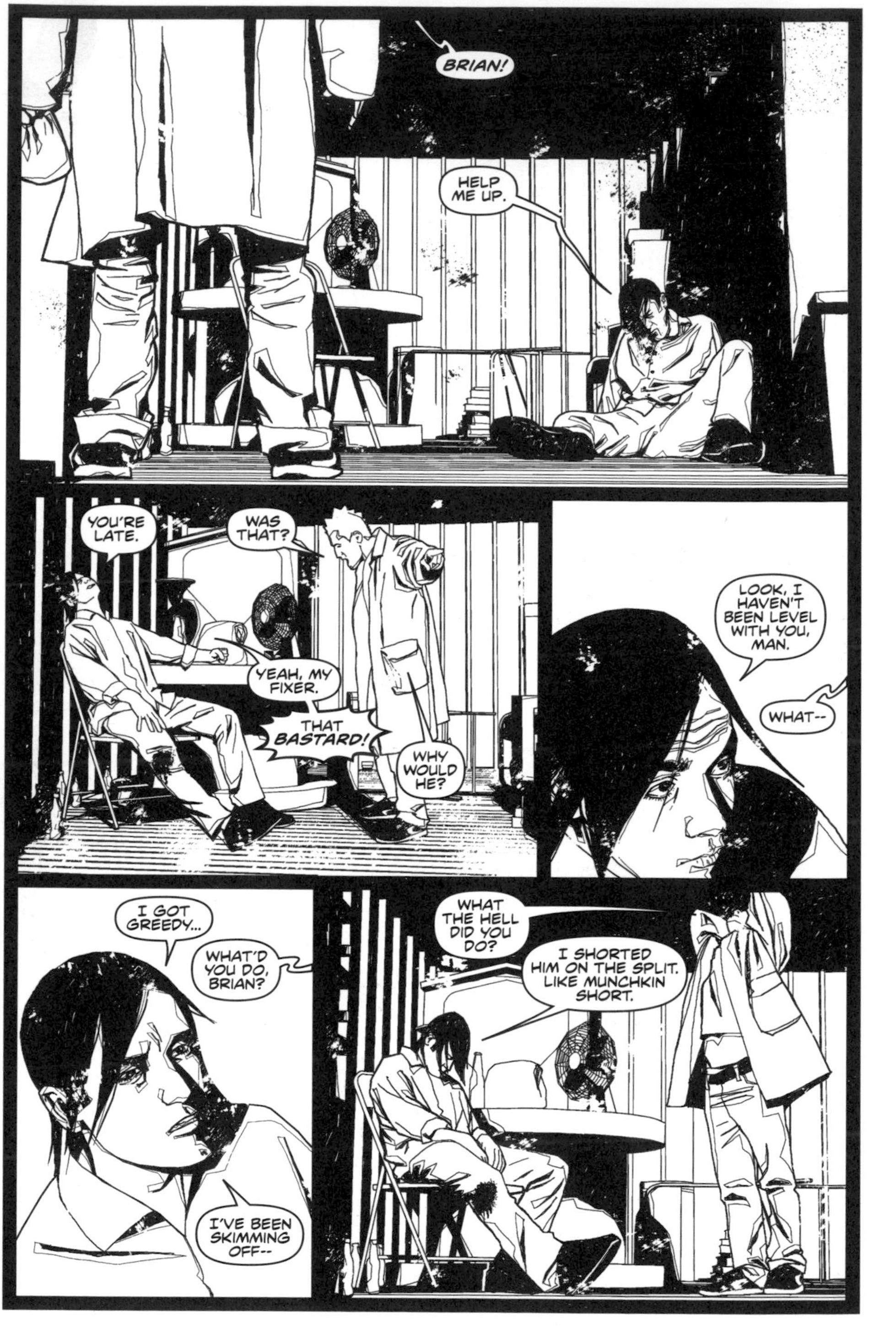
BRIAN!
HELP ME UP.
YOU'RE LATE.
WAS THAT?
YEAH, MY FIXER.
THAT BASTARD!
WHY WOULD HE?
LOOK, I HAVEN'T BEEN LEVEL WITH YOU, MAN.
WHAT--
I GOT GREEDY...
WHAT'D YOU DO, BRIAN?
I'VE BEEN SKIMMING OFF--
WHAT THE HELL DID YOU DO?
I SHORTED HIM ON THE SPLIT. LIKE MUNCHKIN SHORT.

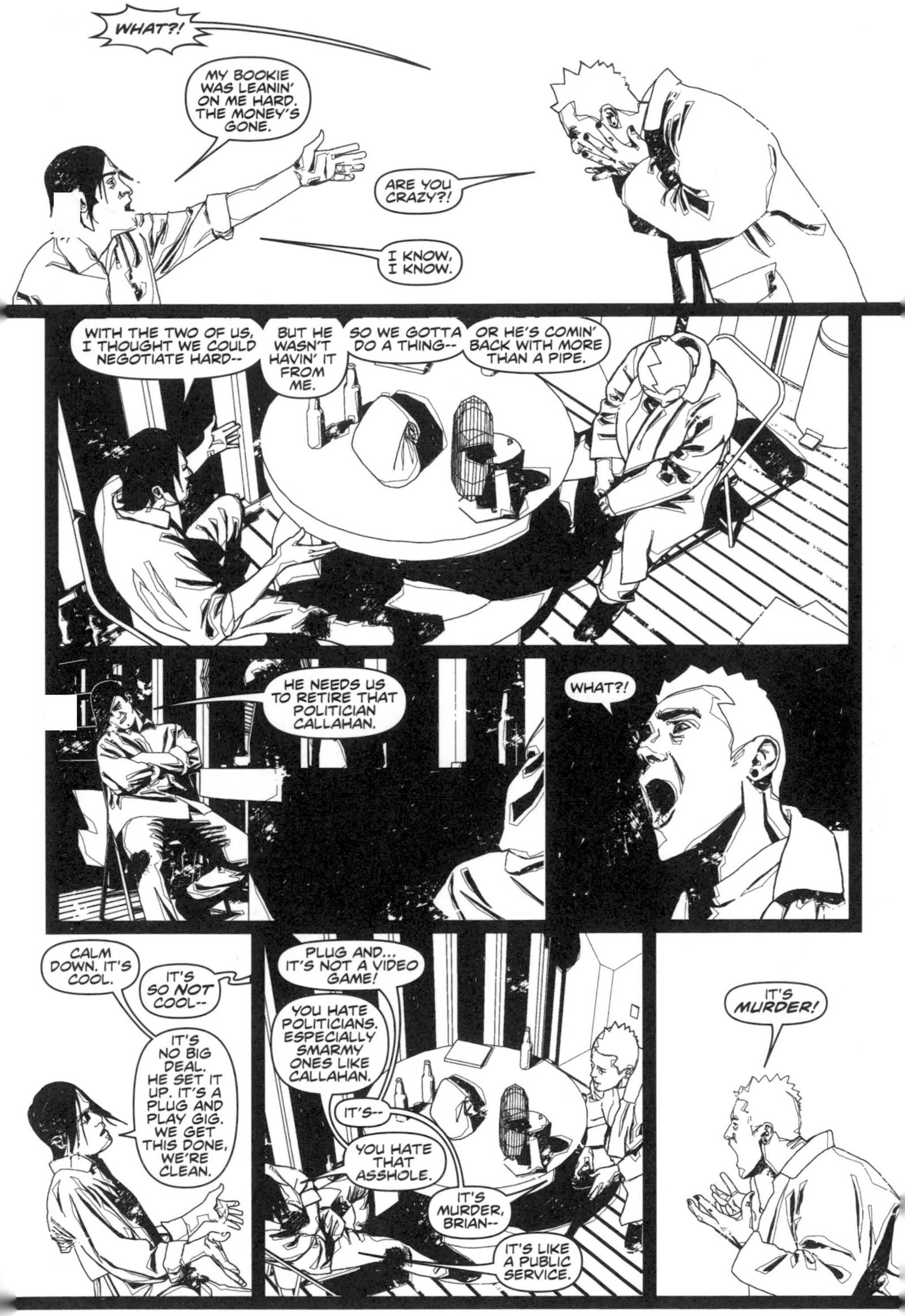
WHAT?!
MY BOOKIE WAS LEANIN' ON ME HARD. THE MONEY'S GONE.
ARE YOU CRAZY?!
I KNOW, I KNOW.
WITH THE TWO OF US, I THOUGHT WE COULD NEGOTIATE HARD--
BUT HE WASN'T HAVIN' IT FROM ME.
SO WE GOTTA DO A THING--
OR HE'S COMIN' BACK WITH MORE THAN A PIPE.
HE NEEDS US TO RETIRE THAT POLITICIAN CALLAHAN.
WHAT?!
CALM DOWN. IT'S COOL.
IT'S SO NOT COOL--
IT'S NO BIG DEAL. HE SET IT UP. IT'S A PLUG AND PLAY GIG. WE GET THIS DONE, WE'RE CLEAN.
PLUG AND... IT'S NOT A VIDEO GAME!
YOU HATE POLITICIANS. ESPECIALLY SMARMY ONES LIKE CALLAHAN.
IT'S--
YOU HATE THAT ASSHOLE.
IT'S MURDER, BRIAN--
IT'S LIKE A PUBLIC SERVICE.
IT'S MURDER!

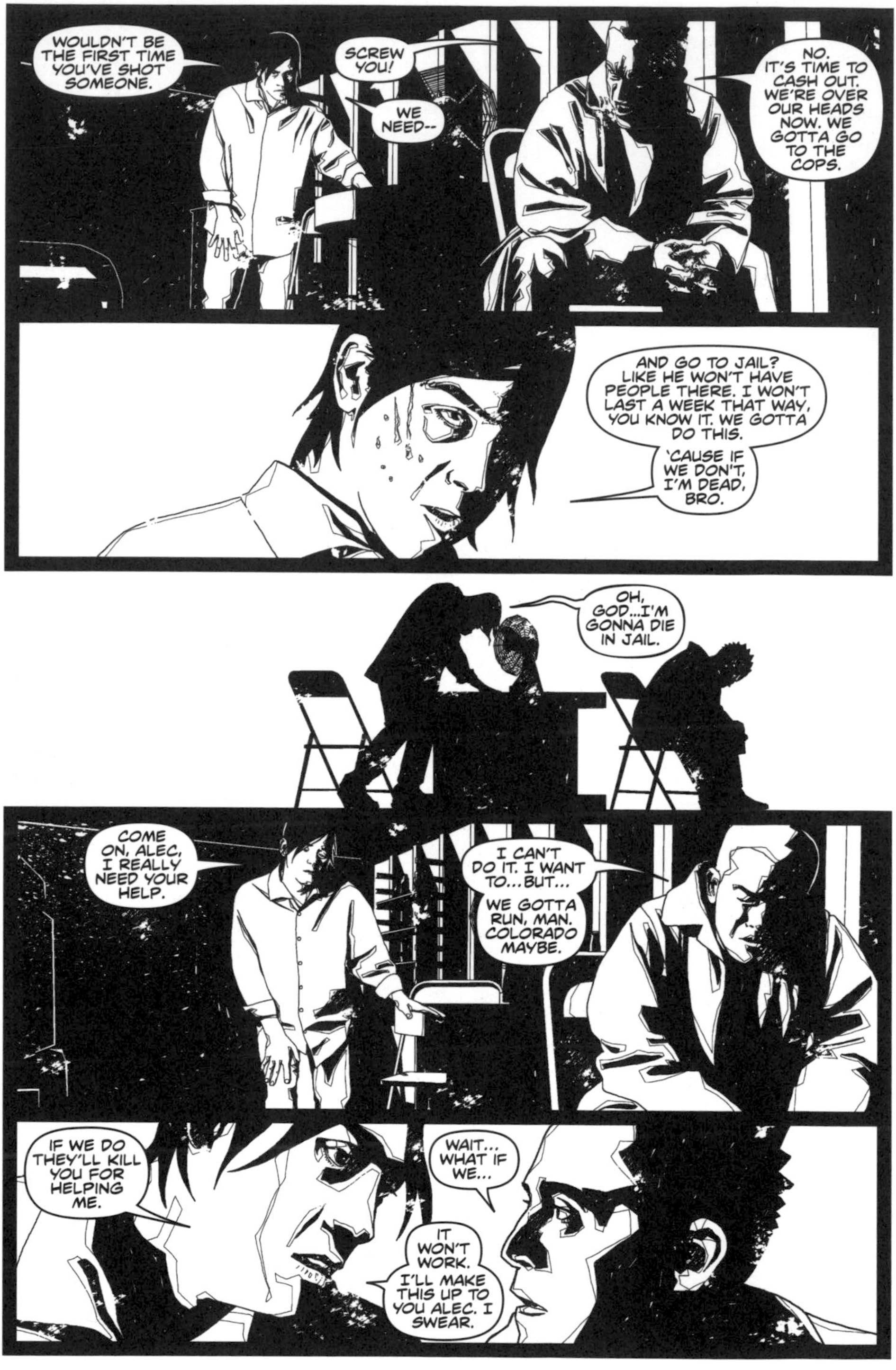
WOULDN'T BE THE FIRST TIME YOU'VE SHOT SOMEONE.
SCREW YOU!
WE NEED--
NO. IT'S TIME TO CASH OUT. WE'RE OVER OUR HEADS NOW. WE GOTTA GO TO THE COPS.
AND GO TO JAIL? LIKE HE WON'T HAVE PEOPLE THERE. I WON'T LAST A WEEK THAT WAY, YOU KNOW IT. WE GOTTA DO THIS.
'CAUSE IF WE DON'T, I'M DEAD, BRO.
OH, GOD...I'M GONNA DIE IN JAIL.
COME ON, ALEC, I REALLY NEED YOUR HELP.
I CAN'T DO IT. I WANT TO...BUT...
WE GOTTA RUN, MAN. COLORADO MAYBE.
IF WE DO THEY'LL KILL YOU FOR HELPING ME.
WAIT... WHAT IF WE...
IT WON'T WORK. I'LL MAKE THIS UP TO YOU ALEC. I SWEAR.

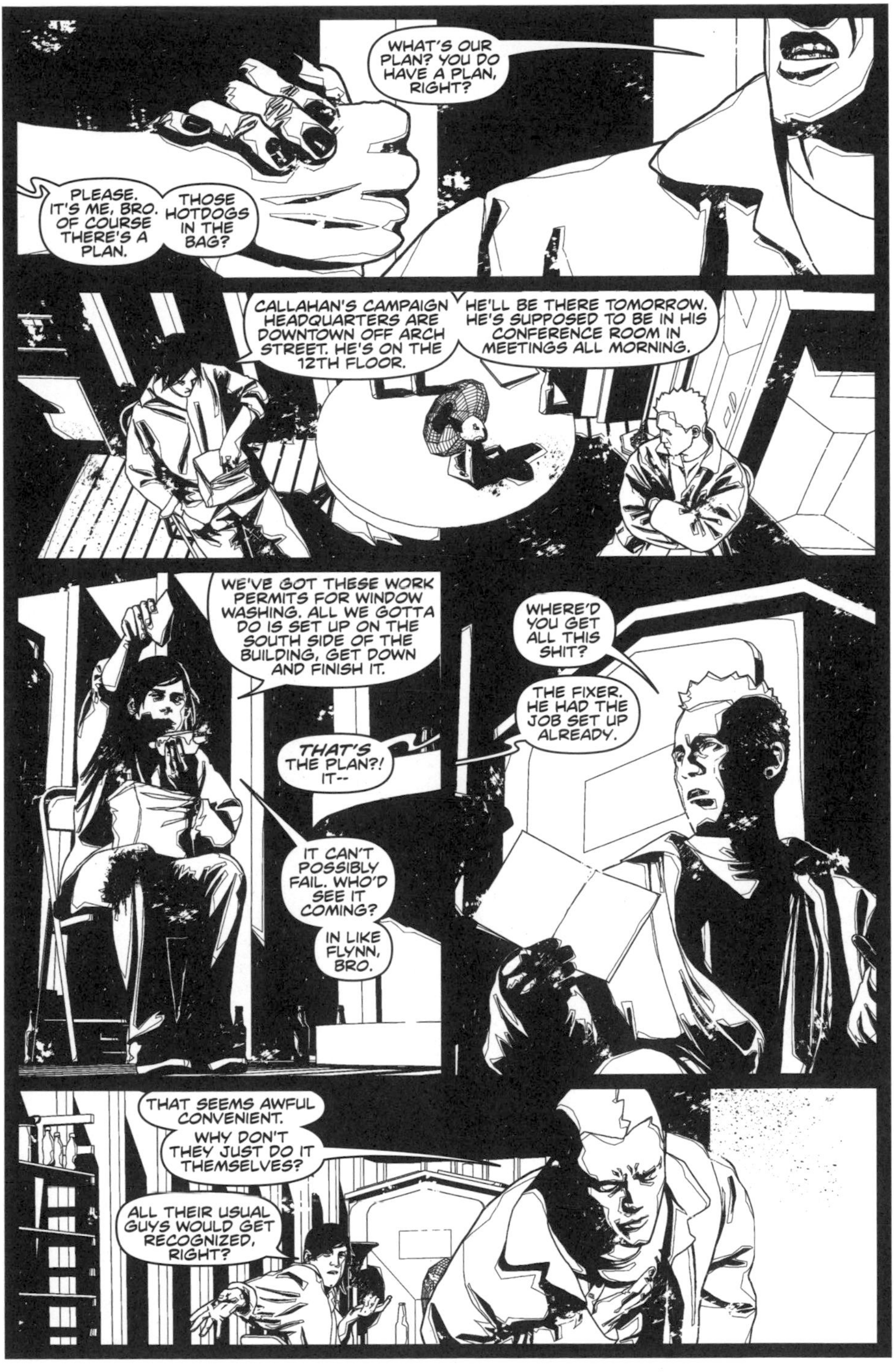
WHAT'S OUR PLAN? YOU DO HAVE A PLAN, RIGHT?
PLEASE. IT'S ME, BRO. OF COURSE THERE'S A PLAN.
THOSE HOTDOGS IN THE BAG?
CALLAHAN'S CAMPAIGN HEADQUARTERS ARE DOWNTOWN OFF ARCH STREET. HE'S ON THE 12TH FLOOR.
HE'LL BE THERE TOMORROW. HE'S SUPPOSED TO BE IN HIS CONFERENCE ROOM IN MEETINGS ALL MORNING.
WE'VE GOT THESE WORK PERMITS FOR WINDOW WASHING. ALL WE GOTTA DO IS SET UP ON THE SOUTH SIDE OF THE BUILDING, GET DOWN AND FINISH IT.
THAT'S THE PLAN?! IT--
IT CAN'T POSSIBLY FAIL. WHO'D SEE IT COMING?
IN LIKE FLYNN, BRO.
WHERE'D YOU GET ALL THIS SHIT?
THE FIXER. HE HAD THE JOB SET UP ALREADY.
THAT SEEMS AWFUL CONVENIENT.
WHY DON'T THEY JUST DO IT THEMSELVES?
ALL THEIR USUAL GUYS WOULD GET RECOGNIZED, RIGHT?

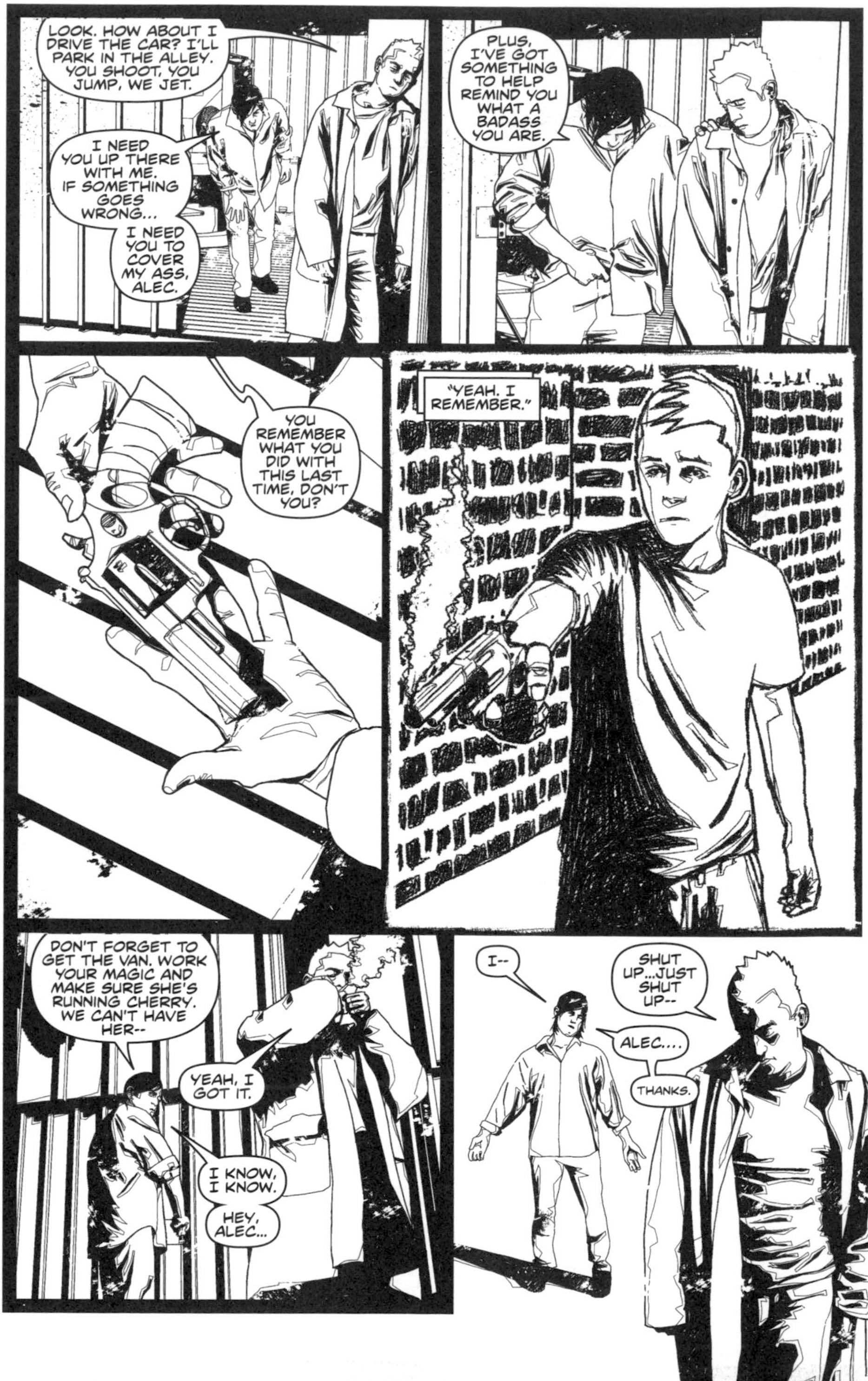
LOOK. HOW ABOUT I DRIVE THE CAR? I'LL PARK IN THE ALLEY. YOU SHOOT, YOU JUMP, WE JET.
I NEED YOU UP THERE WITH ME. IF SOMETHING GOES WRONG...
I NEED YOU TO COVER MY ASS, ALEC.
PLUS, I'VE GOT SOMETHING TO HELP REMIND YOU WHAT A BADASS YOU ARE.
YOU REMEMBER WHAT YOU DID WITH THIS LAST TIME, DON'T YOU?
"YEAH. I REMEMBER."
DON'T FORGET TO GET THE VAN. WORK YOUR MAGIC AND MAKE SURE SHE'S RUNNING CHERRY. WE CAN'T HAVE HER--
YEAH, I GOT IT.
I KNOW, I KNOW.
HEY, ALEC...
I--
SHUT UP...JUST SHUT UP--
ALEC....
THANKS.

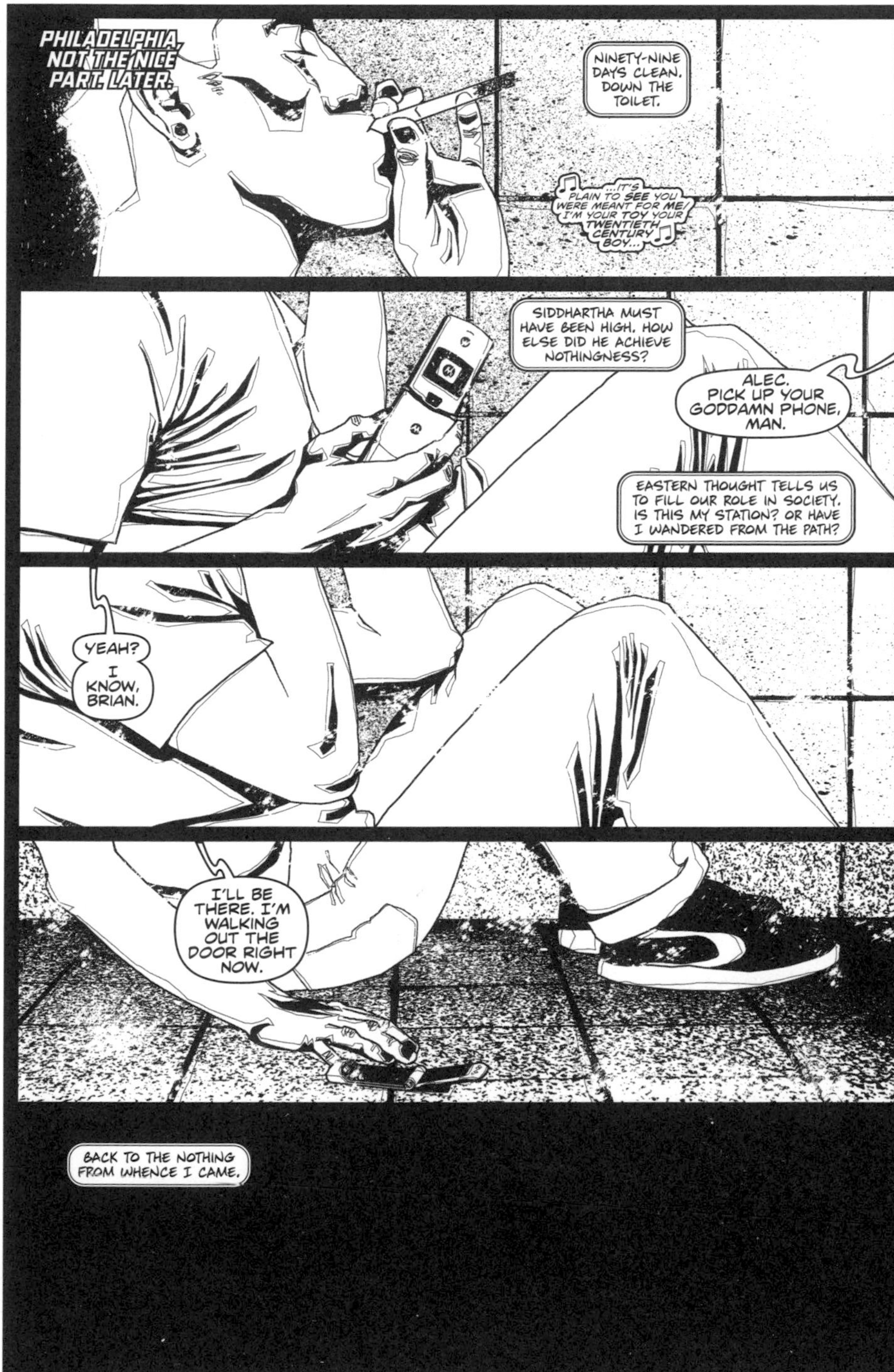
PHILADELPHIA, NOT THE NICE PART. LATER.
NINETY-NINE DAYS CLEAN. DOWN THE TOILET.
♪...IT'S PLAIN TO SEE YOU WERE MEANT FOR ME! I'M YOUR TOY YOUR TWENTIETH CENTURY BOY...♪
SIDDHARTHA MUST HAVE BEEN HIGH. HOW ELSE DID HE ACHIEVE NOTHINGNESS?
ALEC. PICK UP YOUR GODDAMN PHONE, MAN.
EASTERN THOUGHT TELLS US TO FILL OUR ROLE IN SOCIETY. IS THIS MY STATION? OR HAVE I WANDERED FROM THE PATH?
YEAH? I KNOW, BRIAN.
I'LL BE THERE. I'M WALKING OUT THE DOOR RIGHT NOW.
BACK TO THE NOTHING FROM WHENCE I CAME.

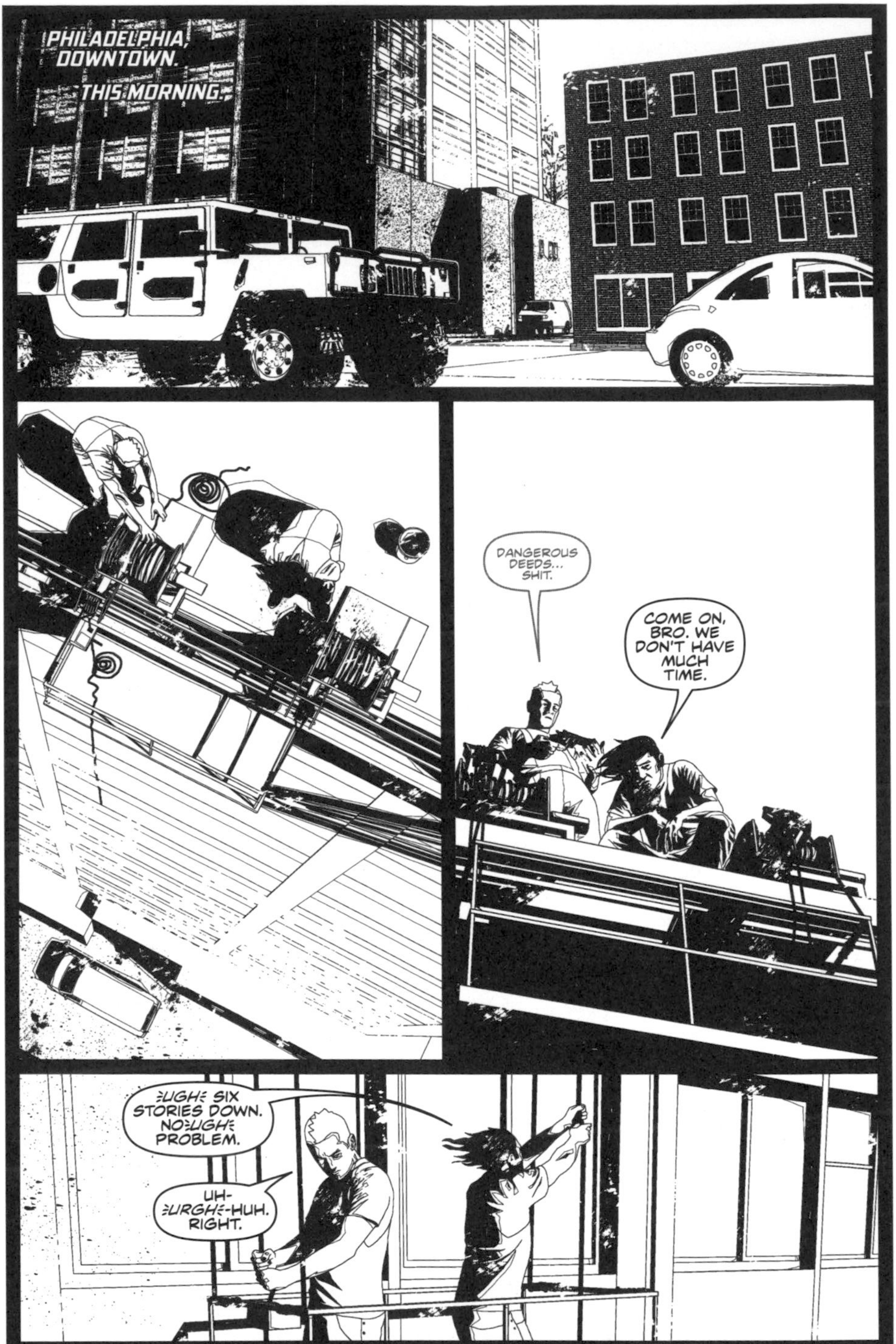
PHILADELPHIA, DOWNTOWN.
THIS MORNING.
DANGEROUS DEEDS... SHIT.
COME ON, BRO. WE DON'T HAVE MUCH TIME.
UGH SIX STORIES DOWN. NO UGH PROBLEM.
UH- URGH -HUH. RIGHT.

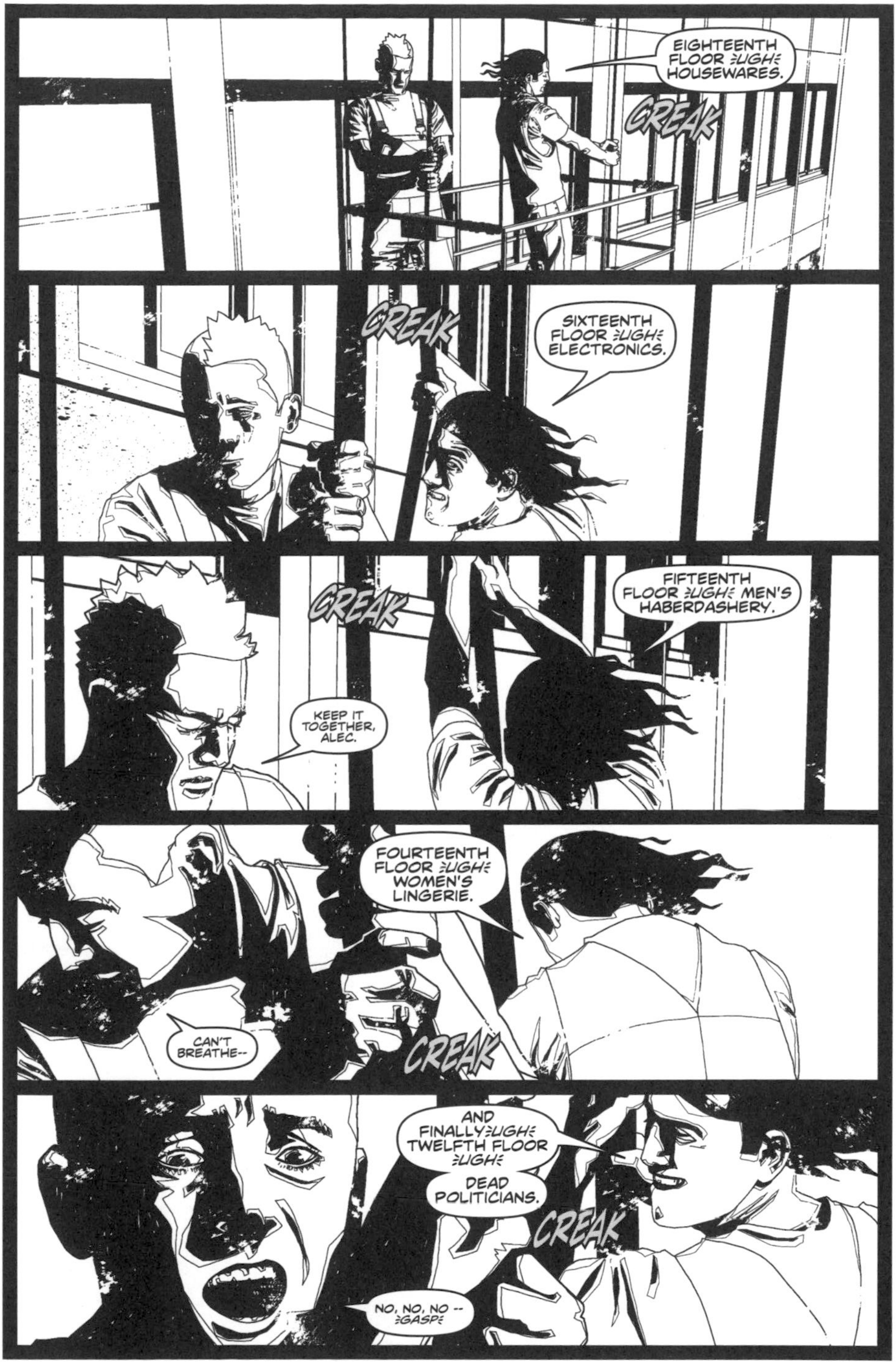
EIGHTEENTH FLOOR UGH HOUSEWARES.
CREAK
CREAK
SIXTEENTH FLOOR UGH ELECTRONICS.
CREAK
FIFTEENTH FLOOR UGH MEN'S HABERDASHERY.
KEEP IT TOGETHER, ALEC.
FOURTEENTH FLOOR UGH WOMEN'S LINGERIE.
CAN'T BREATHE--
CREAK
AND FINALLY UGH TWELFTH FLOOR UGH DEAD POLITICIANS.
CREAK
NO, NO, NO -- GASP

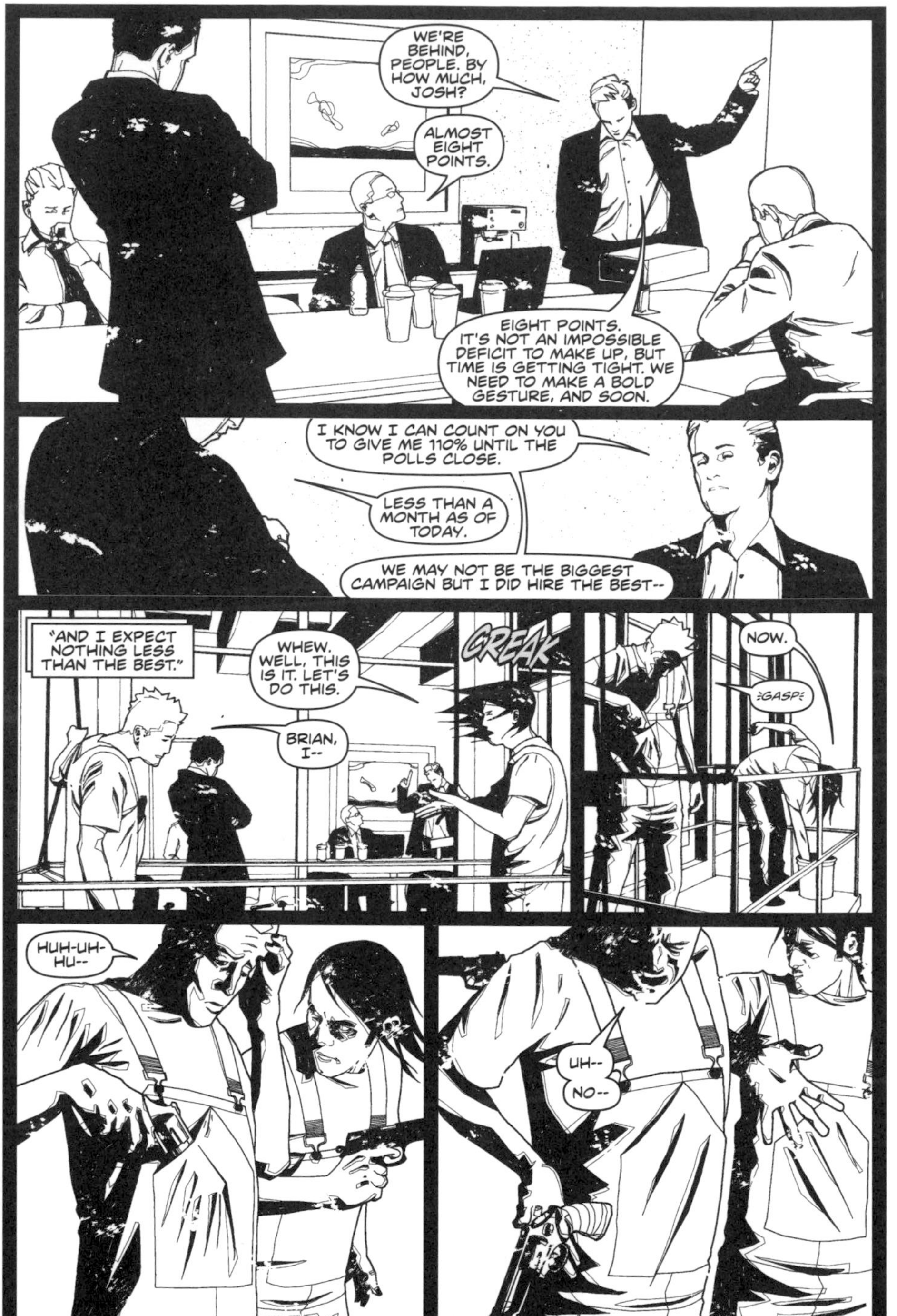
WE'RE BEHIND, PEOPLE. BY HOW MUCH, JOSH?
ALMOST EIGHT POINTS.
EIGHT POINTS. IT'S NOT AN IMPOSSIBLE DEFICIT TO MAKE UP, BUT TIME IS GETTING TIGHT. WE NEED TO MAKE A BOLD GESTURE, AND SOON.
I KNOW I CAN COUNT ON YOU TO GIVE ME 110% UNTIL THE POLLS CLOSE.
LESS THAN A MONTH AS OF TODAY.
WE MAY NOT BE THE BIGGEST CAMPAIGN BUT I DID HIRE THE BEST--
"AND I EXPECT NOTHING LESS THAN THE BEST."
WHEW. WELL, THIS IS IT. LET'S DO THIS.
BRIAN, I--
CREAK
NOW.
GASP
HUH-UH-HU--
UH--
NO--

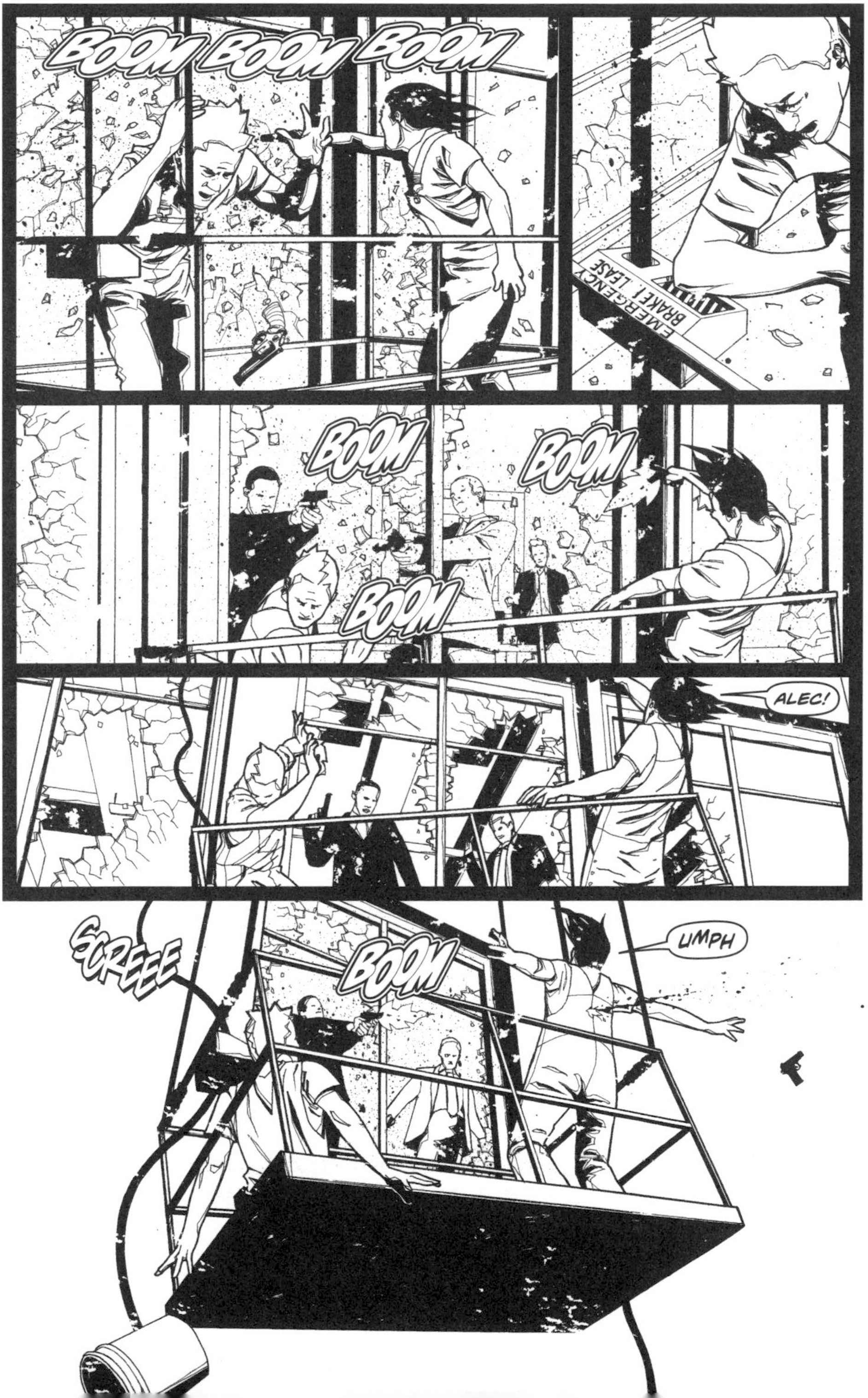
BOOM BOOM BOOM
BOOM
BOOM
BOOM
ALEC!
SCREEE
BOOM
UMPH

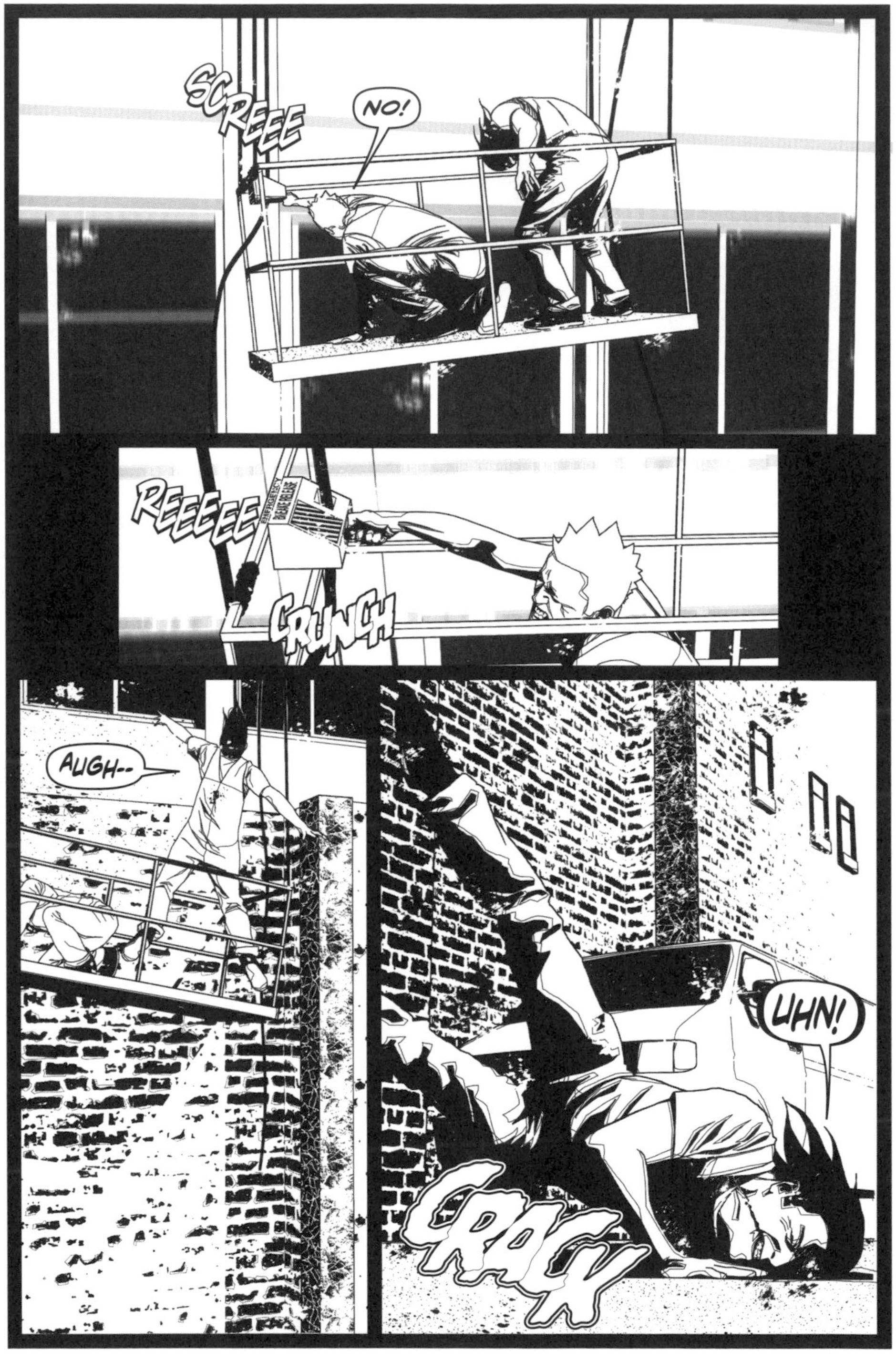
SCREEE
NO!
REEEEE
CRUNCH
AUGH--
UHN!
CRACK

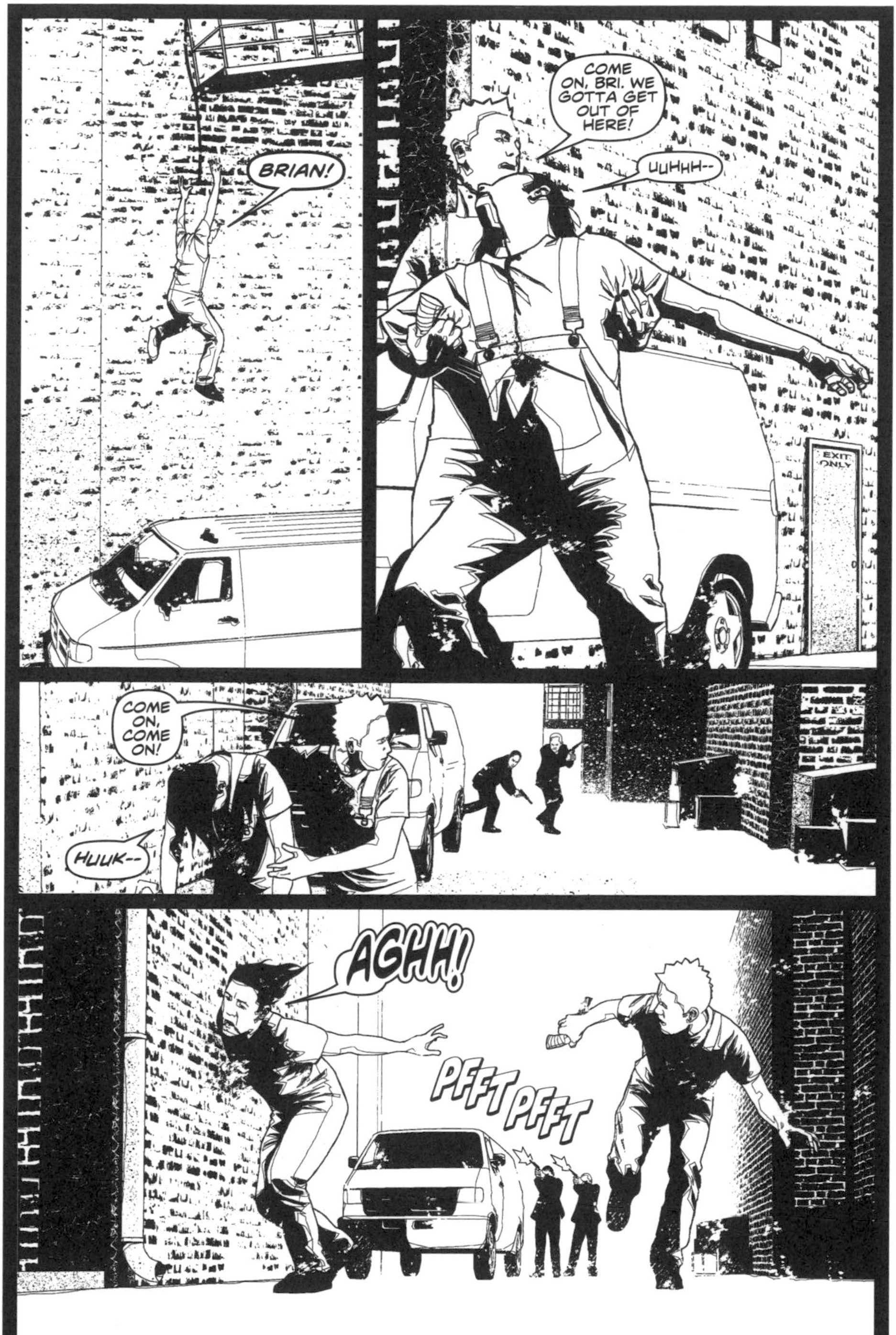
BRIAN!
COME ON, BRI. WE GOTTA GET OUT OF HERE!
UUHHH--
EXIT ONLY
COME ON, COME ON!
HUUK--
AGHH!
PFFT PFFT

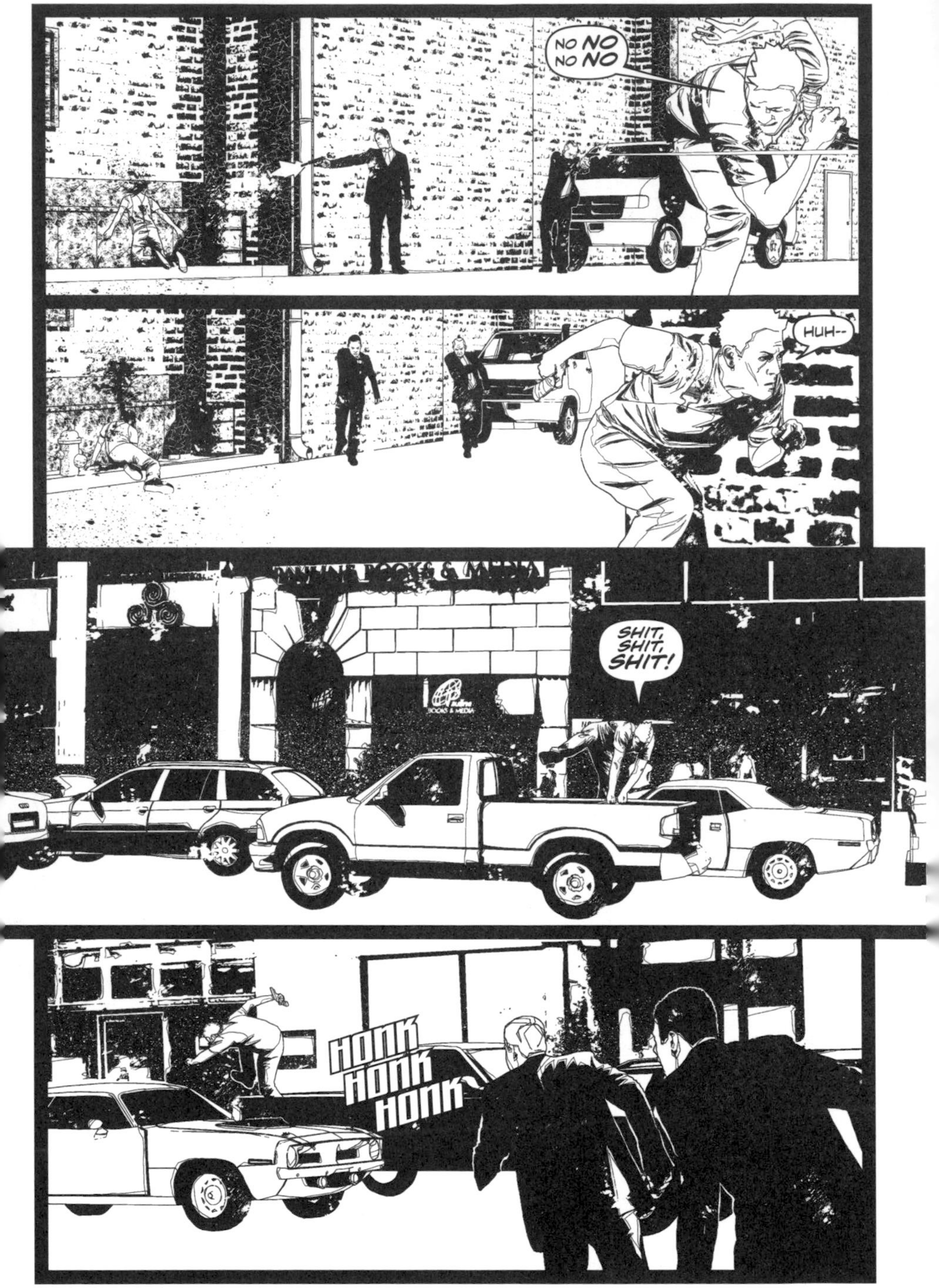
NO NO
NO NO
HUH--
SHIT, SHIT, SHIT!
HONK HONK HONK

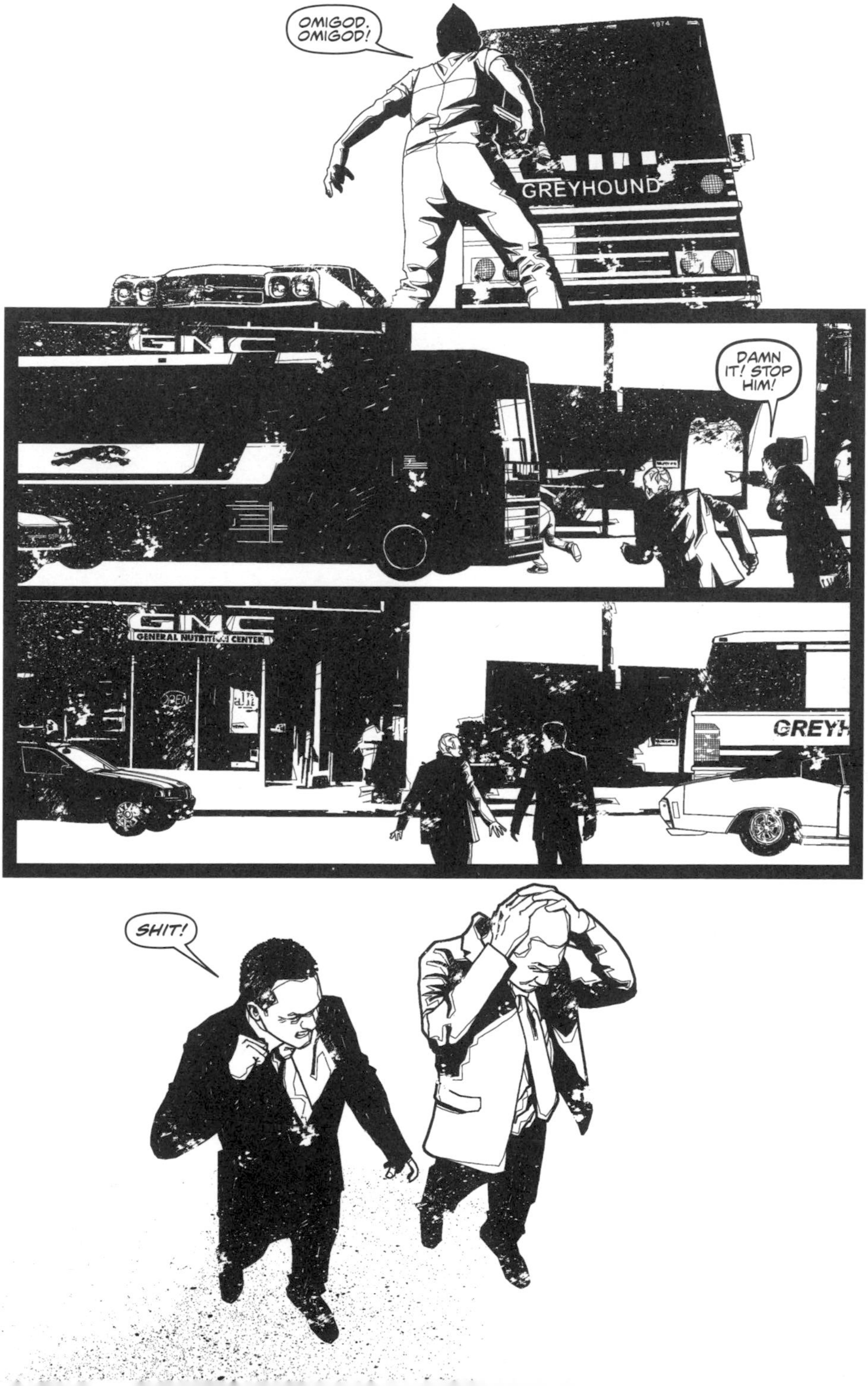
OMIGOD. OMIGOD!
1974
GREYHOUND
GMC
DAMN IT! STOP HIM!
GMC
GENERAL NUTRITION CENTER
OPEN
GREYH
SHIT!

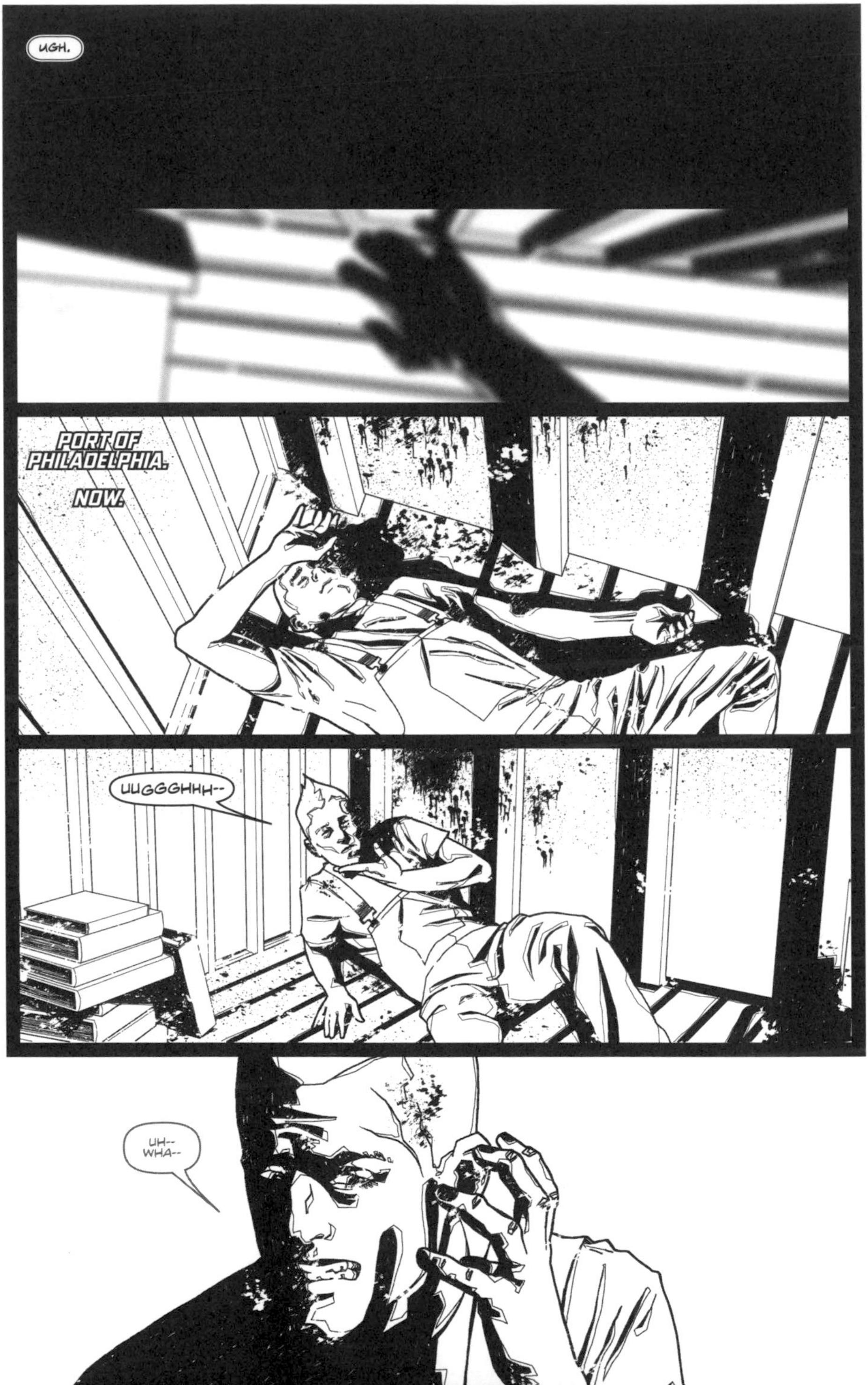
UGH.
PORT OF PHILADELPHIA.
NOW.
UUGGGHHH--
UH-- WHA--

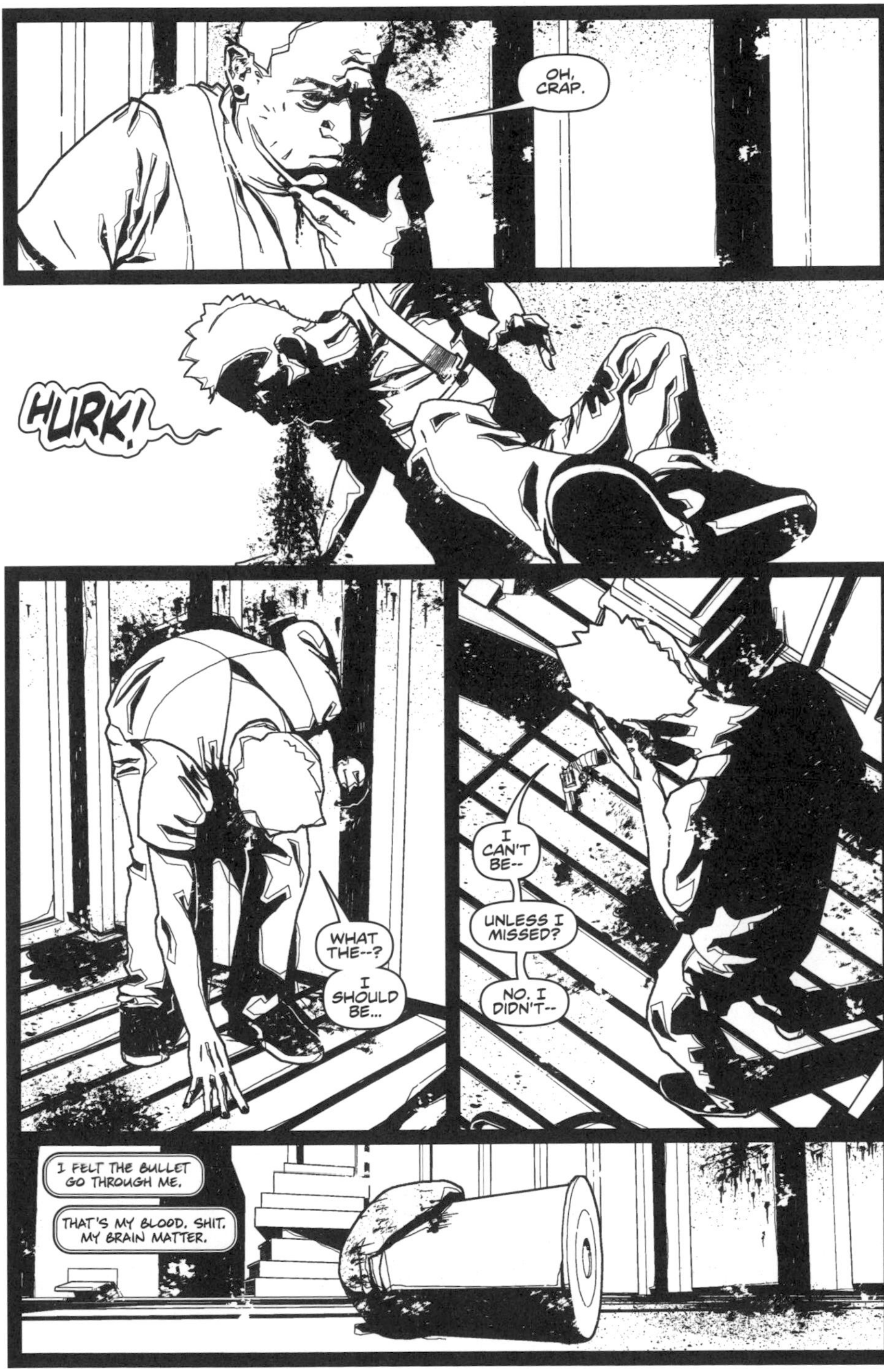
OH, CRAP.
HURK!
WHAT THE--?
I SHOULD BE...
I CAN'T BE--
UNLESS I MISSED?
NO. I DIDN'T--
I FELT THE BULLET GO THROUGH ME.
THAT'S MY BLOOD. SHIT. MY BRAIN MATTER.

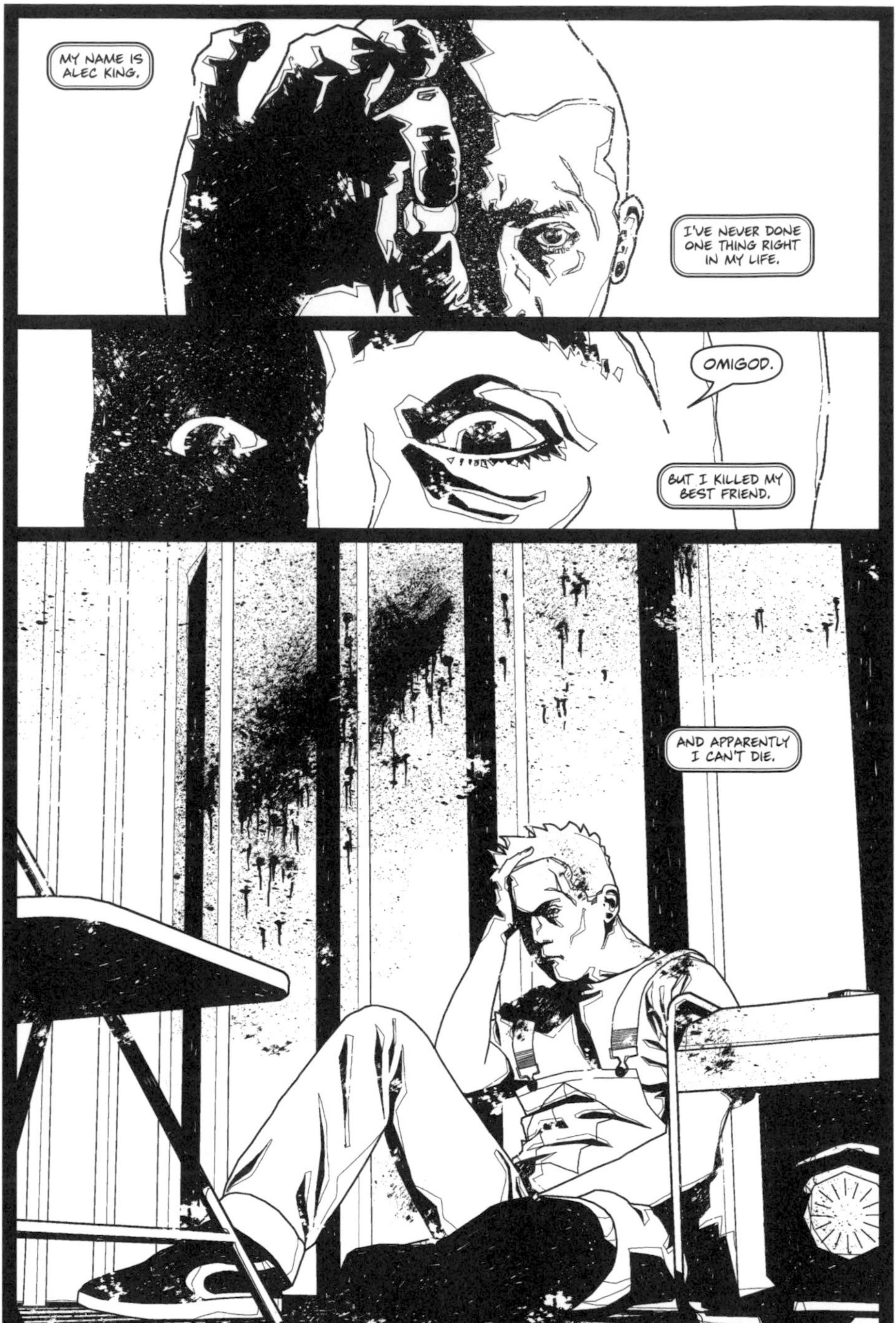
MY NAME IS ALEC KING.
I'VE NEVER DONE ONE THING RIGHT IN MY LIFE.
OMIGOD.
BUT I KILLED MY BEST FRIEND.
AND APPARENTLY I CAN'T DIE.

LAST MORTAL

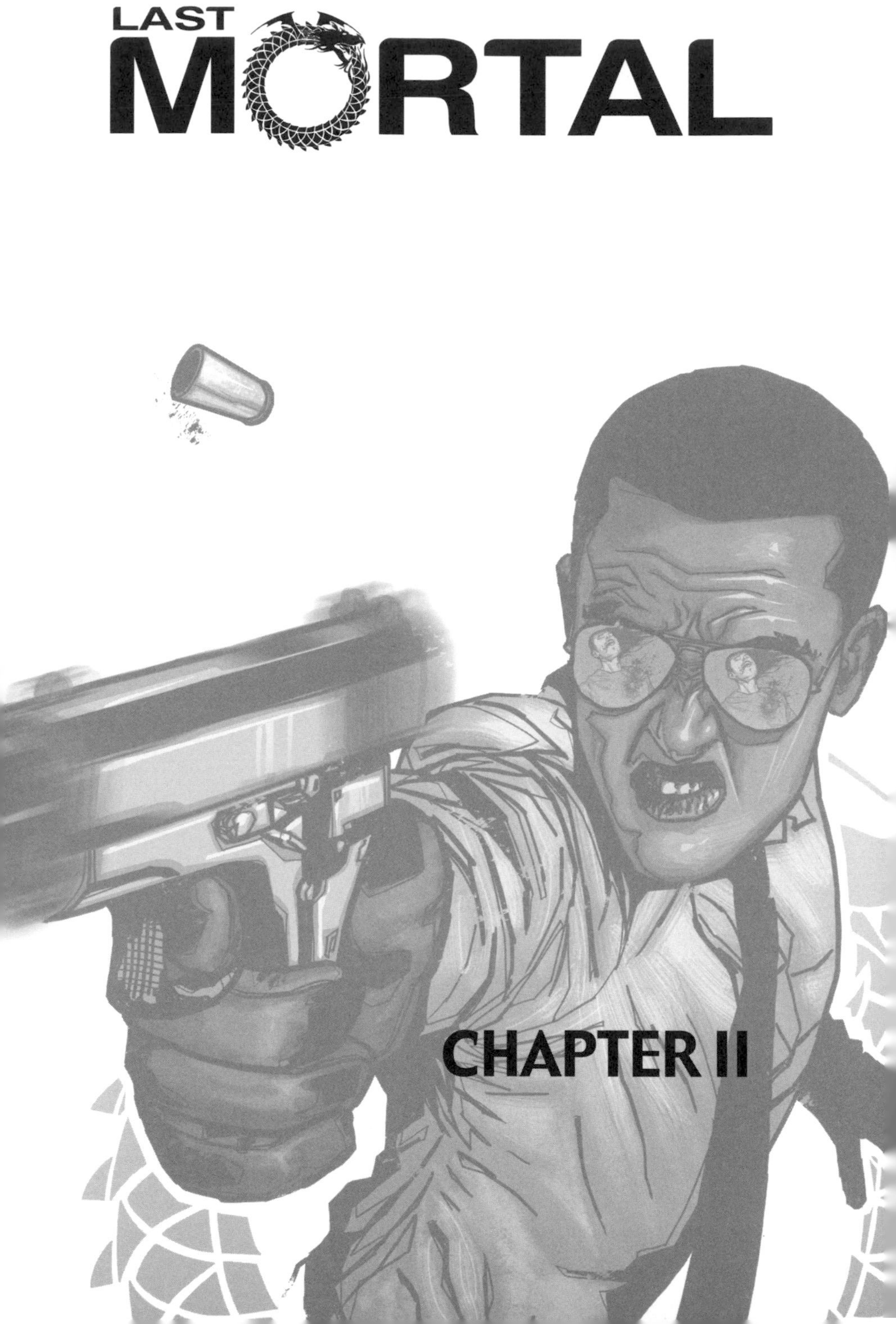

CHAPTER II

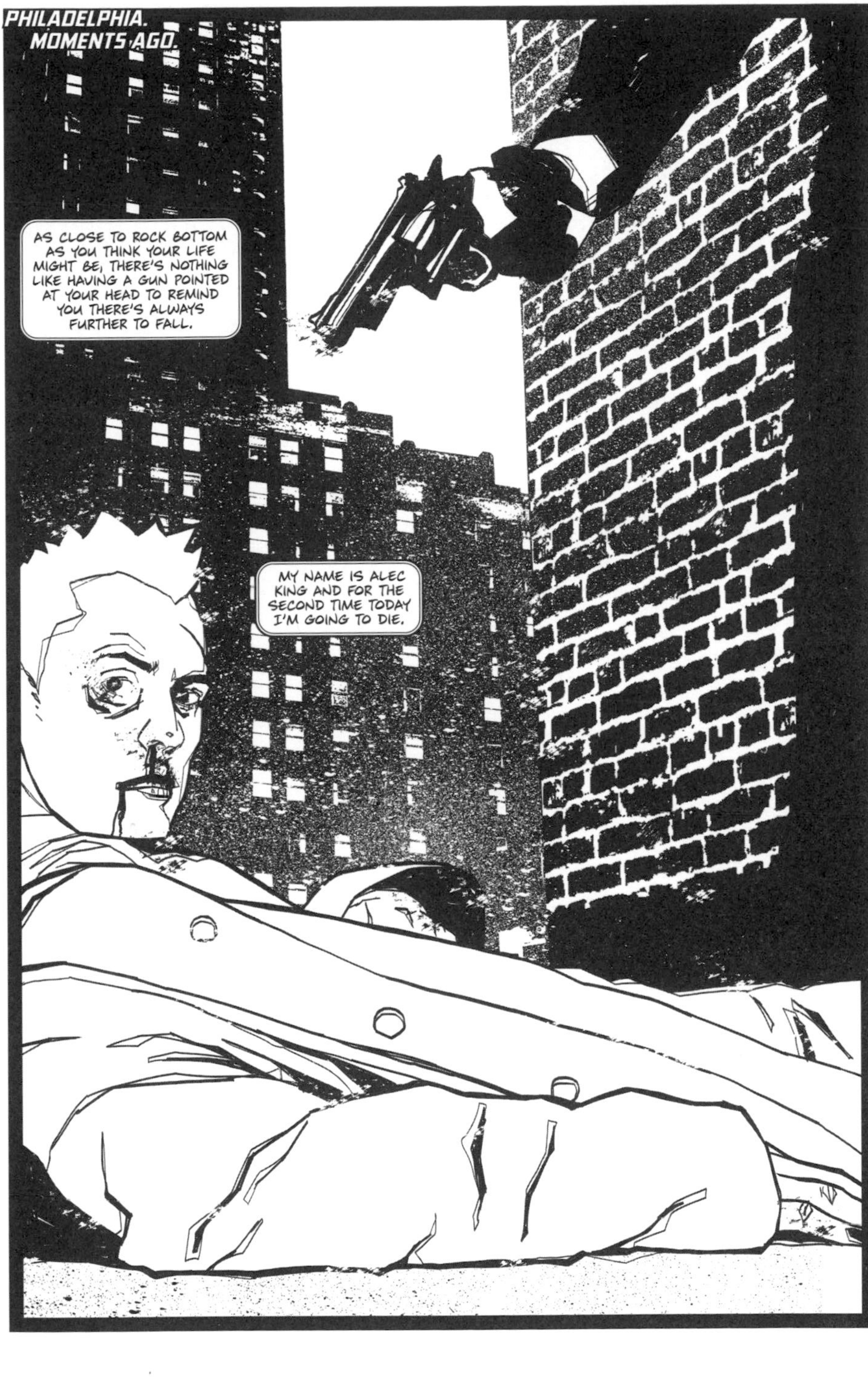
PHILADELPHIA. MOMENTS AGO.
AS CLOSE TO ROCK BOTTOM AS YOU THINK YOUR LIFE MIGHT BE, THERE'S NOTHING LIKE HAVING A GUN POINTED AT YOUR HEAD TO REMIND YOU THERE'S ALWAYS FURTHER TO FALL.
MY NAME IS ALEC KING AND FOR THE SECOND TIME TODAY I'M GOING TO DIE.

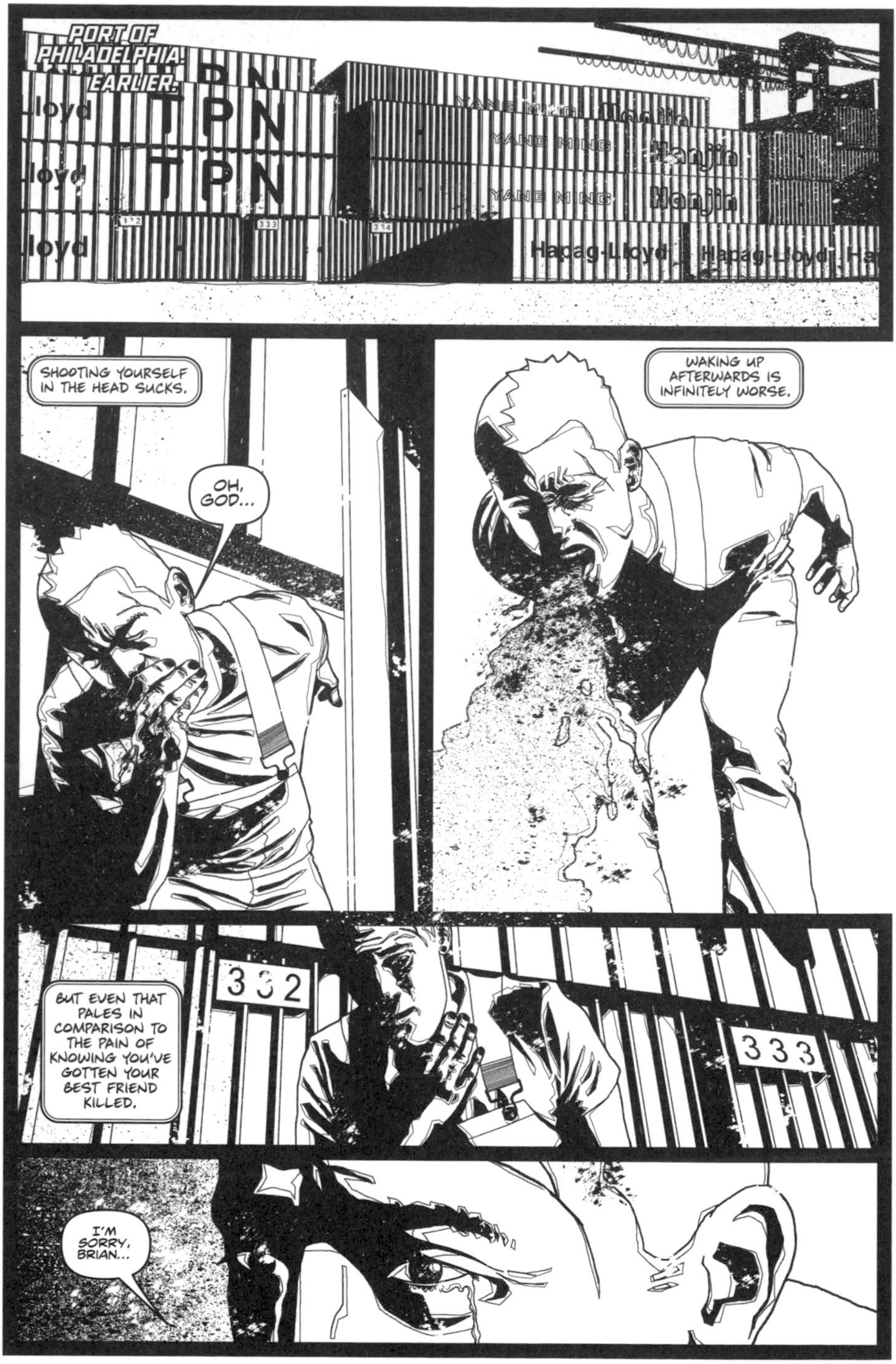
PORT OF PHILADELPHIA. EARLIER.
SHOOTING YOURSELF IN THE HEAD SUCKS.
OH, GOD...
WAKING UP AFTERWARDS IS INFINITELY WORSE.
BUT EVEN THAT PALES IN COMPARISON TO THE PAIN OF KNOWING YOU'VE GOTTEN YOUR BEST FRIEND KILLED.
I'M SORRY, BRIAN...

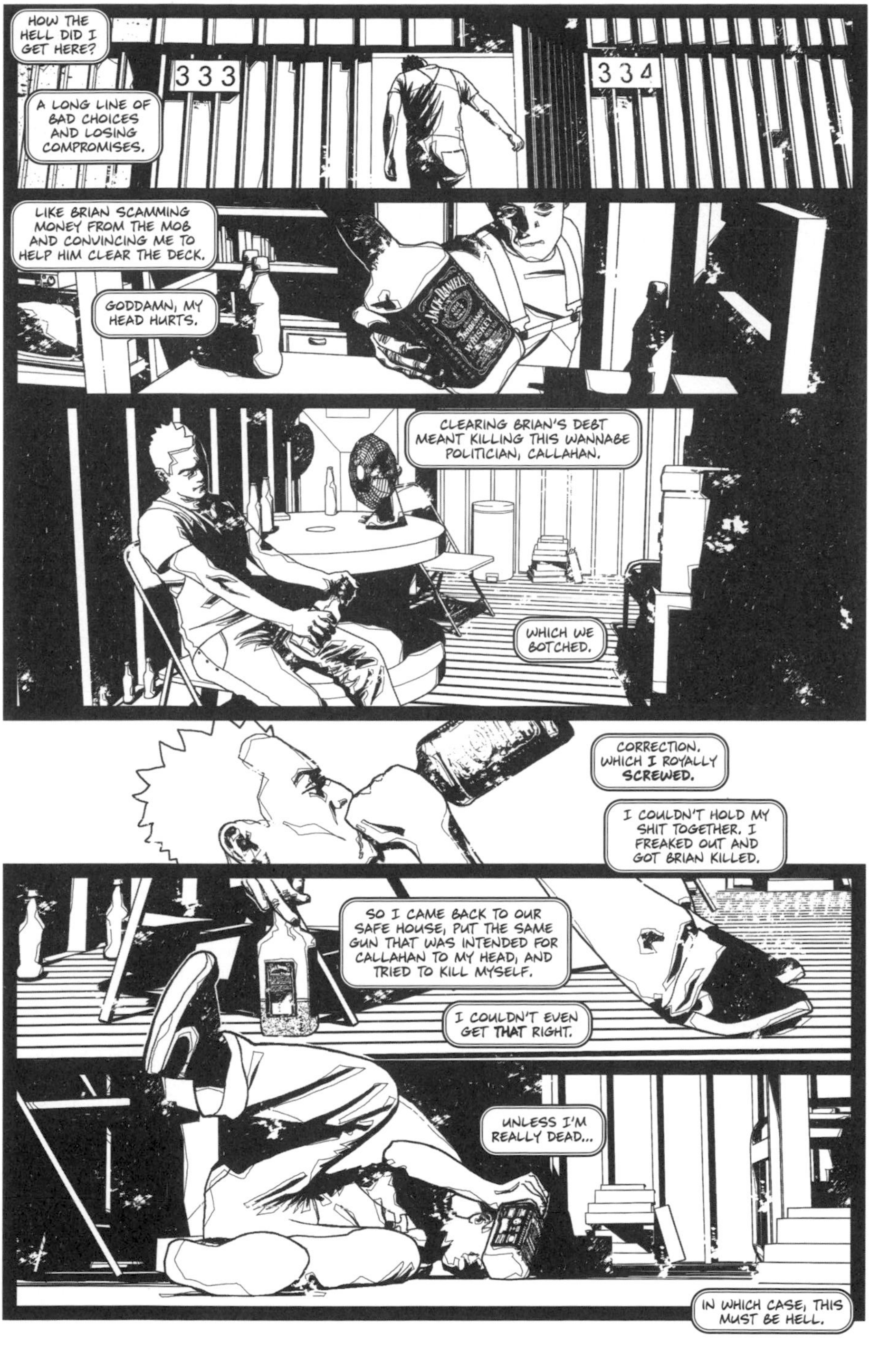
HOW THE HELL DID I GET HERE?
333
334
A LONG LINE OF BAD CHOICES AND LOSING COMPROMISES.
LIKE BRIAN SCAMMING MONEY FROM THE MOB AND CONVINCING ME TO HELP HIM CLEAR THE DECK.
GODDAMN, MY HEAD HURTS.
CLEARING BRIAN'S DEBT MEANT KILLING THIS WANNABE POLITICIAN, CALLAHAN.
WHICH WE BOTCHED.
CORRECTION. WHICH I ROYALLY **SCREWED.**
I COULDN'T HOLD MY SHIT TOGETHER. I FREAKED OUT AND GOT BRIAN KILLED.
SO I CAME BACK TO OUR SAFE HOUSE, PUT THE SAME GUN THAT WAS INTENDED FOR CALLAHAN TO MY HEAD, AND TRIED TO KILL MYSELF.
I COULDN'T EVEN GET **THAT** RIGHT.
UNLESS I'M REALLY DEAD...
IN WHICH CASE, THIS MUST BE HELL.

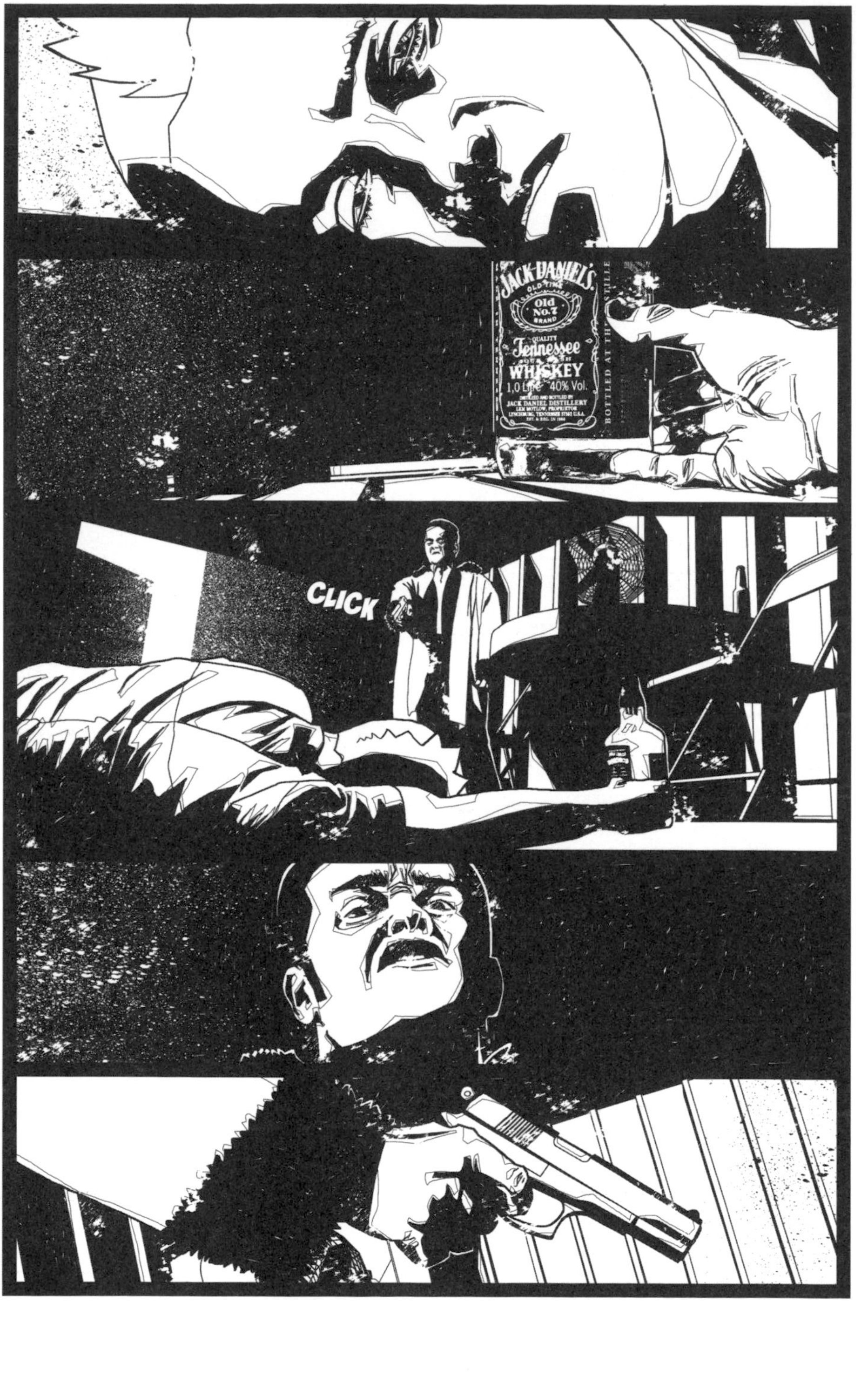

JACK DANIEL'S
OLD TIME
Old No.7
BRAND
QUALITY
Tennessee
WHISKEY
40% Vol.
JACK DANIEL DISTILLERY
CLICK

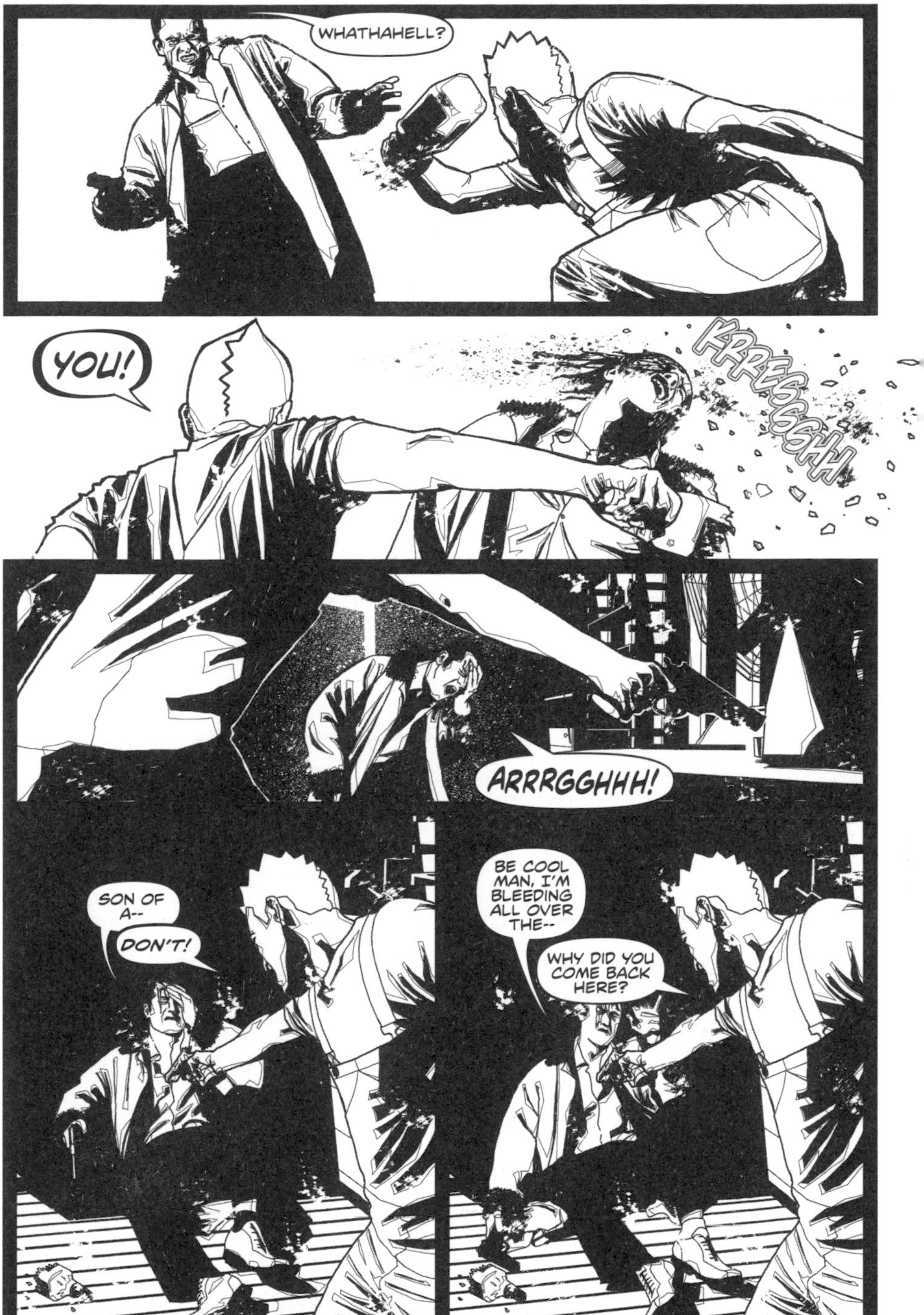
WHATHAHELL?
YOU!
KRRESSHH
ARRRGGHHH!
SON OF A--
DON'T!
BE COOL MAN, I'M BLEEDING ALL OVER THE--
WHY DID YOU COME BACK HERE?

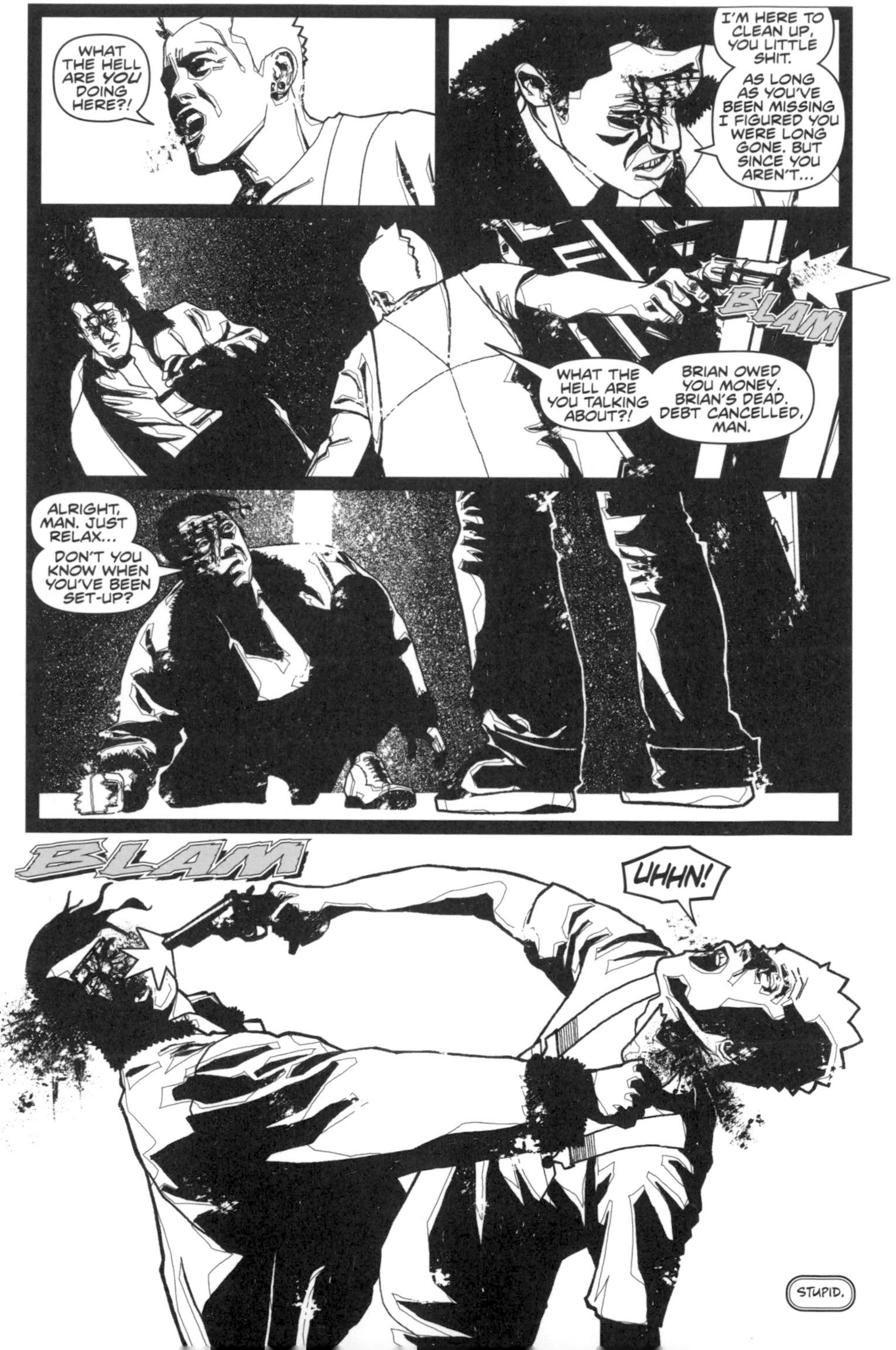
WHAT THE HELL ARE YOU DOING HERE?!
I'M HERE TO CLEAN UP, YOU LITTLE SHIT.
AS LONG AS YOU'VE BEEN MISSING I FIGURED YOU WERE LONG GONE. BUT SINCE YOU AREN'T...
BLAM
WHAT THE HELL ARE YOU TALKING ABOUT?!
BRIAN OWED YOU MONEY. BRIAN'S DEAD. DEBT CANCELLED, MAN.
ALRIGHT, MAN. JUST RELAX...
DON'T YOU KNOW WHEN YOU'VE BEEN SET-UP?
BLAM
UHHN!
STUPID.

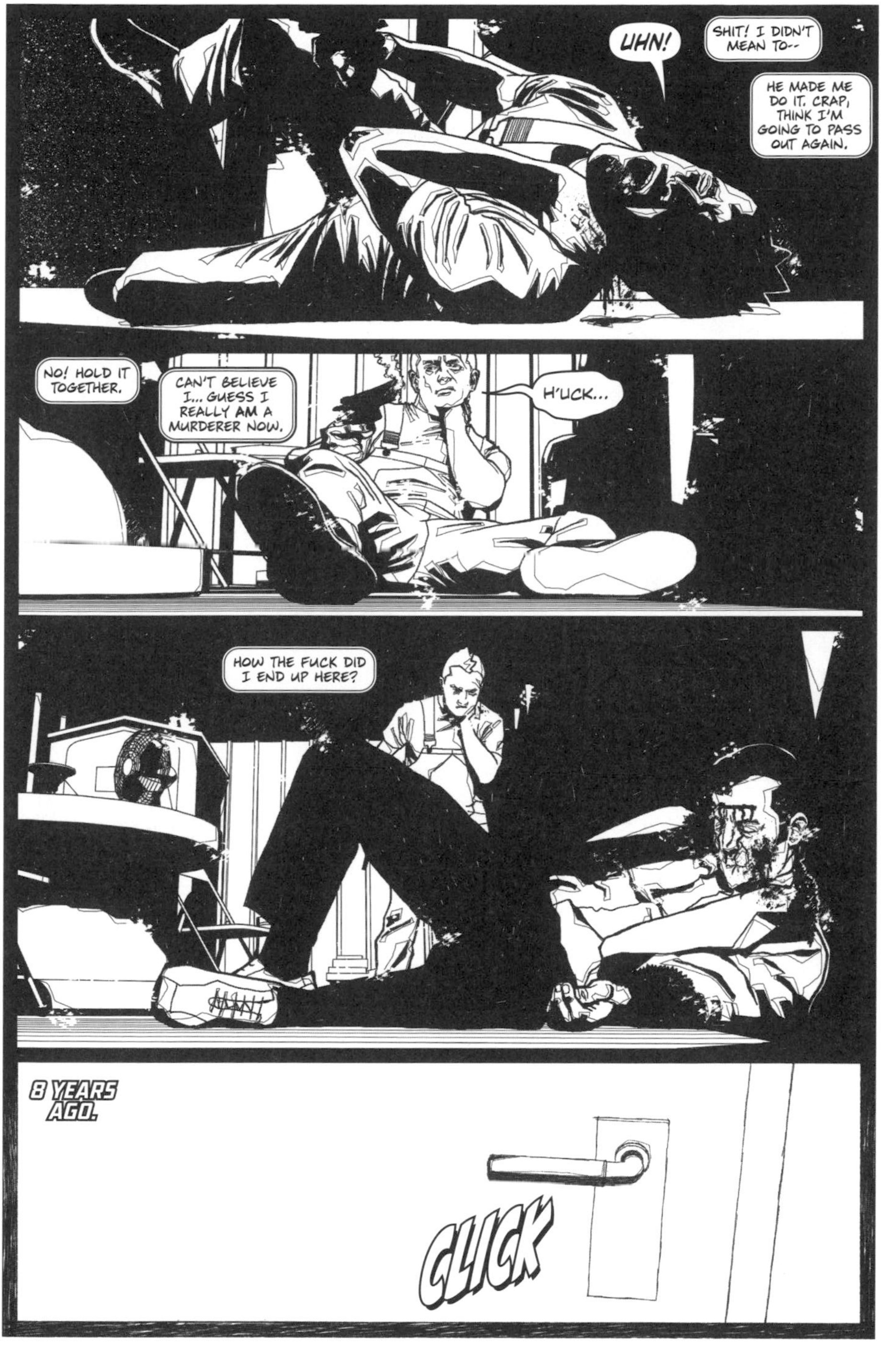

UHN!
SHIT! I DIDN'T MEAN TO--
HE MADE ME DO IT. CRAP, THINK I'M GOING TO PASS OUT AGAIN.
NO! HOLD IT TOGETHER.
CAN'T BELIEVE I... GUESS I REALLY AM A MURDERER NOW.
H'UCK...
HOW THE FUCK DID I END UP HERE?
8 YEARS AGO.
CLICK

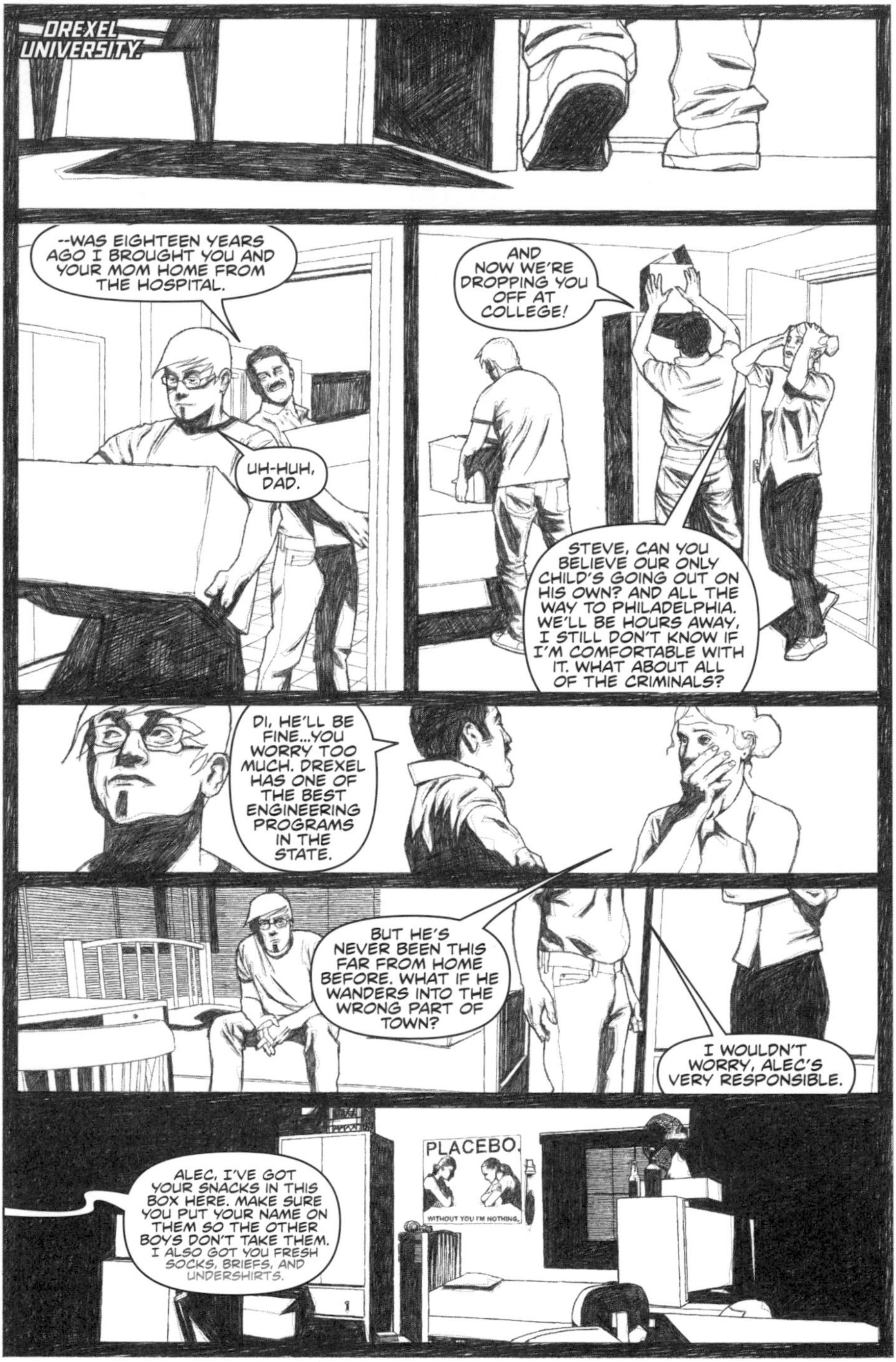
DREXEL UNIVERSITY.
--WAS EIGHTEEN YEARS AGO I BROUGHT YOU AND YOUR MOM HOME FROM THE HOSPITAL.
UH-HUH, DAD.
AND NOW WE'RE DROPPING YOU OFF AT COLLEGE!
STEVE, CAN YOU BELIEVE OUR ONLY CHILD'S GOING OUT ON HIS OWN? AND ALL THE WAY TO PHILADELPHIA. WE'LL BE HOURS AWAY, I STILL DON'T KNOW IF I'M COMFORTABLE WITH IT. WHAT ABOUT ALL OF THE CRIMINALS?
DI, HE'LL BE FINE...YOU WORRY TOO MUCH. DREXEL HAS ONE OF THE BEST ENGINEERING PROGRAMS IN THE STATE.
BUT HE'S NEVER BEEN THIS FAR FROM HOME BEFORE. WHAT IF HE WANDERS INTO THE WRONG PART OF TOWN?
I WOULDN'T WORRY, ALEC'S VERY RESPONSIBLE.
ALEC, I'VE GOT YOUR SNACKS IN THIS BOX HERE. MAKE SURE YOU PUT YOUR NAME ON THEM SO THE OTHER BOYS DON'T TAKE THEM. I ALSO GOT YOU FRESH SOCKS, BRIEFS, AND UNDERSHIRTS.
PLACEBO.
WITHOUT YOU I'M NOTHING.

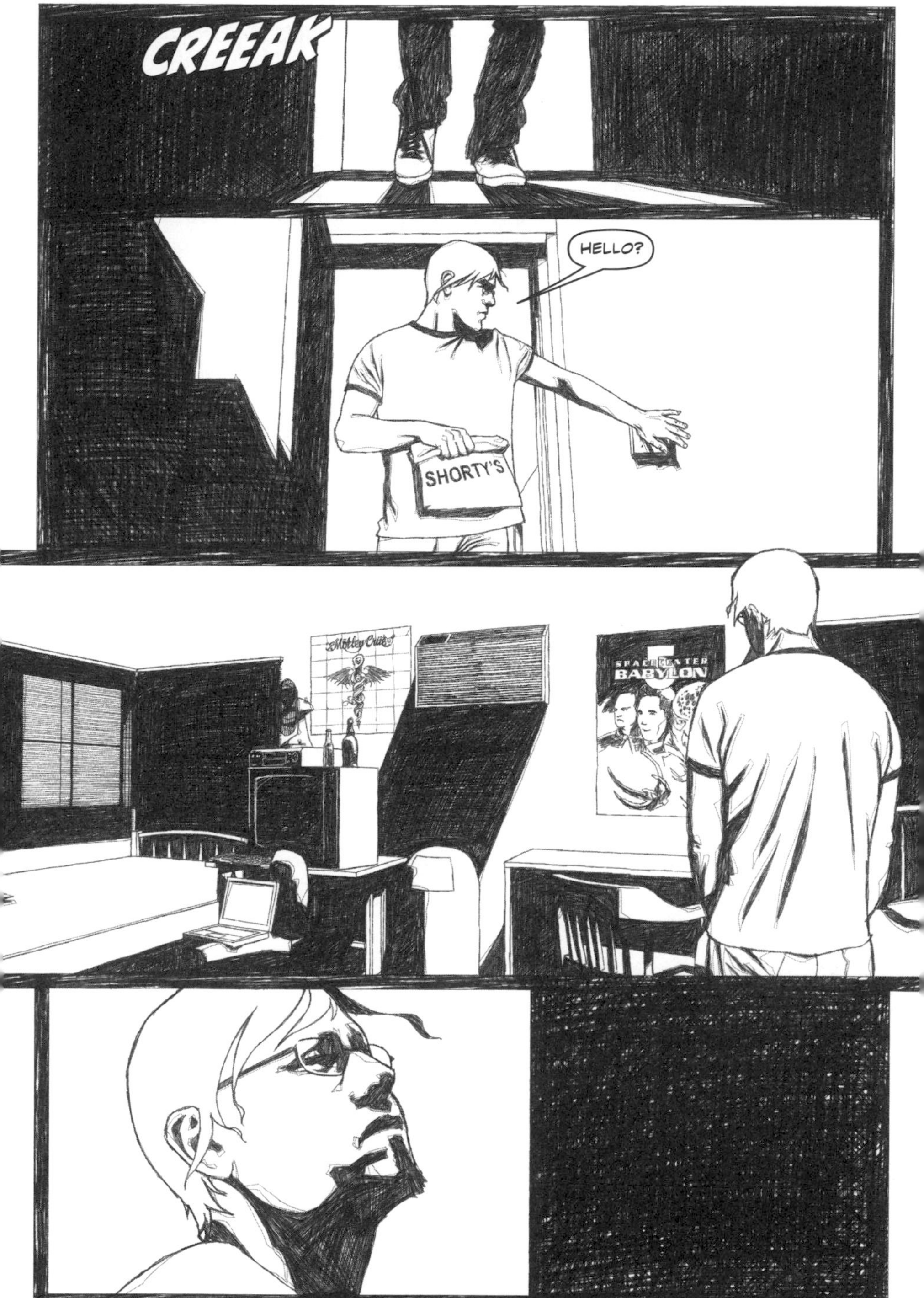
CREEAK
HELLO?
SHORTY'S
BABYLON

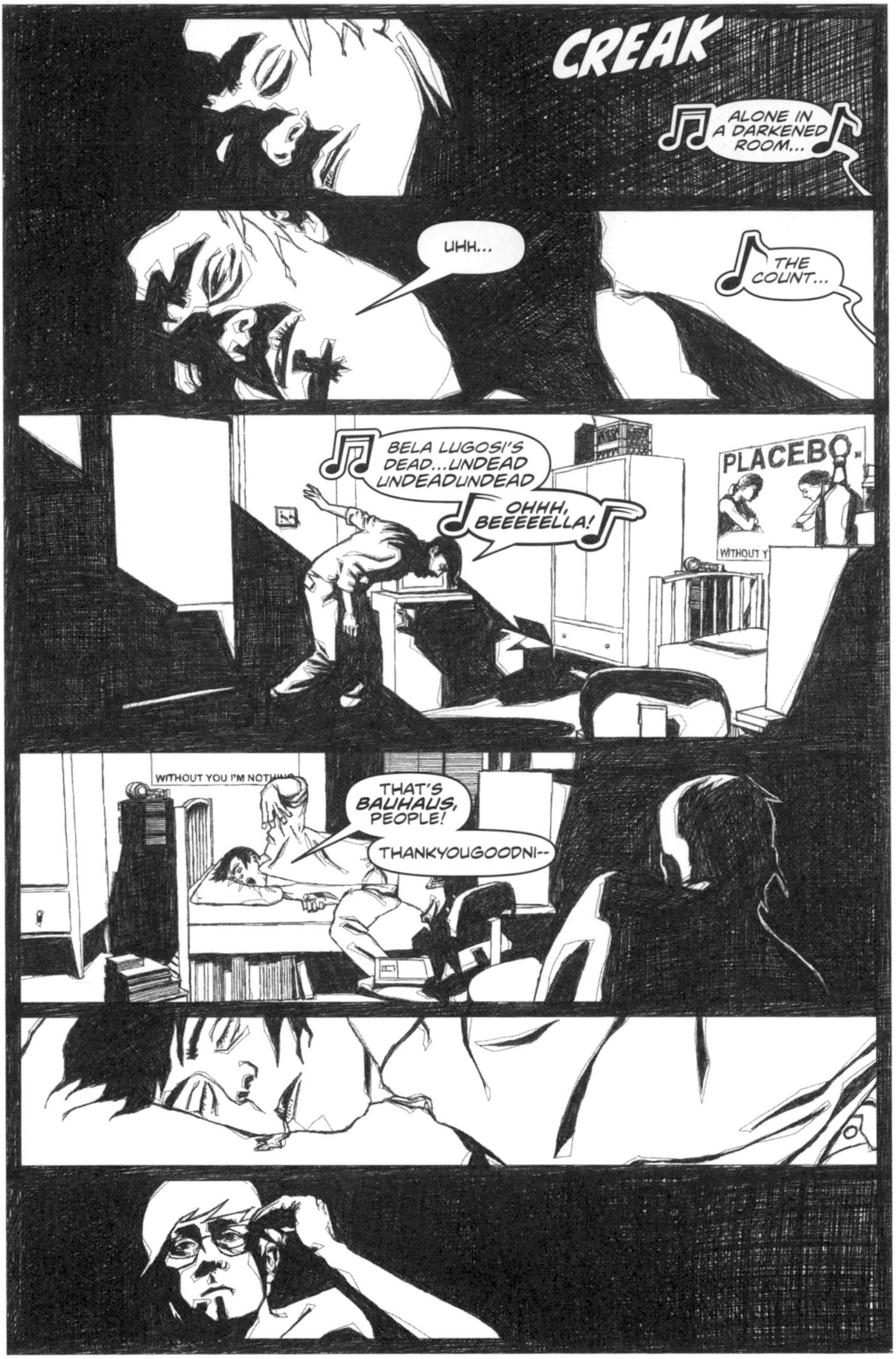
CREAK
ALONE IN A DARKENED ROOM...
UHH...
THE COUNT...
BELA LUGOSI'S DEAD...UNDEAD UNDEADUNDEAD
OHHH, BEEEEELLA!
PLACEBO
WITHOUT Y
WITHOUT YOU I'M NOTHING
THAT'S BAUHAUS, PEOPLE!
THANKYOUGOODNI--

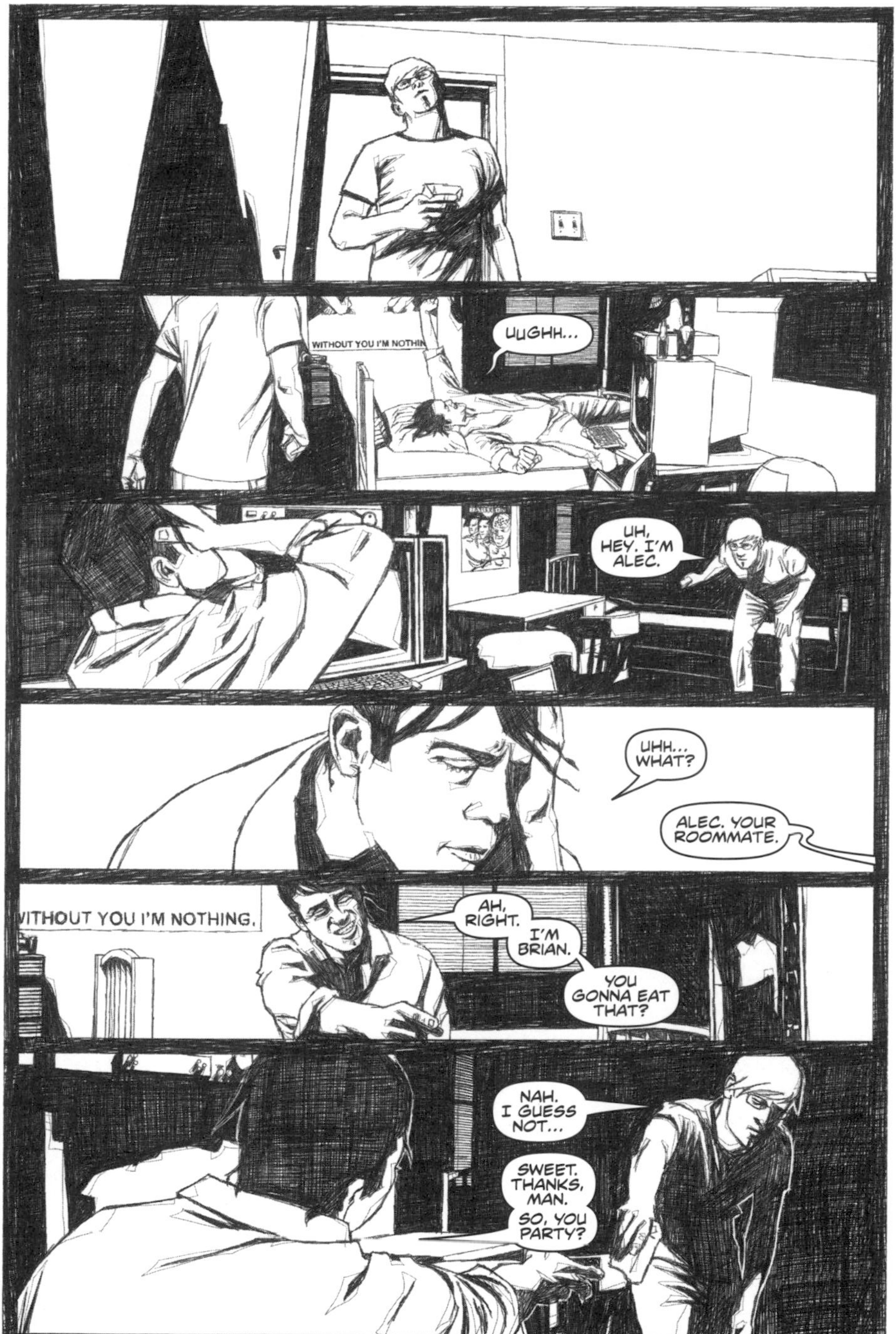
WITHOUT YOU I'M NOTHIN
UUGHH...
UH, HEY. I'M ALEC.
UHH... WHAT?
ALEC. YOUR ROOMMATE.
WITHOUT YOU I'M NOTHING.
AH, RIGHT.
I'M BRIAN.
YOU GONNA EAT THAT?
NAH. I GUESS NOT...
SWEET. THANKS, MAN.
SO, YOU PARTY?

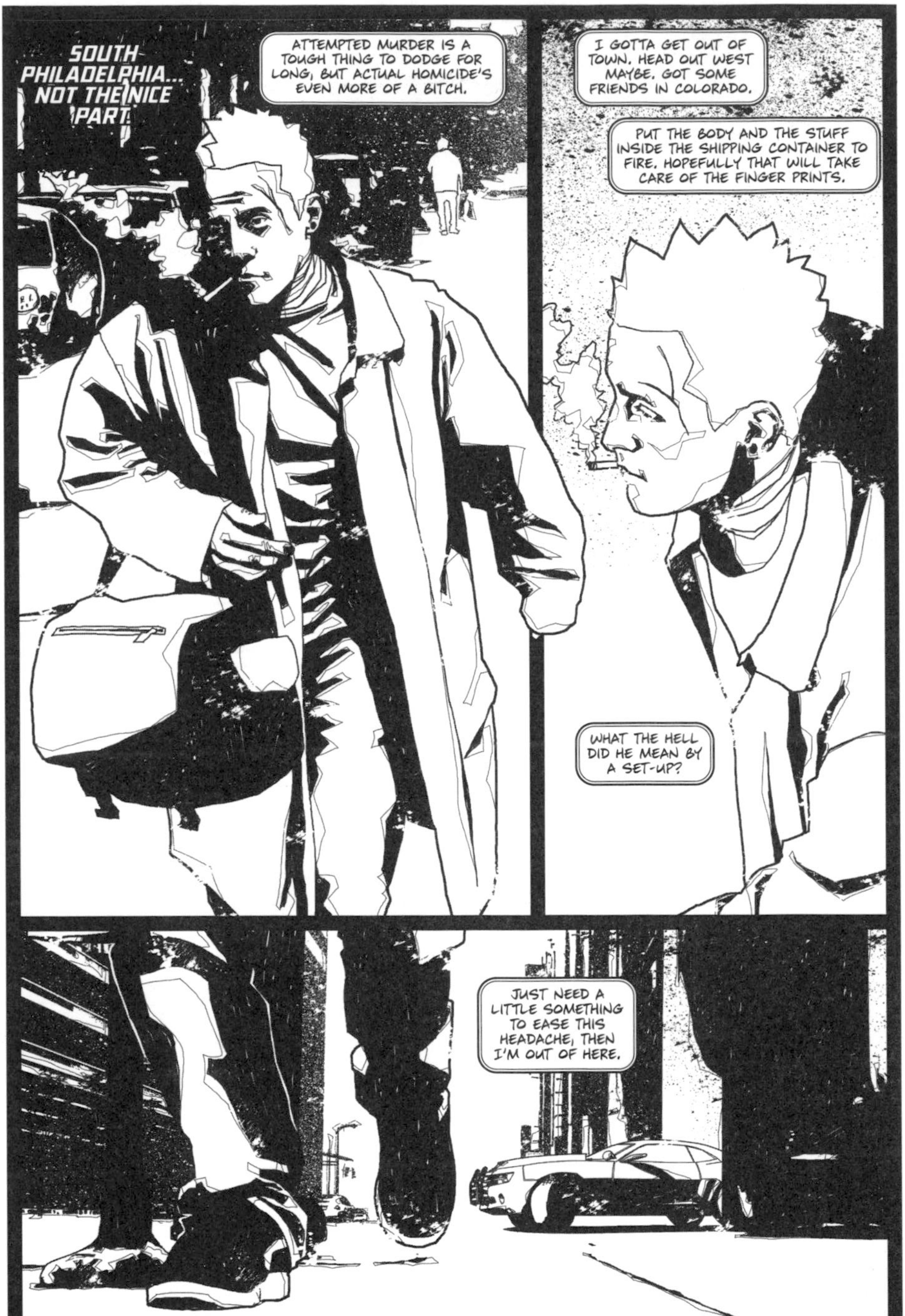
SOUTH PHILADELPHIA... NOT THE NICE PART
ATTEMPTED MURDER IS A TOUGH THING TO DODGE FOR LONG, BUT ACTUAL HOMICIDE'S EVEN MORE OF A BITCH.
I GOTTA GET OUT OF TOWN. HEAD OUT WEST MAYBE. GOT SOME FRIENDS IN COLORADO.
PUT THE BODY AND THE STUFF INSIDE THE SHIPPING CONTAINER TO FIRE. HOPEFULLY THAT WILL TAKE CARE OF THE FINGER PRINTS.
WHAT THE HELL DID HE MEAN BY A SET-UP?
JUST NEED A LITTLE SOMETHING TO EASE THIS HEADACHE, THEN I'M OUT OF HERE.

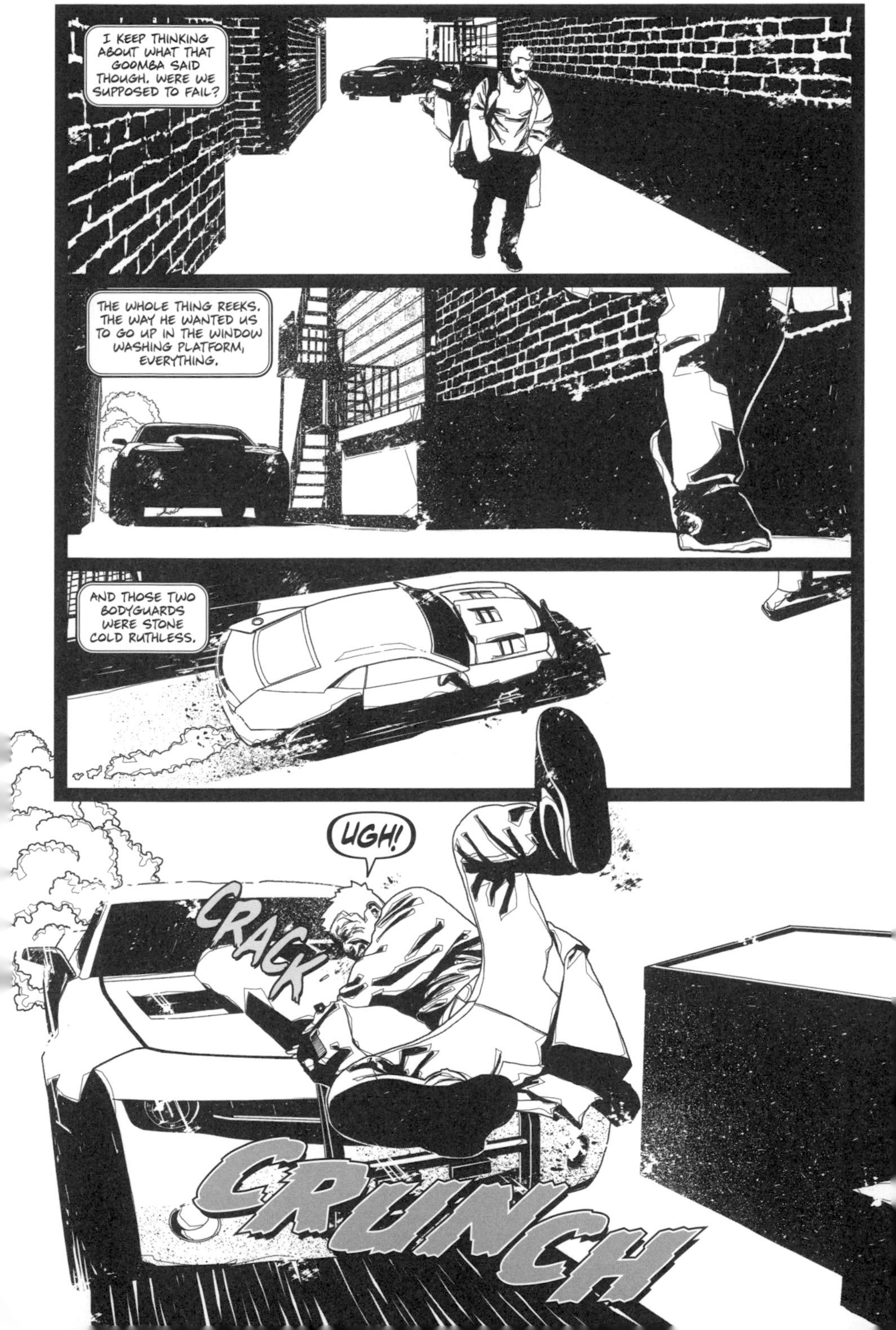
I KEEP THINKING ABOUT WHAT THAT GOOMBA SAID THOUGH. WERE WE SUPPOSED TO FAIL?
THE WHOLE THING REEKS. THE WAY HE WANTED US TO GO UP IN THE WINDOW WASHING PLATFORM, EVERYTHING.
AND THOSE TWO BODYGUARDS WERE STONE COLD RUTHLESS.
UGH!
CRACK
CRUNCH

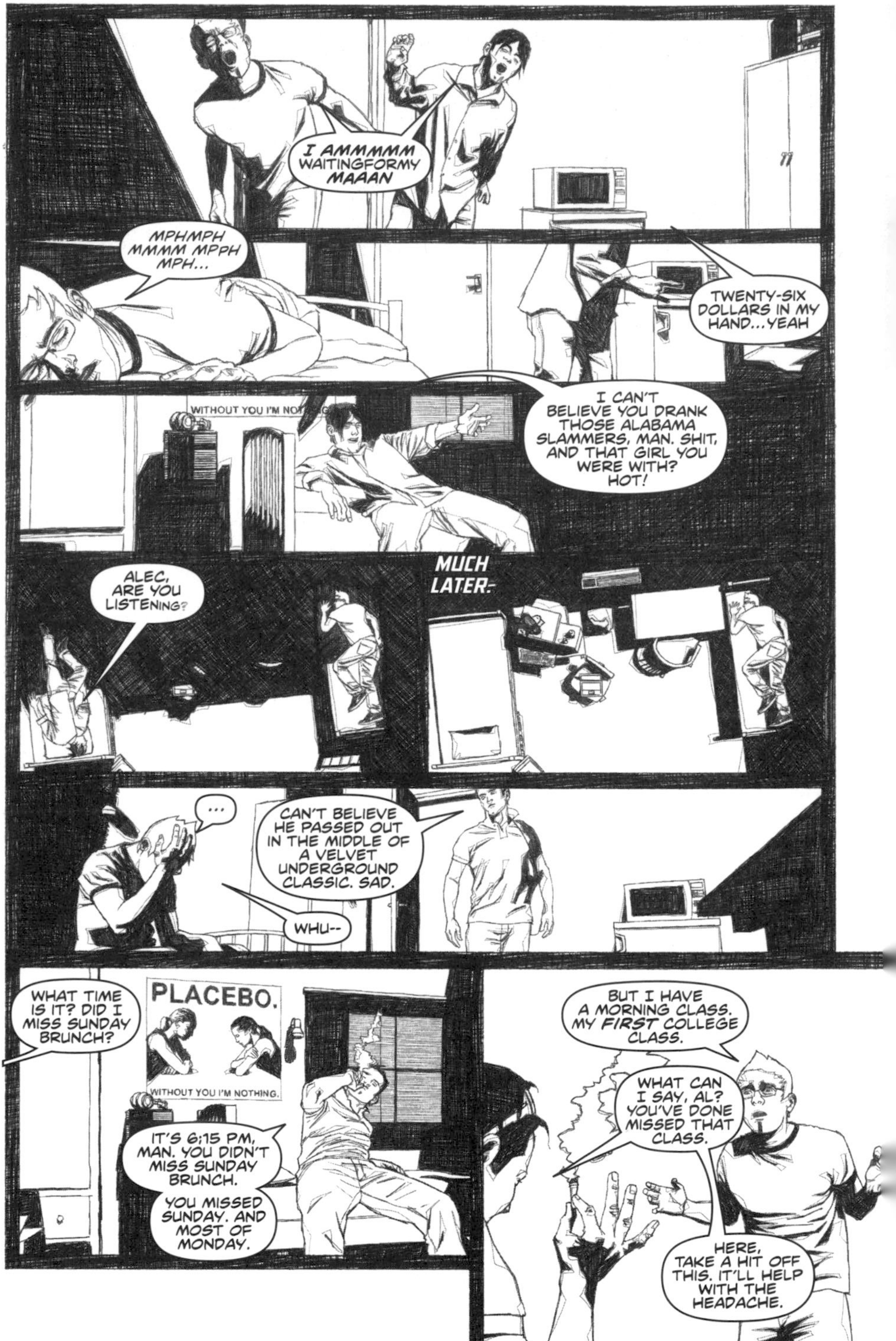
I AMMMMM WAITINGFORMY MAAAN
MPHMPH MMMM MPPH MPH...
TWENTY-SIX DOLLARS IN MY HAND...YEAH
WITHOUT YOU I'M NO
I CAN'T BELIEVE YOU DRANK THOSE ALABAMA SLAMMERS, MAN. SHIT, AND THAT GIRL YOU WERE WITH? HOT!
ALEC, ARE YOU LISTENING?
MUCH LATER-
...
CAN'T BELIEVE HE PASSED OUT IN THE MIDDLE OF A VELVET UNDERGROUND CLASSIC. SAD.
WHU--
WHAT TIME IS IT? DID I MISS SUNDAY BRUNCH?
PLACEBO.
WITHOUT YOU I'M NOTHING.
IT'S 6;15 PM, MAN. YOU DIDN'T MISS SUNDAY BRUNCH.
YOU MISSED SUNDAY. AND MOST OF MONDAY.
BUT I HAVE A MORNING CLASS. MY FIRST COLLEGE CLASS.
WHAT CAN I SAY, AL? YOU'VE DONE MISSED THAT CLASS.
HERE, TAKE A HIT OFF THIS. IT'LL HELP WITH THE HEADACHE.

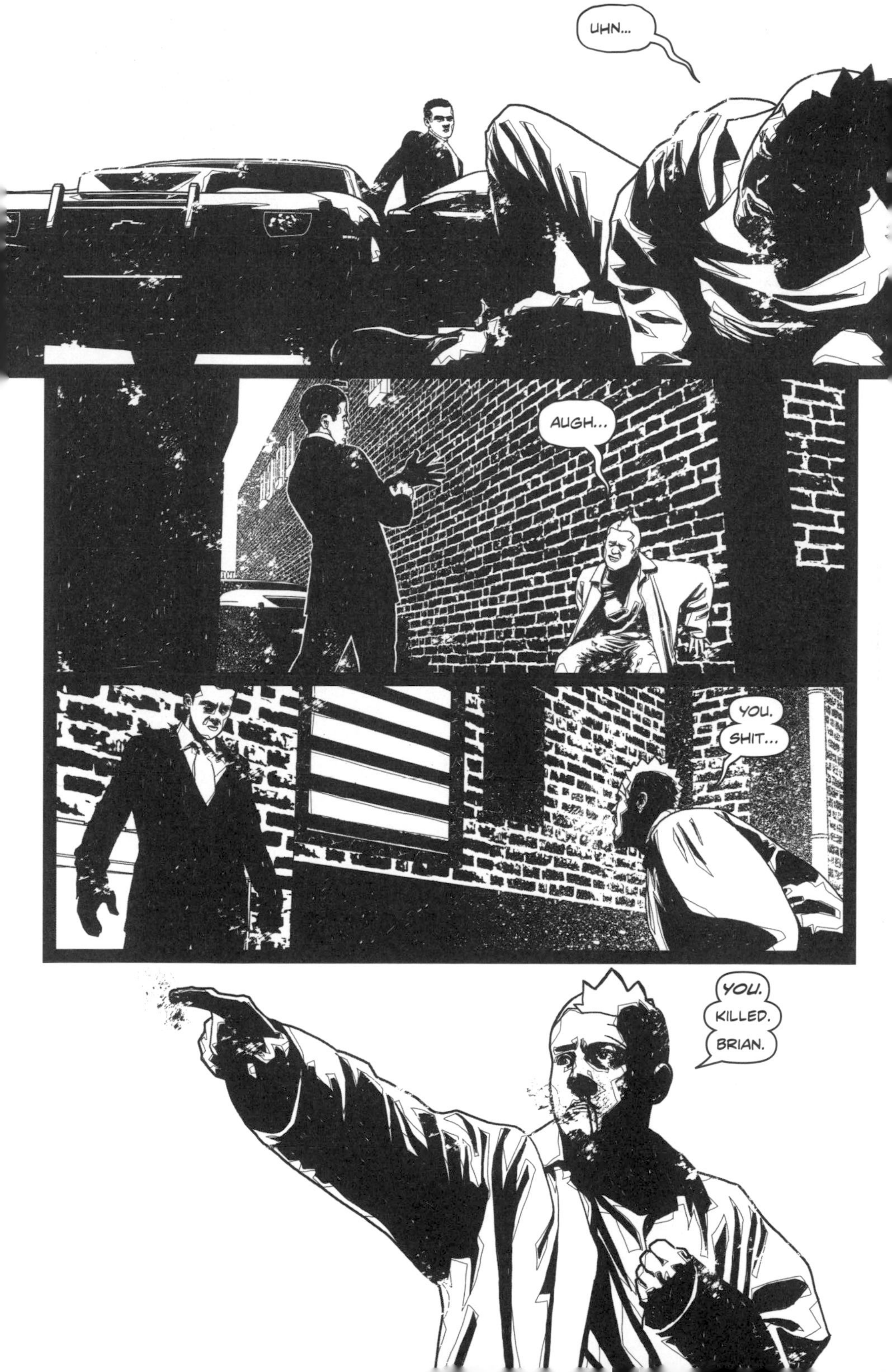
UHN...
AUGH...
YOU. SHIT...
YOU. KILLED. BRIAN.

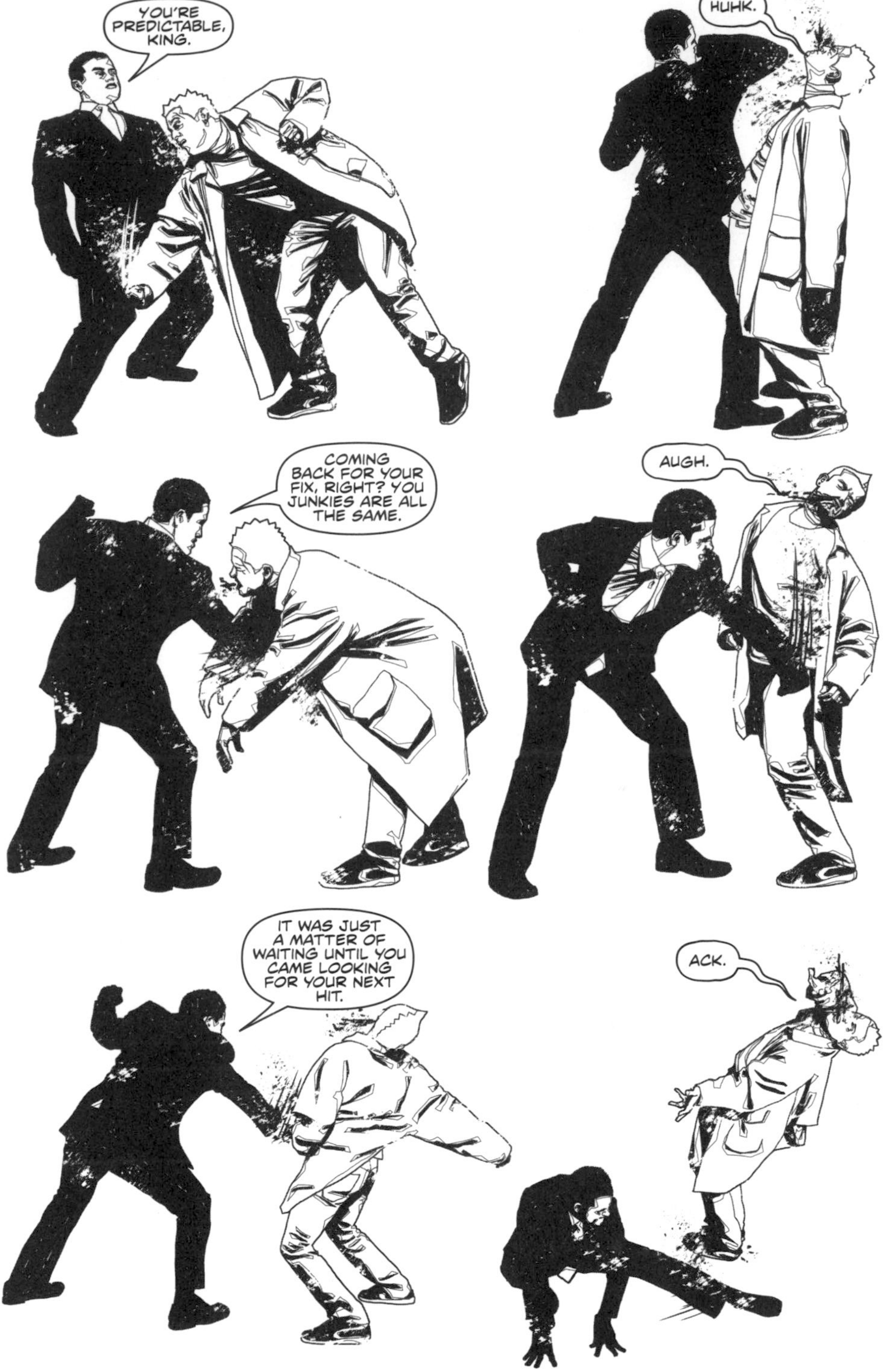
YOU'RE PREDICTABLE, KING.
HUHK.
COMING BACK FOR YOUR FIX, RIGHT? YOU JUNKIES ARE ALL THE SAME.
AUGH.
IT WAS JUST A MATTER OF WAITING UNTIL YOU CAME LOOKING FOR YOUR NEXT HIT.
ACK.

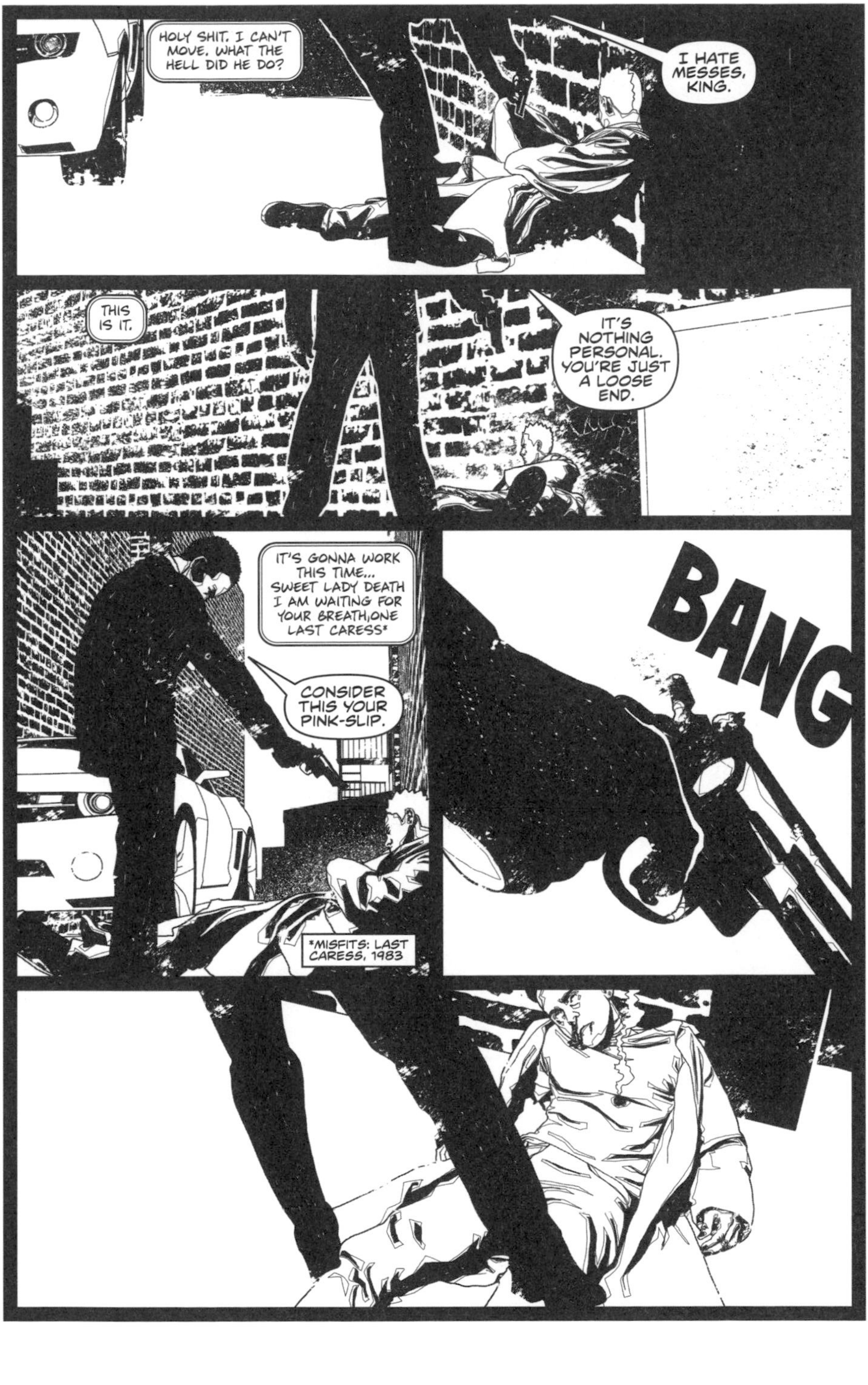
HOLY SHIT. I CAN'T MOVE. WHAT THE HELL DID HE DO?
I HATE MESSES, KING.
THIS IS IT.
IT'S NOTHING PERSONAL. YOU'RE JUST A LOOSE END.
IT'S GONNA WORK THIS TIME... SWEET LADY DEATH I AM WAITING FOR YOUR BREATH, ONE LAST CARESS*
CONSIDER THIS YOUR PINK-SLIP.
*MISFITS: LAST CARESS, 1983
BANG

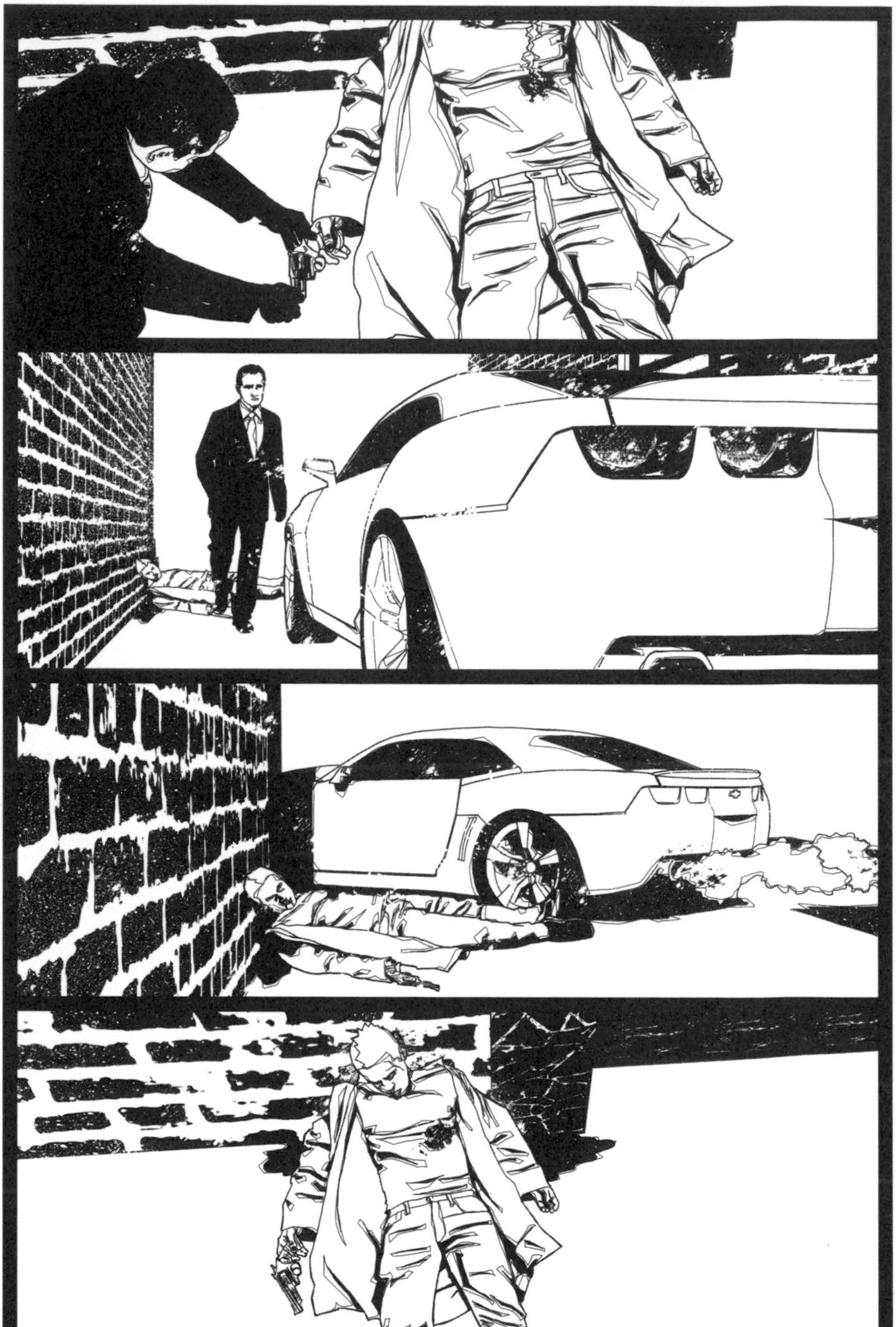

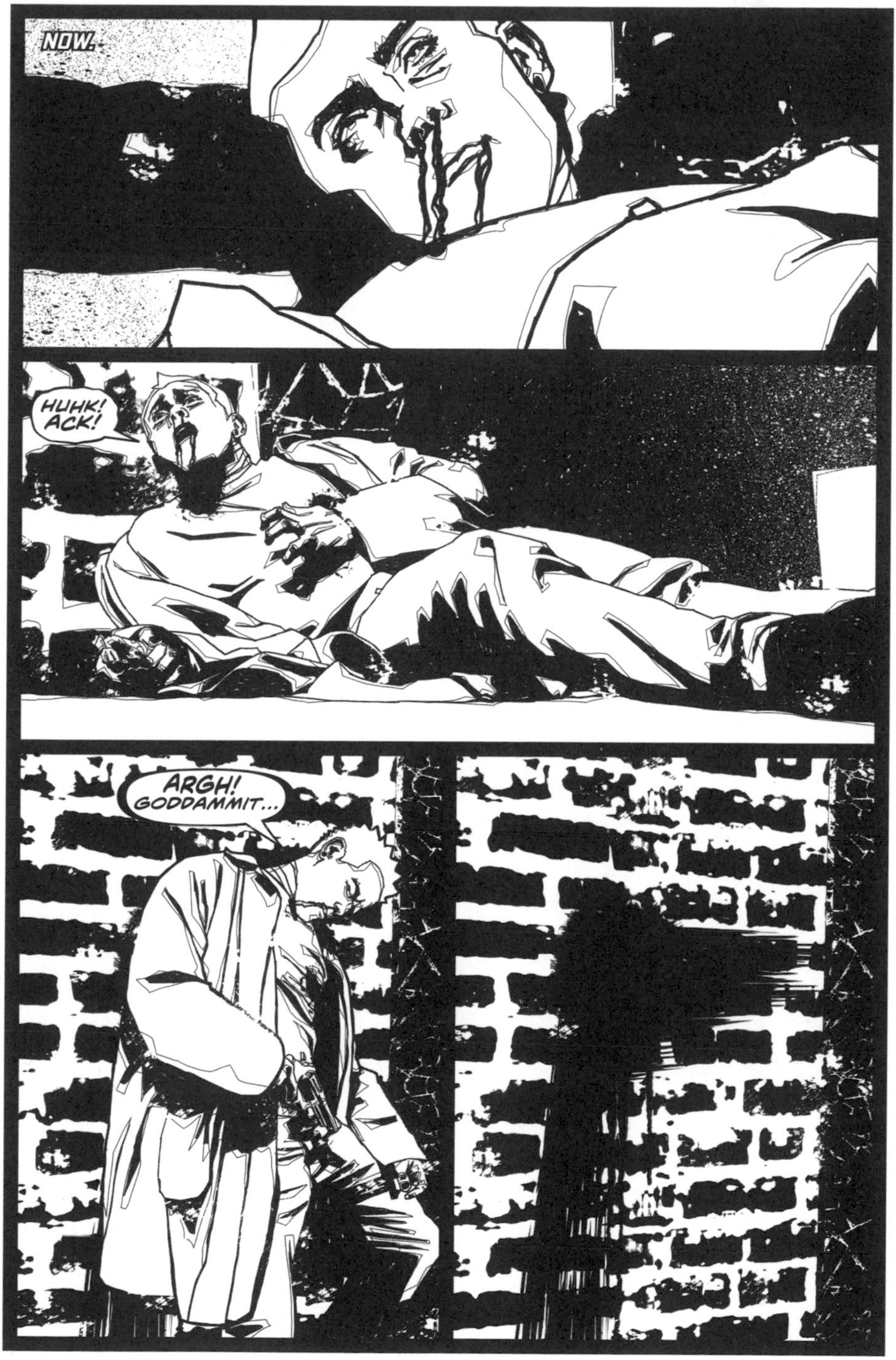
NOW.
HUHK! ACK!
ARGH! GODDAMMIT...

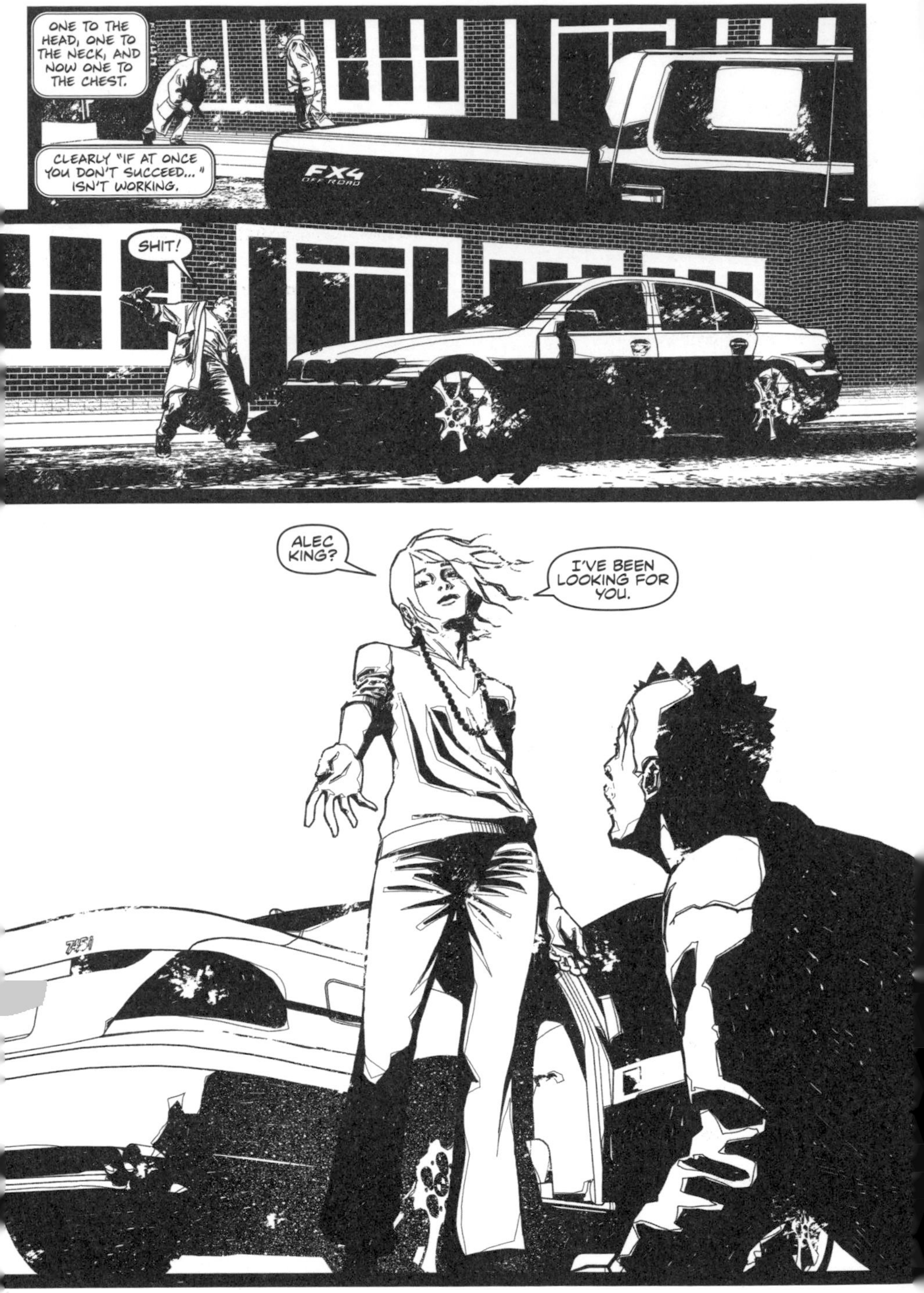
ONE TO THE HEAD, ONE TO THE NECK, AND NOW ONE TO THE CHEST.
CLEARLY "IF AT ONCE YOU DON'T SUCCEED..." ISN'T WORKING.
FX4 OFF ROAD
SHIT!
ALEC KING?
I'VE BEEN LOOKING FOR YOU.

LAST MORTAL

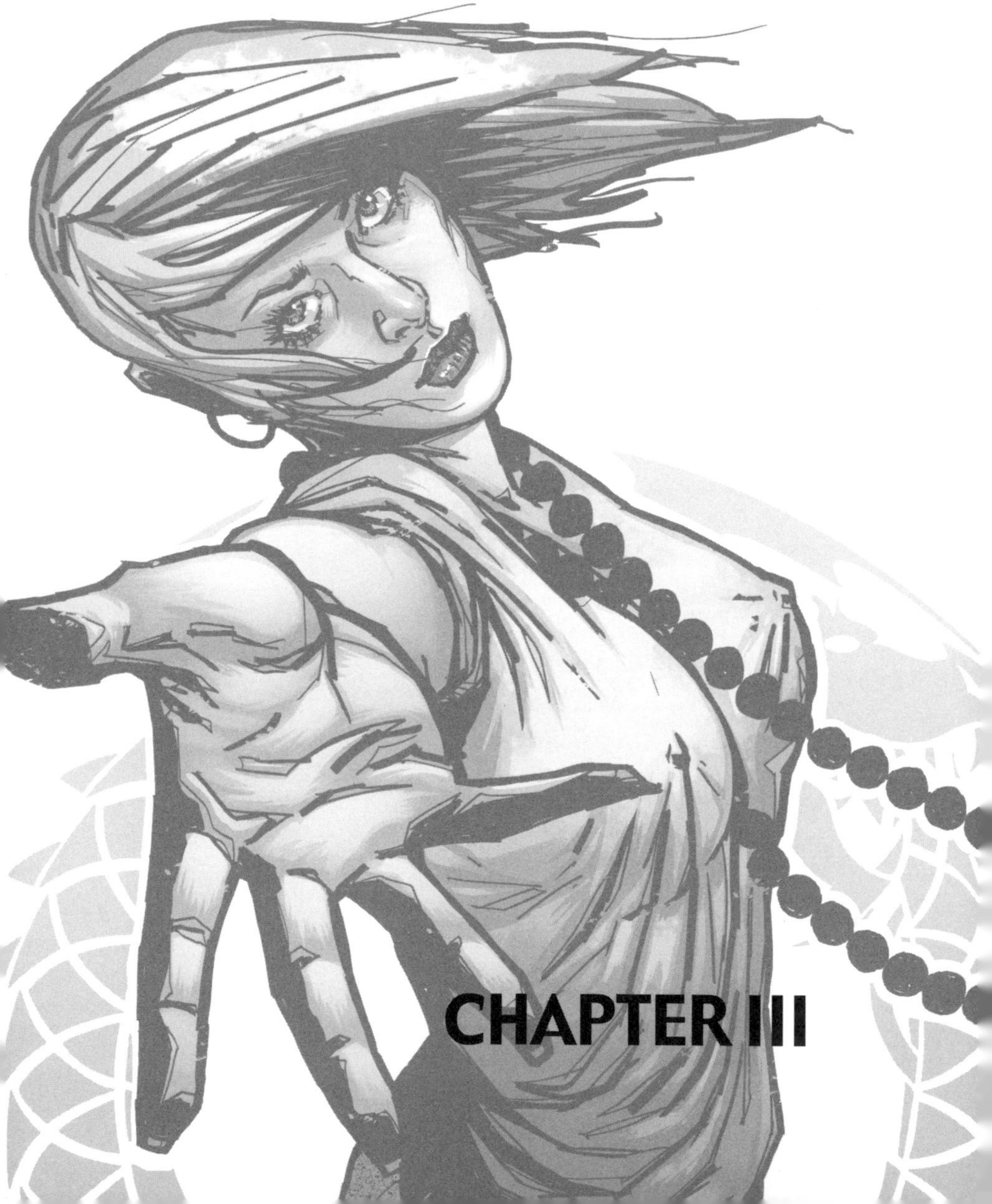

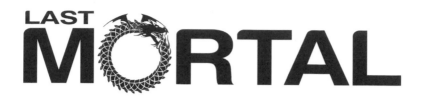

CHAPTER III

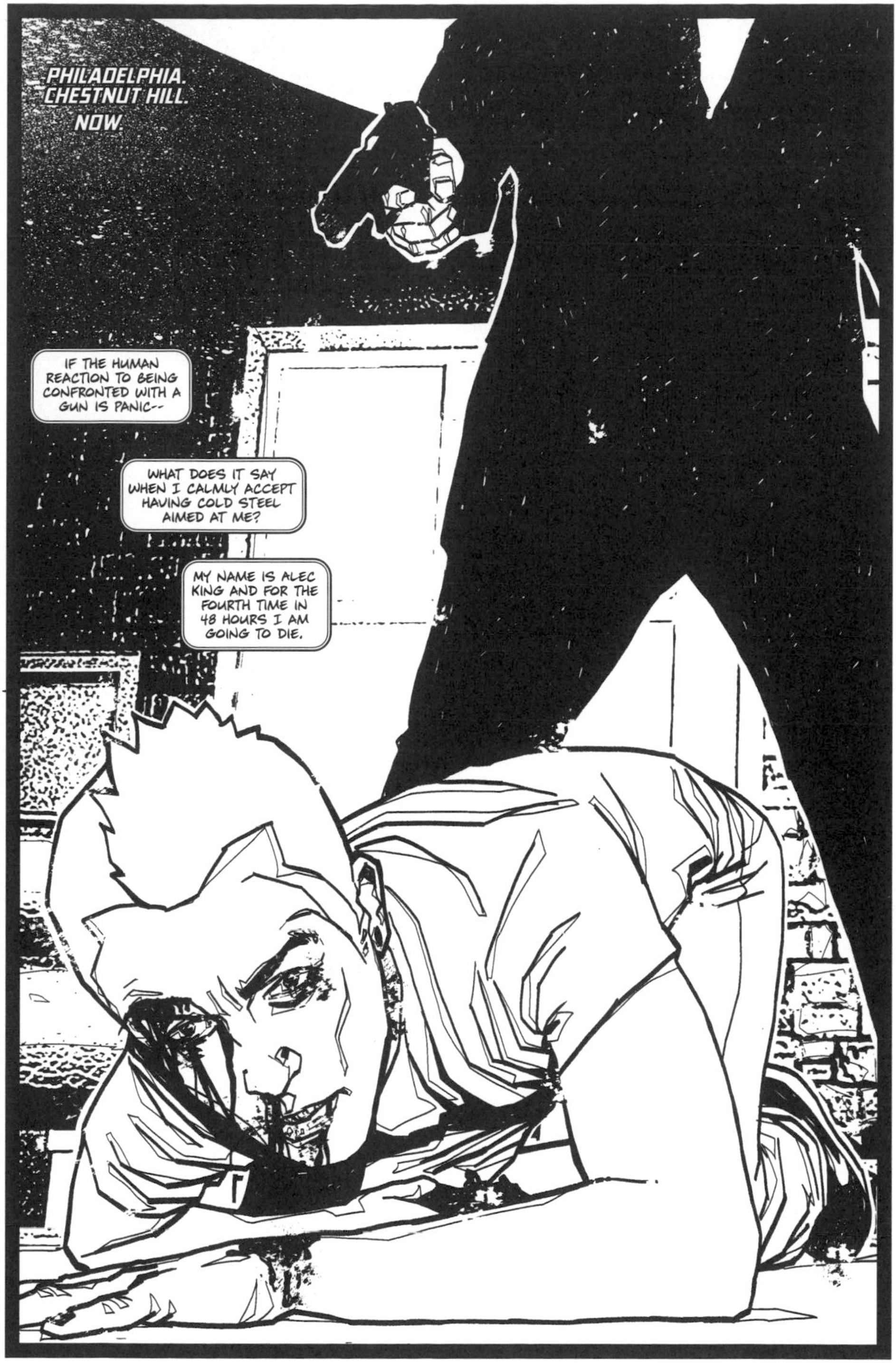
PHILADELPHIA. CHESTNUT HILL. NOW.
IF THE HUMAN REACTION TO BEING CONFRONTED WITH A GUN IS PANIC--
WHAT DOES IT SAY WHEN I CALMLY ACCEPT HAVING COLD STEEL AIMED AT ME?
MY NAME IS ALEC KING AND FOR THE FOURTH TIME IN 48 HOURS I AM GOING TO DIE.

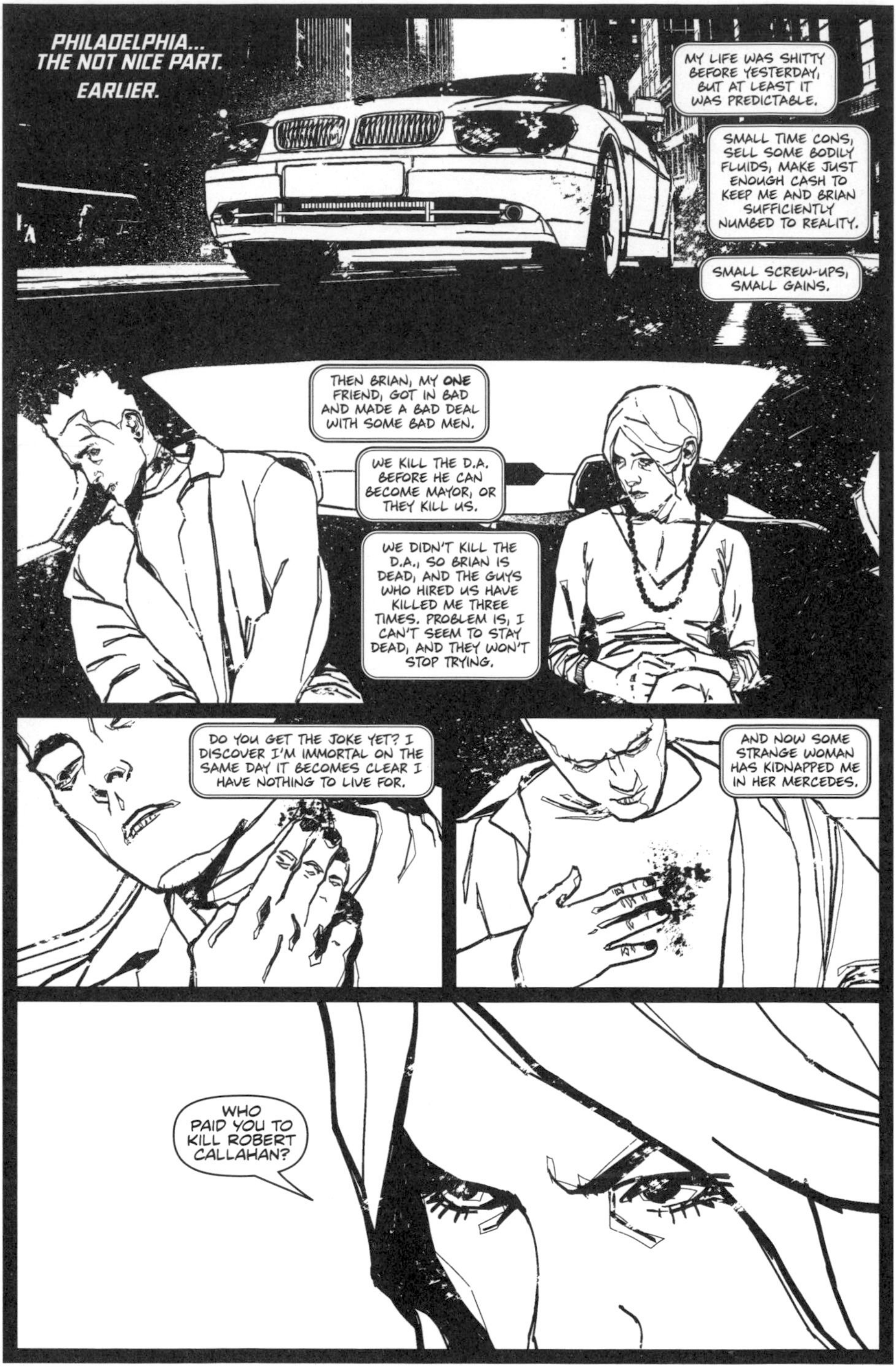
PHILADELPHIA... THE NOT NICE PART.
EARLIER.
MY LIFE WAS SHITTY BEFORE YESTERDAY, BUT AT LEAST IT WAS PREDICTABLE.
SMALL TIME CONS, SELL SOME BODILY FLUIDS, MAKE JUST ENOUGH CASH TO KEEP ME AND BRIAN SUFFICIENTLY NUMBED TO REALITY.
SMALL SCREW-UPS, SMALL GAINS.
THEN BRIAN, MY **ONE** FRIEND, GOT IN BAD AND MADE A BAD DEAL WITH SOME BAD MEN.
WE KILL THE D.A. BEFORE HE CAN BECOME MAYOR, OR THEY KILL US.
WE DIDN'T KILL THE D.A., SO BRIAN IS DEAD, AND THE GUYS WHO HIRED US HAVE KILLED ME THREE TIMES. PROBLEM IS, I CAN'T SEEM TO STAY DEAD, AND THEY WON'T STOP TRYING.
DO YOU GET THE JOKE YET? I DISCOVER I'M IMMORTAL ON THE SAME DAY IT BECOMES CLEAR I HAVE NOTHING TO LIVE FOR.
AND NOW SOME STRANGE WOMAN HAS KIDNAPPED ME IN HER MERCEDES.
WHO PAID YOU TO KILL ROBERT CALLAHAN?

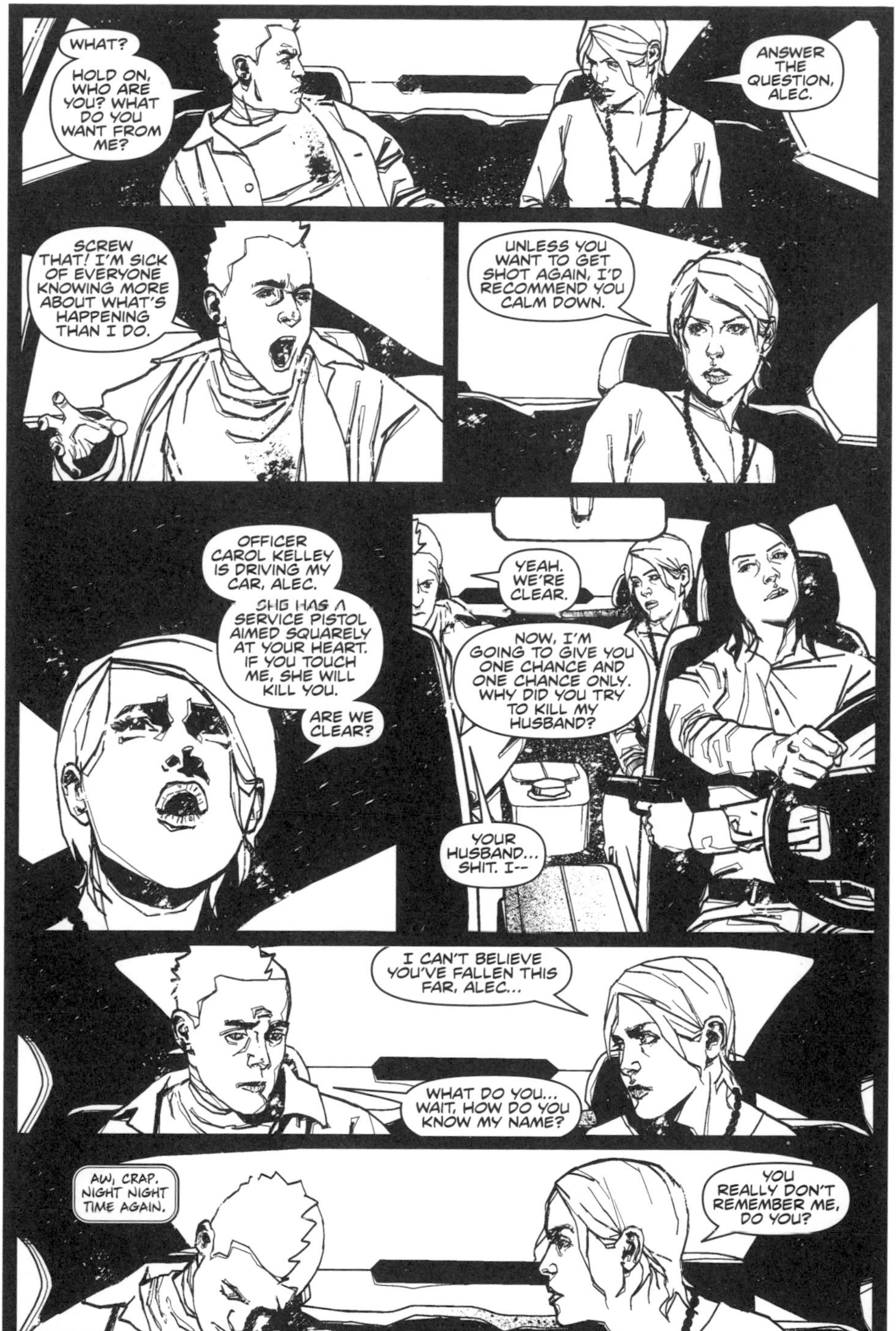
WHAT?
HOLD ON, WHO ARE YOU? WHAT DO YOU WANT FROM ME?
ANSWER THE QUESTION, ALEC.
SCREW THAT! I'M SICK OF EVERYONE KNOWING MORE ABOUT WHAT'S HAPPENING THAN I DO.
UNLESS YOU WANT TO GET SHOT AGAIN, I'D RECOMMEND YOU CALM DOWN.
OFFICER CAROL KELLEY IS DRIVING MY CAR, ALEC.
SHE HAS A SERVICE PISTOL AIMED SQUARELY AT YOUR HEART. IF YOU TOUCH ME, SHE WILL KILL YOU.
ARE WE CLEAR?
YEAH. WE'RE CLEAR.
NOW, I'M GOING TO GIVE YOU ONE CHANCE AND ONE CHANCE ONLY. WHY DID YOU TRY TO KILL MY HUSBAND?
YOUR HUSBAND... SHIT. I--
I CAN'T BELIEVE YOU'VE FALLEN THIS FAR, ALEC...
WHAT DO YOU... WAIT, HOW DO YOU KNOW MY NAME?
AW, CRAP. NIGHT NIGHT TIME AGAIN.
YOU REALLY DON'T REMEMBER ME, DO YOU?

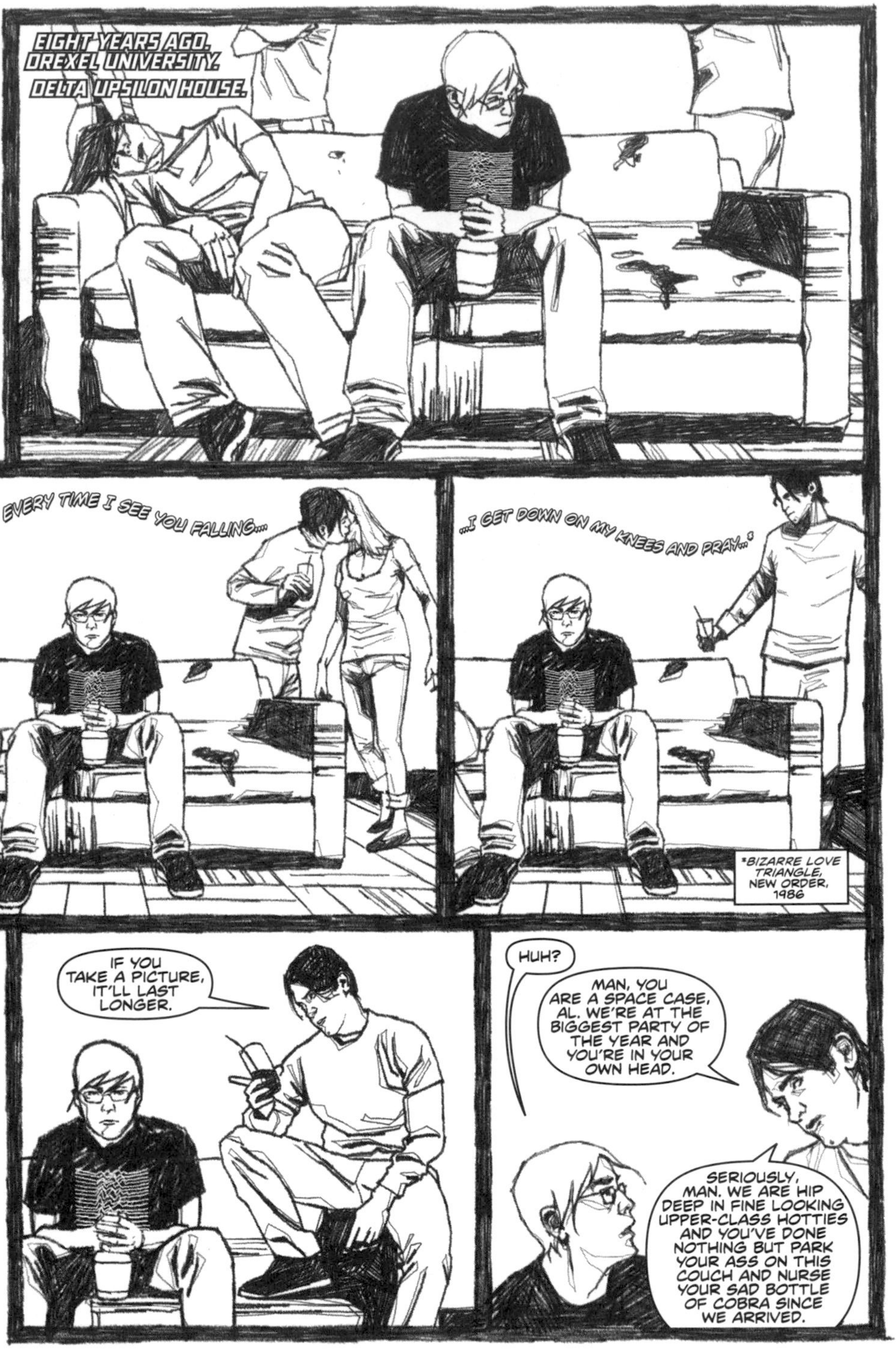
EIGHT YEARS AGO. DREXEL UNIVERSITY.
DELTA UPSILON HOUSE.
EVERY TIME I SEE YOU FALLING...
...I GET DOWN ON MY KNEES AND PRAY...*
*BIZARRE LOVE TRIANGLE, NEW ORDER, 1986
IF YOU TAKE A PICTURE, IT'LL LAST LONGER.
HUH?
MAN, YOU ARE A SPACE CASE, AL. WE'RE AT THE BIGGEST PARTY OF THE YEAR AND YOU'RE IN YOUR OWN HEAD.
SERIOUSLY, MAN. WE ARE HIP DEEP IN FINE LOOKING UPPER-CLASS HOTTIES AND YOU'VE DONE NOTHING BUT PARK YOUR ASS ON THIS COUCH AND NURSE YOUR SAD BOTTLE OF COBRA SINCE WE ARRIVED.

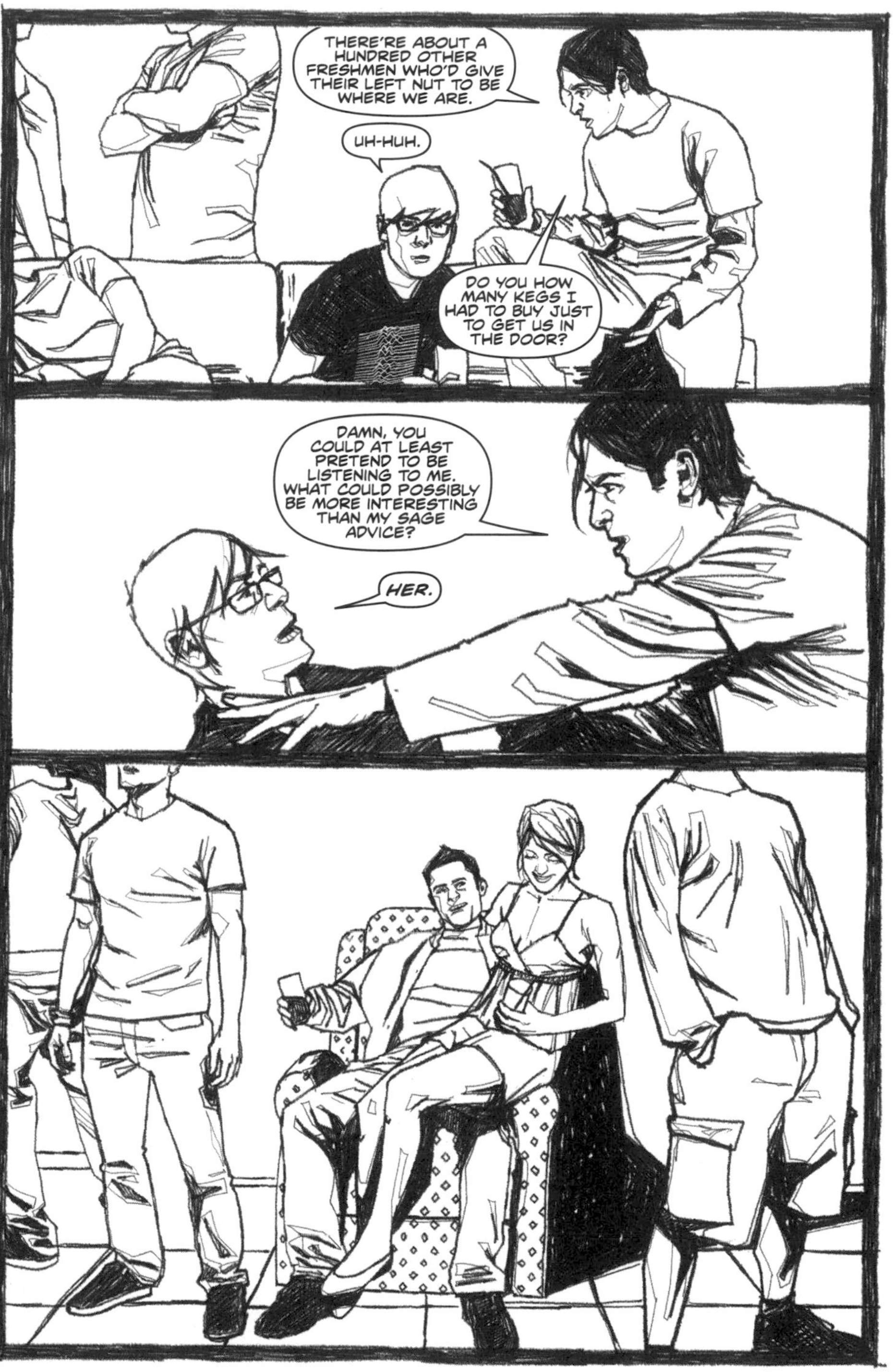
THERE'RE ABOUT A HUNDRED OTHER FRESHMEN WHO'D GIVE THEIR LEFT NUT TO BE WHERE WE ARE.
UH-HUH.
DO YOU HOW MANY KEGS I HAD TO BUY JUST TO GET US IN THE DOOR?
DAMN, YOU COULD AT LEAST PRETEND TO BE LISTENING TO ME. WHAT COULD POSSIBLY BE MORE INTERESTING THAN MY SAGE ADVICE?
HER.

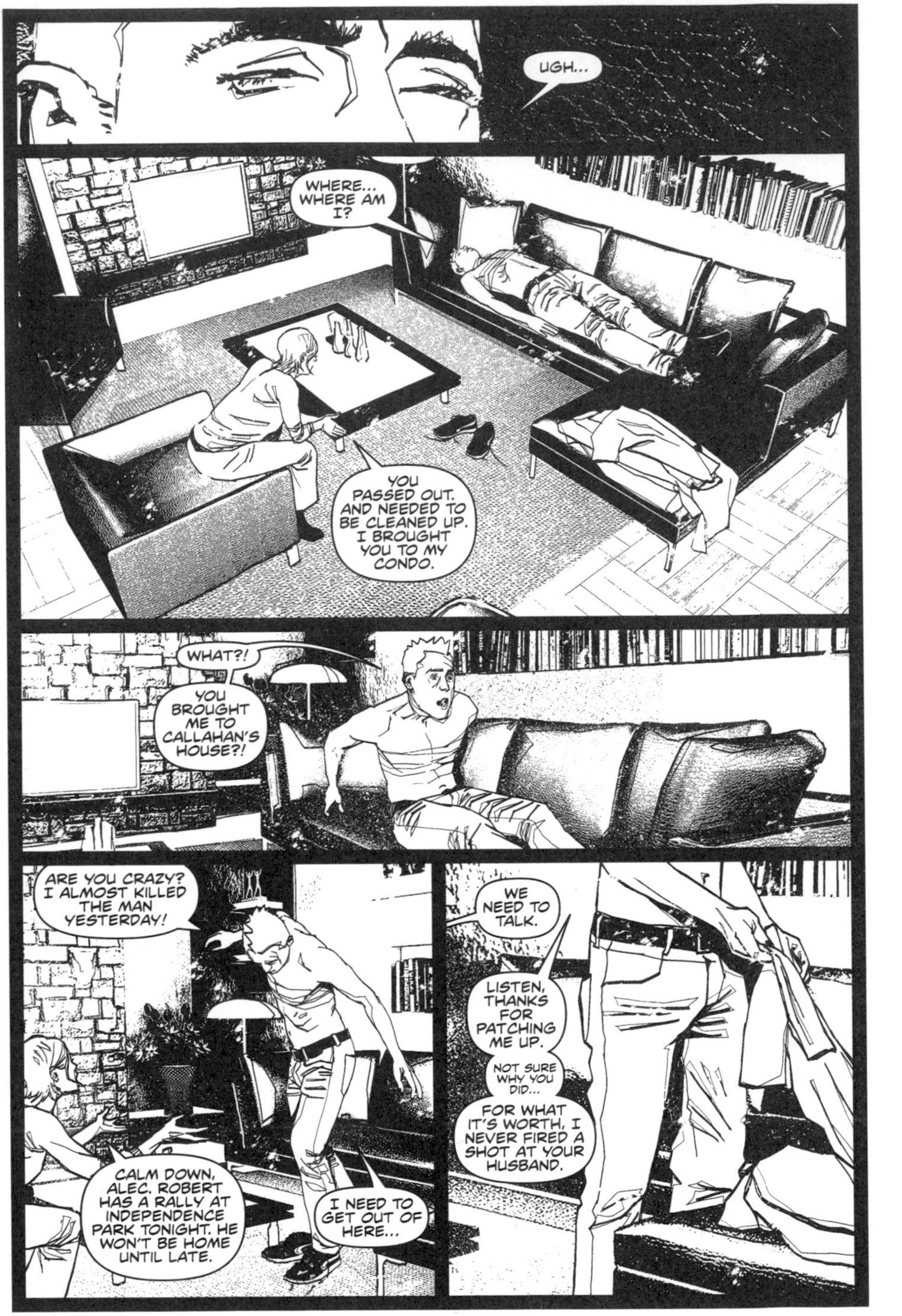
UGH...
WHERE... WHERE AM I?
YOU PASSED OUT. AND NEEDED TO BE CLEANED UP. I BROUGHT YOU TO MY CONDO.
WHAT?!
YOU BROUGHT ME TO CALLAHAN'S HOUSE?!
ARE YOU CRAZY? I ALMOST KILLED THE MAN YESTERDAY!
CALM DOWN, ALEC. ROBERT HAS A RALLY AT INDEPENDENCE PARK TONIGHT. HE WON'T BE HOME UNTIL LATE.
I NEED TO GET OUT OF HERE...
WE NEED TO TALK.
LISTEN, THANKS FOR PATCHING ME UP.
NOT SURE WHY YOU DID...
FOR WHAT IT'S WORTH, I NEVER FIRED A SHOT AT YOUR HUSBAND.

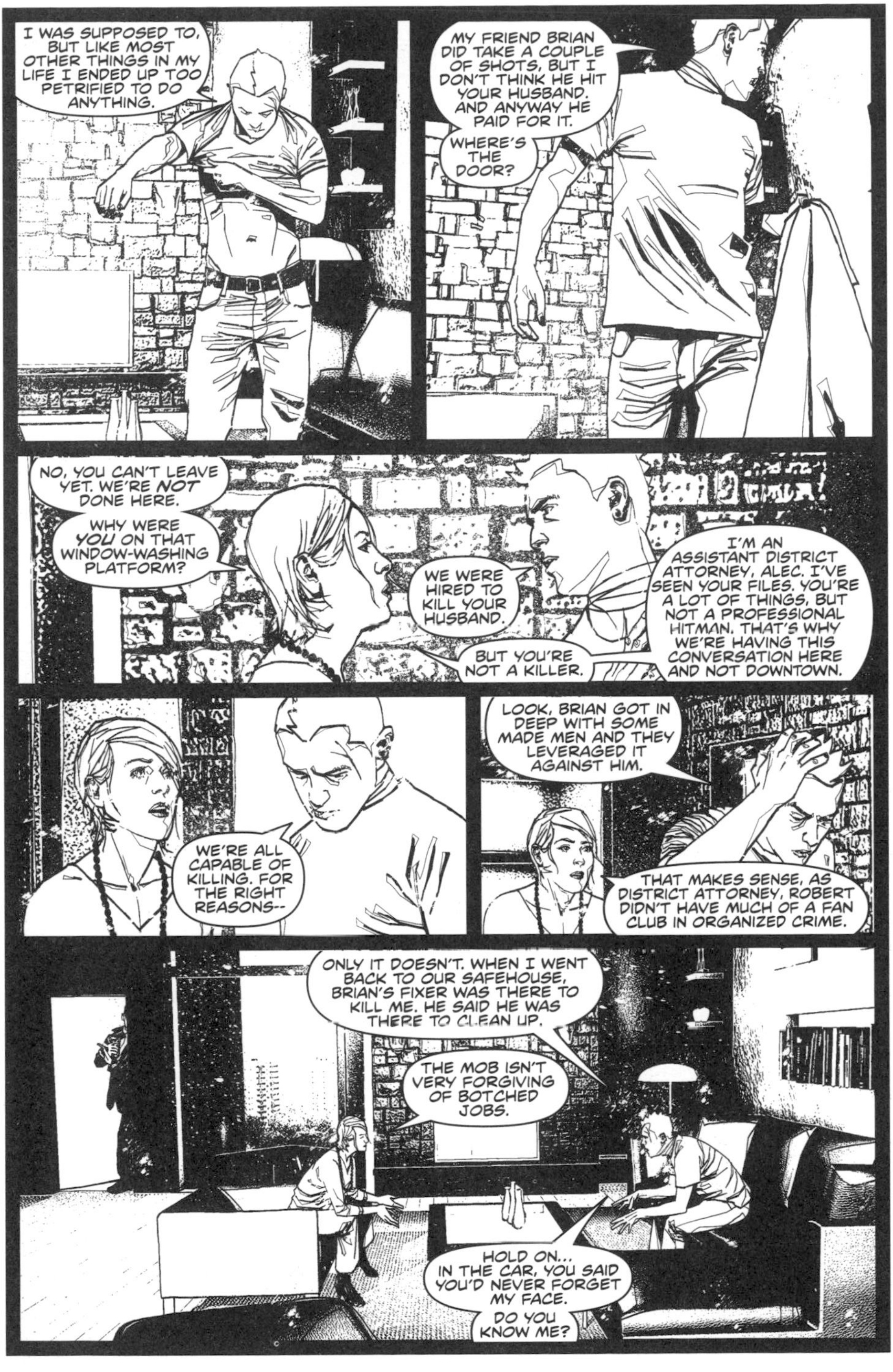
I WAS SUPPOSED TO, BUT LIKE MOST OTHER THINGS IN MY LIFE I ENDED UP TOO PETRIFIED TO DO ANYTHING.
MY FRIEND BRIAN DID TAKE A COUPLE OF SHOTS, BUT I DON'T THINK HE HIT YOUR HUSBAND. AND ANYWAY HE PAID FOR IT.
WHERE'S THE DOOR?
NO, YOU CAN'T LEAVE YET. WE'RE NOT DONE HERE.
WHY WERE YOU ON THAT WINDOW-WASHING PLATFORM?
WE WERE HIRED TO KILL YOUR HUSBAND.
BUT YOU'RE NOT A KILLER.
I'M AN ASSISTANT DISTRICT ATTORNEY, ALEC. I'VE SEEN YOUR FILES. YOU'RE A LOT OF THINGS, BUT NOT A PROFESSIONAL HITMAN. THAT'S WHY WE'RE HAVING THIS CONVERSATION HERE AND NOT DOWNTOWN.
WE'RE ALL CAPABLE OF KILLING. FOR THE RIGHT REASONS--
LOOK, BRIAN GOT IN DEEP WITH SOME MADE MEN AND THEY LEVERAGED IT AGAINST HIM.
THAT MAKES SENSE, AS DISTRICT ATTORNEY, ROBERT DIDN'T HAVE MUCH OF A FAN CLUB IN ORGANIZED CRIME.
ONLY IT DOESN'T. WHEN I WENT BACK TO OUR SAFEHOUSE, BRIAN'S FIXER WAS THERE TO KILL ME. HE SAID HE WAS THERE TO CLEAN UP.
THE MOB ISN'T VERY FORGIVING OF BOTCHED JOBS.
HOLD ON... IN THE CAR, YOU SAID YOU'D NEVER FORGET MY FACE.
DO YOU KNOW ME?

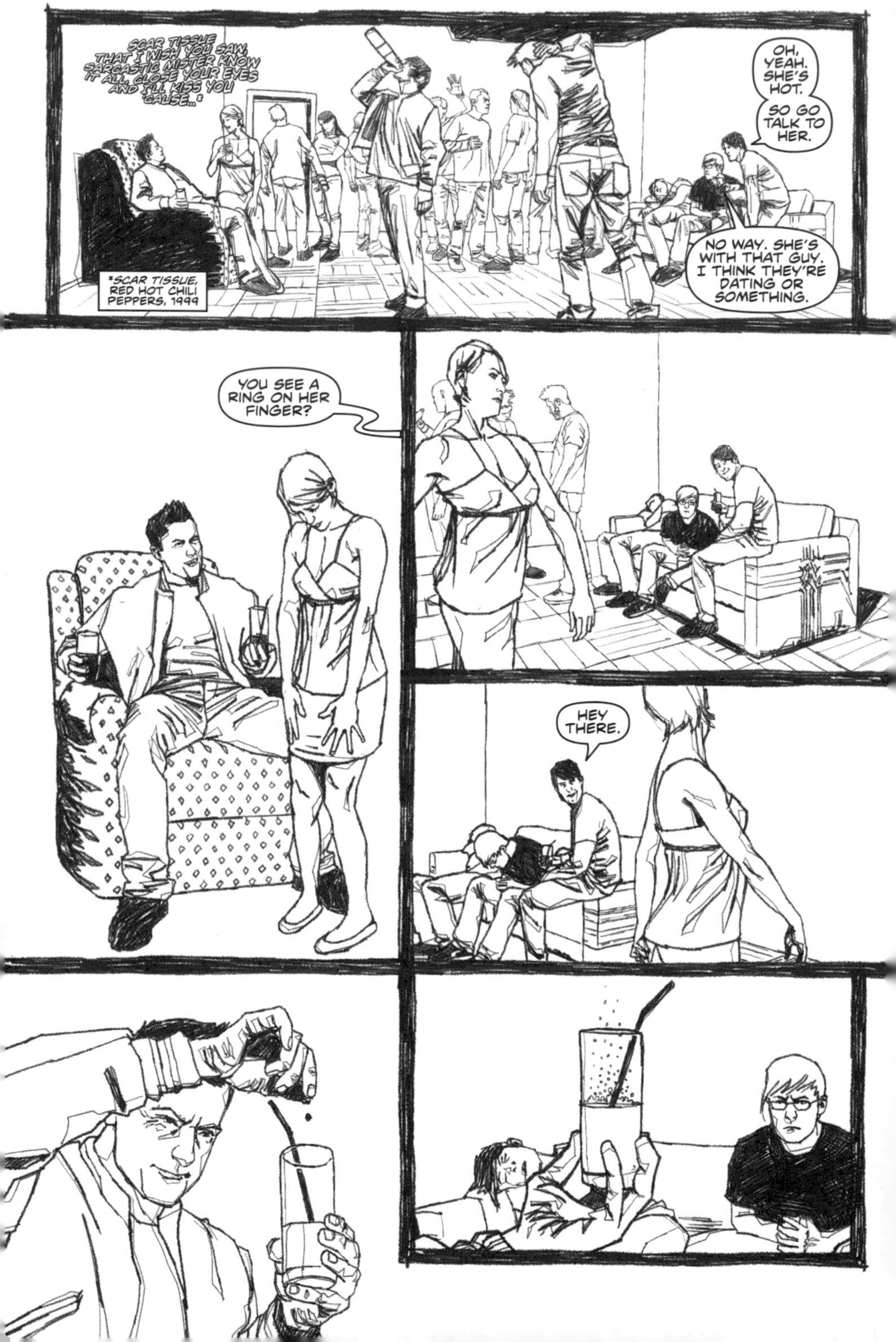
SCAR TISSUE THAT I WISH YOU SAW, SARCASTIC MISTER KNOW IT ALL, CLOSE YOUR EYES AND I'LL KISS YOU 'CAUSE...*
*SCAR TISSUE, RED HOT CHILI PEPPERS, 1999
OH, YEAH. SHE'S HOT.
SO GO TALK TO HER.
NO WAY. SHE'S WITH THAT GUY. I THINK THEY'RE DATING OR SOMETHING.
YOU SEE A RING ON HER FINGER?
HEY THERE.

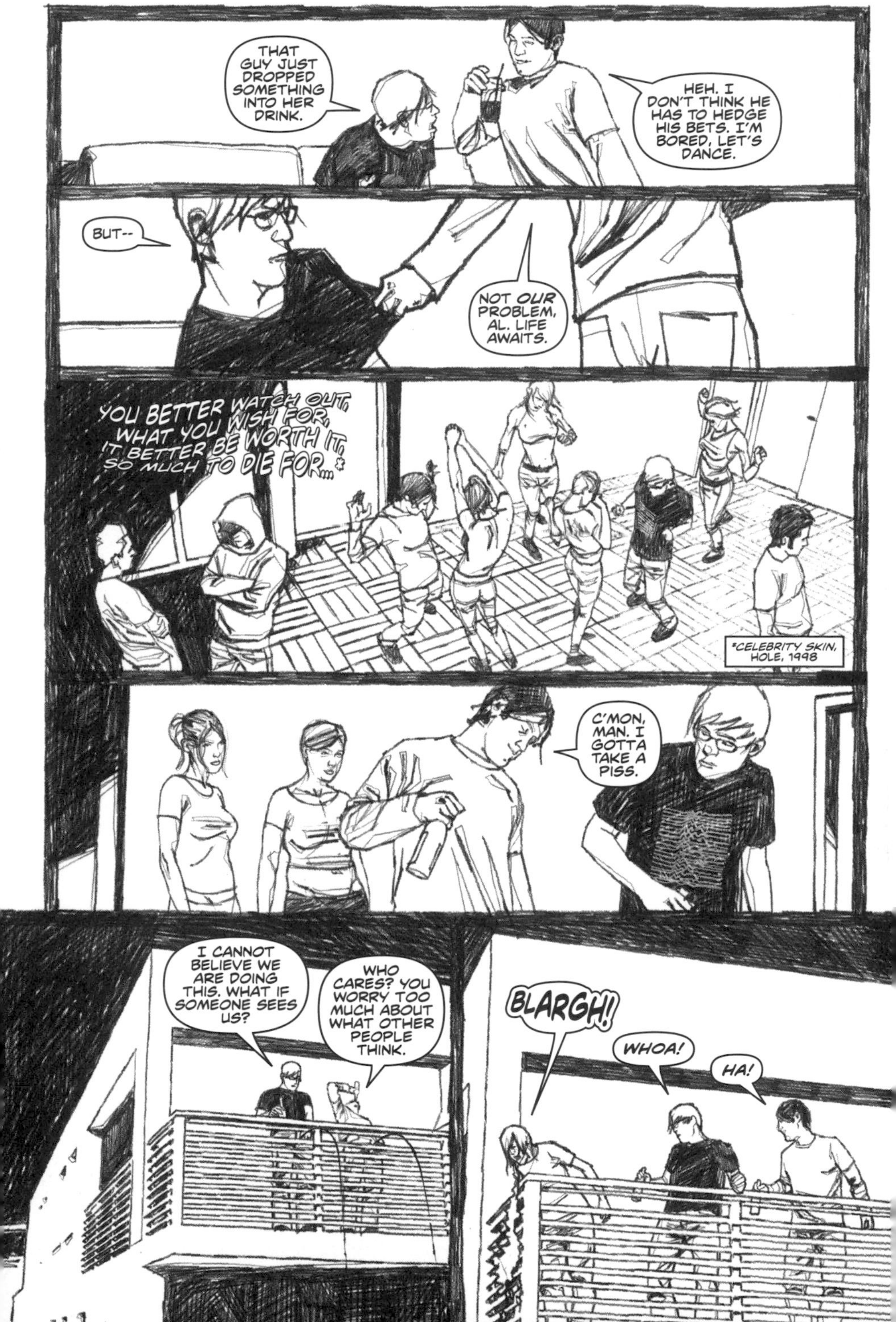
THAT GUY JUST DROPPED SOMETHING INTO HER DRINK.
HEH. I DON'T THINK HE HAS TO HEDGE HIS BETS. I'M BORED, LET'S DANCE.
BUT--
NOT OUR PROBLEM, AL. LIFE AWAITS.
YOU BETTER WATCH OUT, WHAT YOU WISH FOR, IT BETTER BE WORTH IT, SO MUCH TO DIE FOR...*
*CELEBRITY SKIN, HOLE, 1998
C'MON, MAN. I GOTTA TAKE A PISS.
I CANNOT BELIEVE WE ARE DOING THIS. WHAT IF SOMEONE SEES US?
WHO CARES? YOU WORRY TOO MUCH ABOUT WHAT OTHER PEOPLE THINK.
BLARGH!
WHOA!
HA!

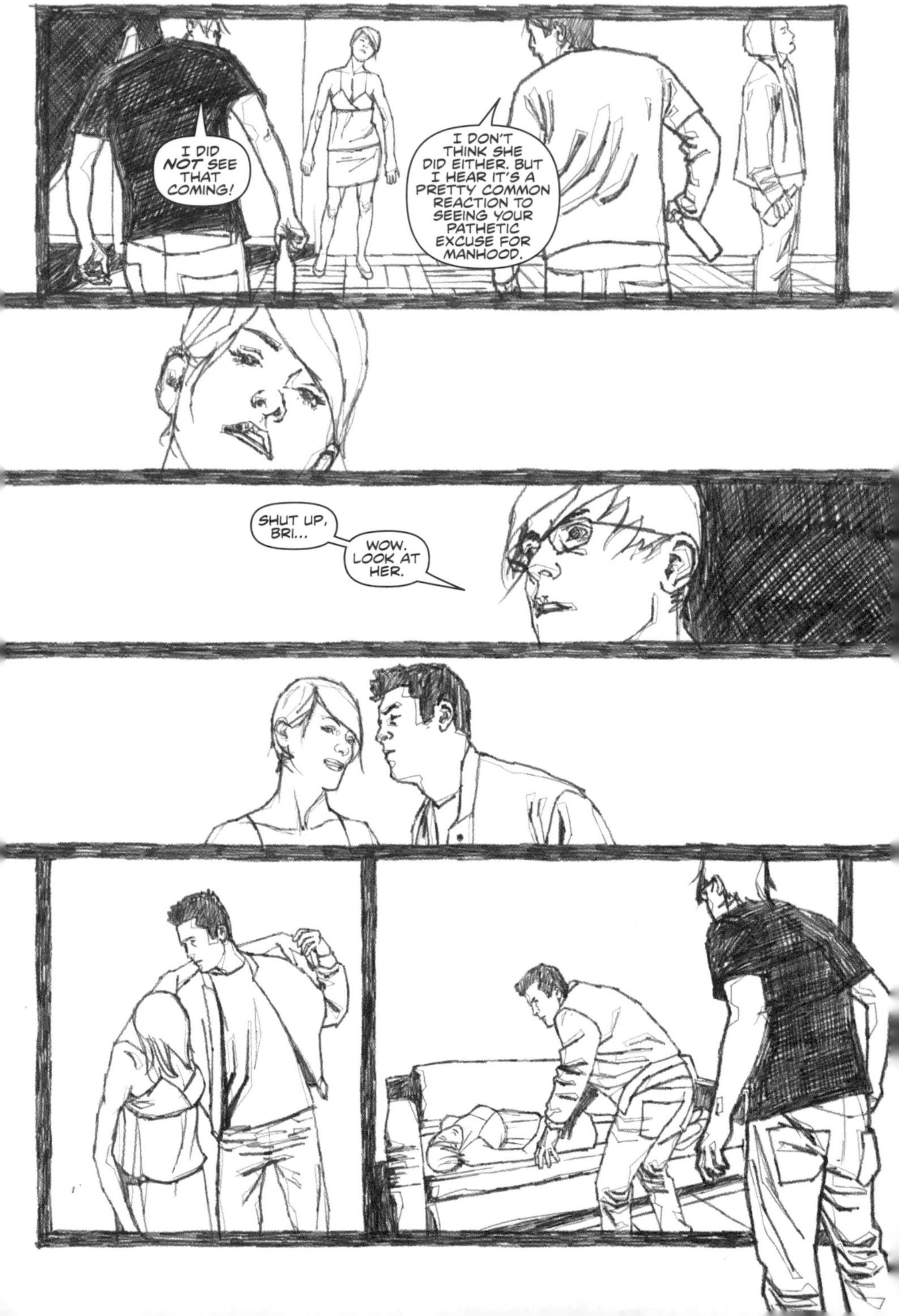
I DID *NOT* SEE THAT COMING!
I DON'T THINK SHE DID EITHER. BUT I HEAR IT'S A PRETTY COMMON REACTION TO SEEING YOUR PATHETIC EXCUSE FOR MANHOOD.
SHUT UP, BRI...
WOW. LOOK AT HER.

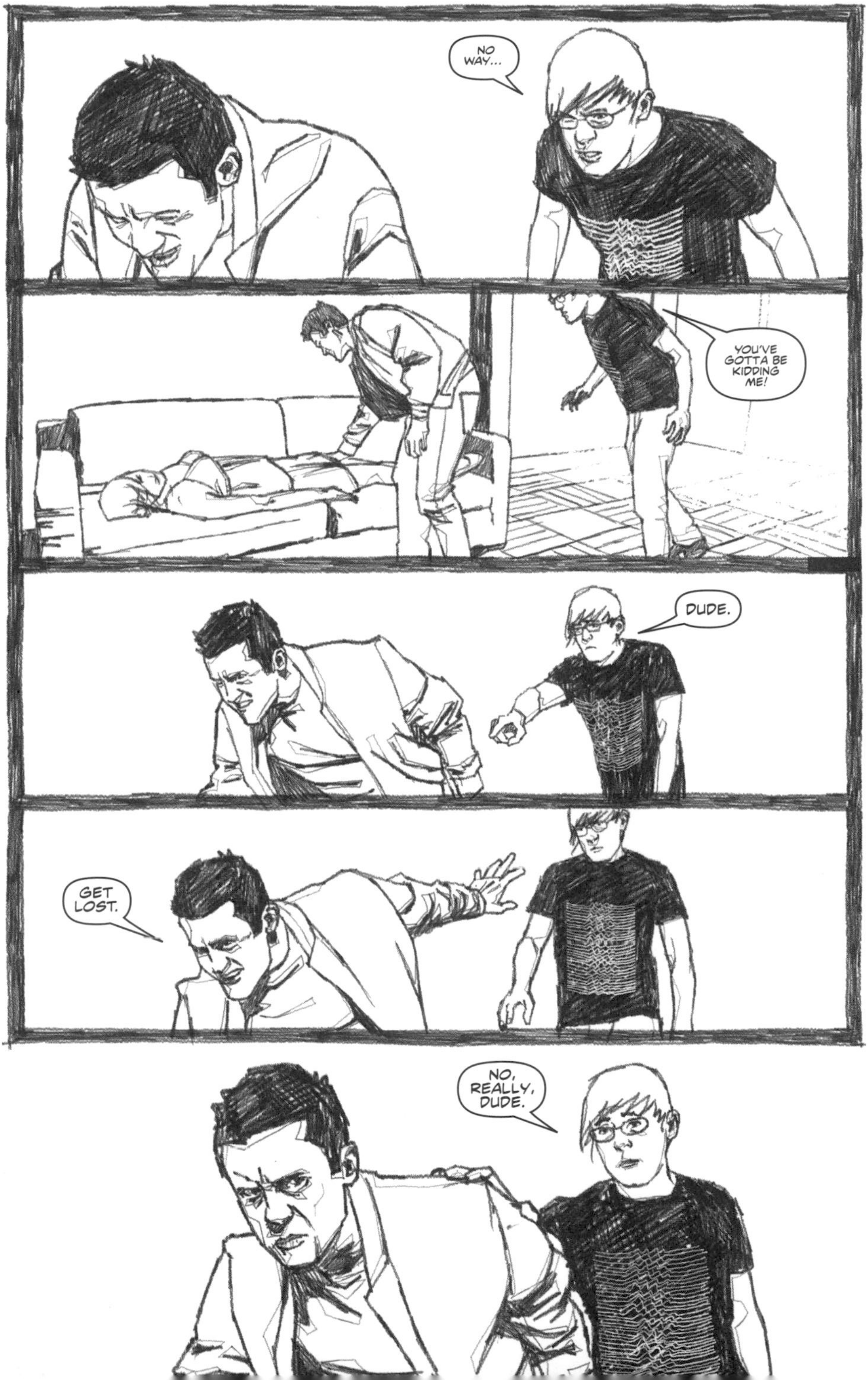
NO WAY...
YOU'VE GOTTA BE KIDDING ME!
DUDE.
GET LOST.
NO, REALLY, DUDE.

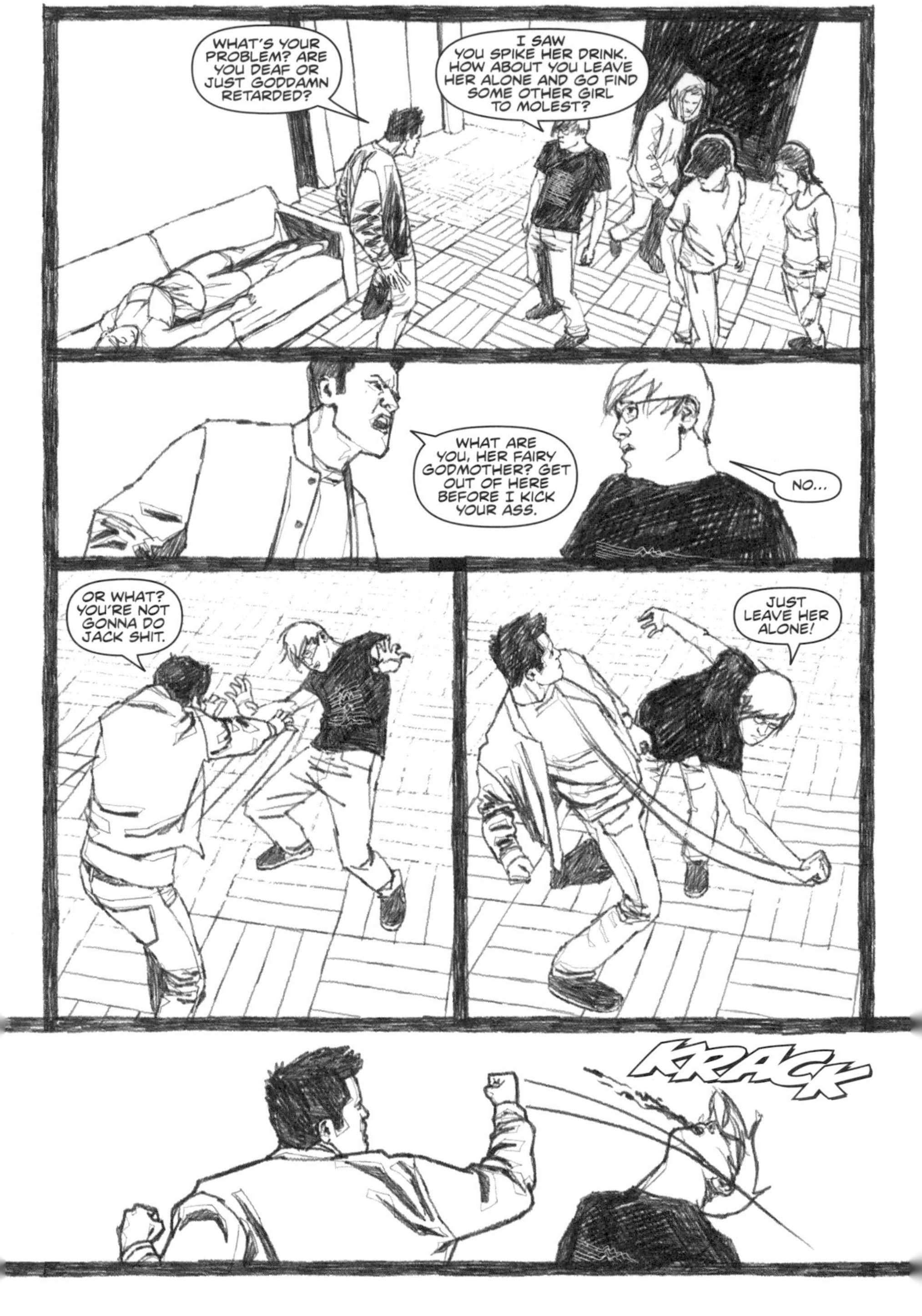
WHAT'S YOUR PROBLEM? ARE YOU DEAF OR JUST GODDAMN RETARDED?
I SAW YOU SPIKE HER DRINK. HOW ABOUT YOU LEAVE HER ALONE AND GO FIND SOME OTHER GIRL TO MOLEST?
WHAT ARE YOU, HER FAIRY GODMOTHER? GET OUT OF HERE BEFORE I KICK YOUR ASS.
NO...
OR WHAT? YOU'RE NOT GONNA DO JACK SHIT.
JUST LEAVE HER ALONE!
KRACK

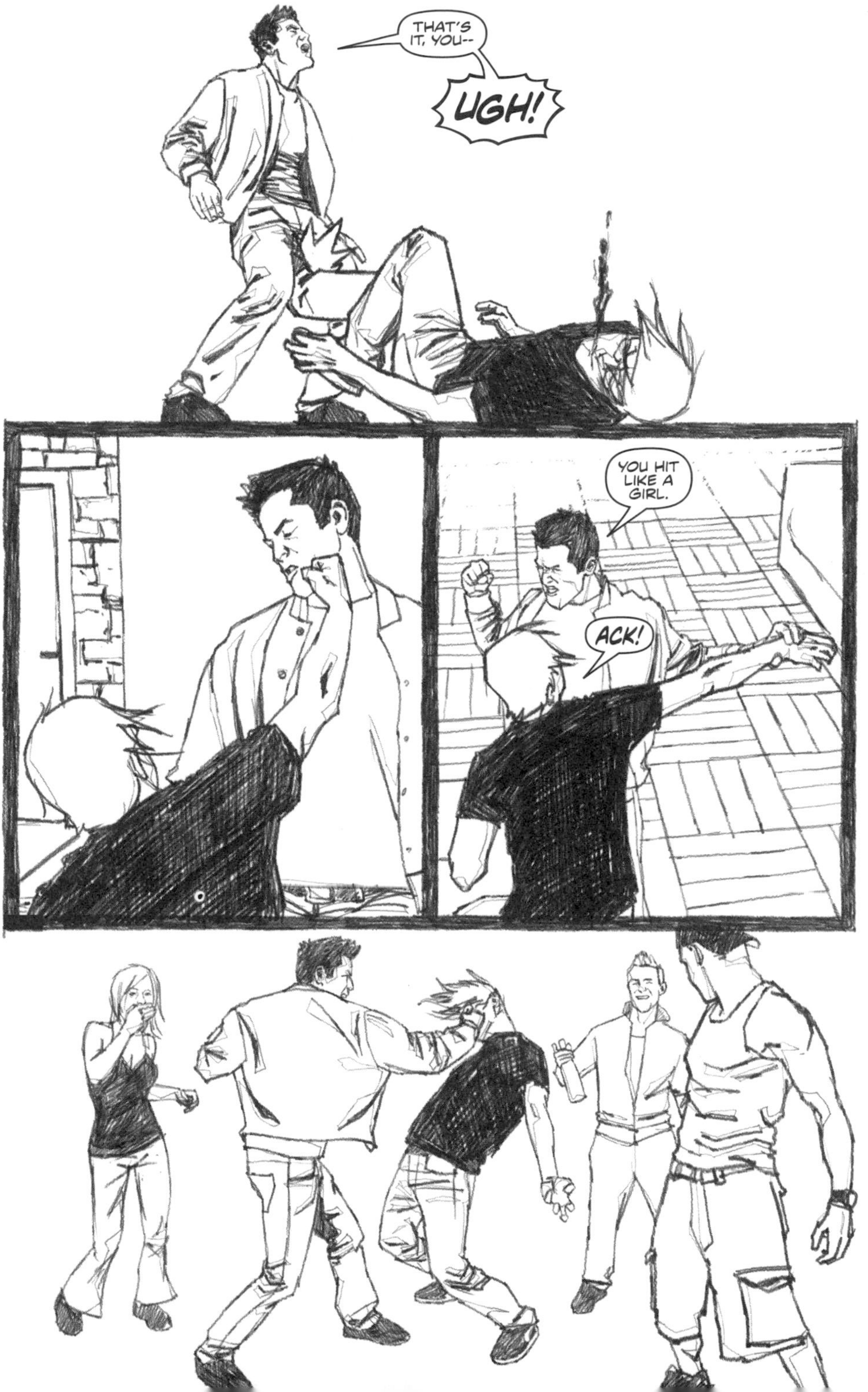
THAT'S IT, YOU--
UGH!
YOU HIT LIKE A GIRL.
ACK!

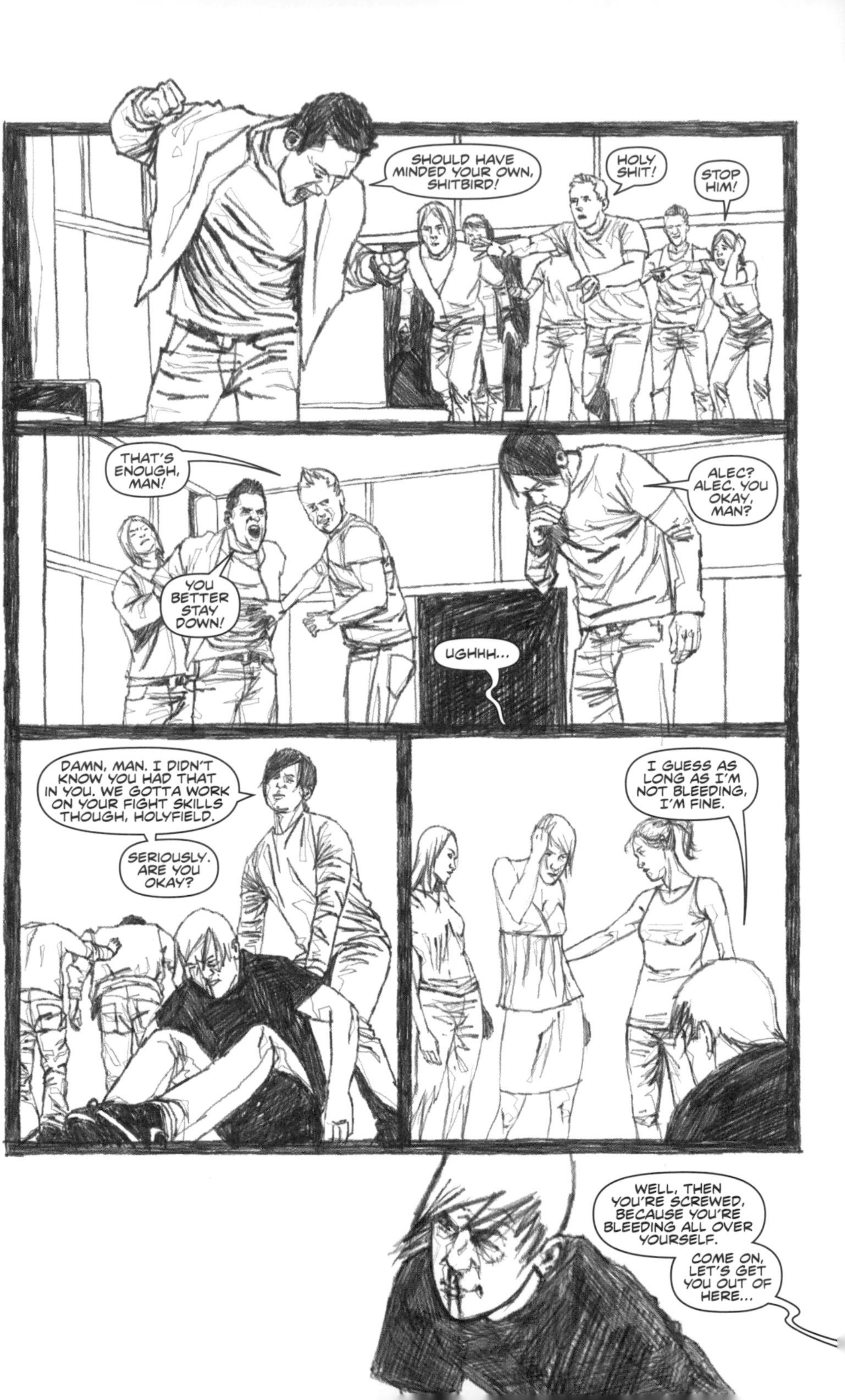
SHOULD HAVE MINDED YOUR OWN, SHITBIRD!
HOLY SHIT!
STOP HIM!
THAT'S ENOUGH, MAN!
YOU BETTER STAY DOWN!
ALEC? ALEC. YOU OKAY, MAN?
UGHHH...
DAMN, MAN. I DIDN'T KNOW YOU HAD THAT IN YOU. WE GOTTA WORK ON YOUR FIGHT SKILLS THOUGH, HOLYFIELD.
SERIOUSLY. ARE YOU OKAY?
I GUESS AS LONG AS I'M NOT BLEEDING, I'M FINE.
WELL, THEN YOU'RE SCREWED, BECAUSE YOU'RE BLEEDING ALL OVER YOURSELF.
COME ON, LET'S GET YOU OUT OF HERE...

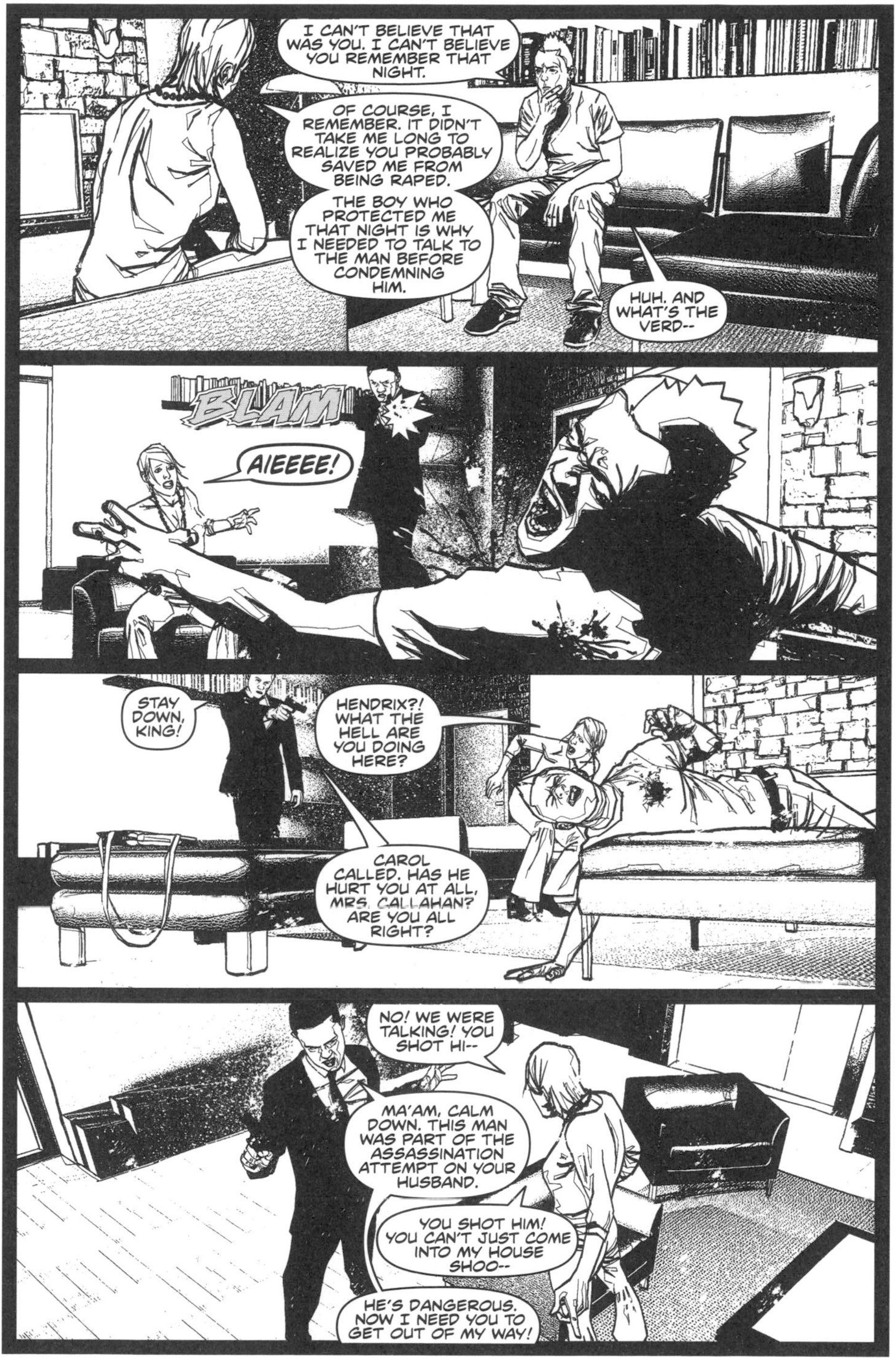
I CAN'T BELIEVE THAT WAS YOU. I CAN'T BELIEVE YOU REMEMBER THAT NIGHT.
OF COURSE, I REMEMBER. IT DIDN'T TAKE ME LONG TO REALIZE YOU PROBABLY SAVED ME FROM BEING RAPED.
THE BOY WHO PROTECTED ME THAT NIGHT IS WHY I NEEDED TO TALK TO THE MAN BEFORE CONDEMNING HIM.
HUH. AND WHAT'S THE VERD--
BLAM
AIEEEE!
STAY DOWN, KING!
HENDRIX?! WHAT THE HELL ARE YOU DOING HERE?
CAROL CALLED. HAS HE HURT YOU AT ALL, MRS. CALLAHAN? ARE YOU ALL RIGHT?
NO! WE WERE TALKING! YOU SHOT HI--
MA'AM, CALM DOWN. THIS MAN WAS PART OF THE ASSASSINATION ATTEMPT ON YOUR HUSBAND.
YOU SHOT HIM! YOU CAN'T JUST COME INTO MY HOUSE SHOO--
HE'S DANGEROUS. NOW I NEED YOU TO GET OUT OF MY WAY!

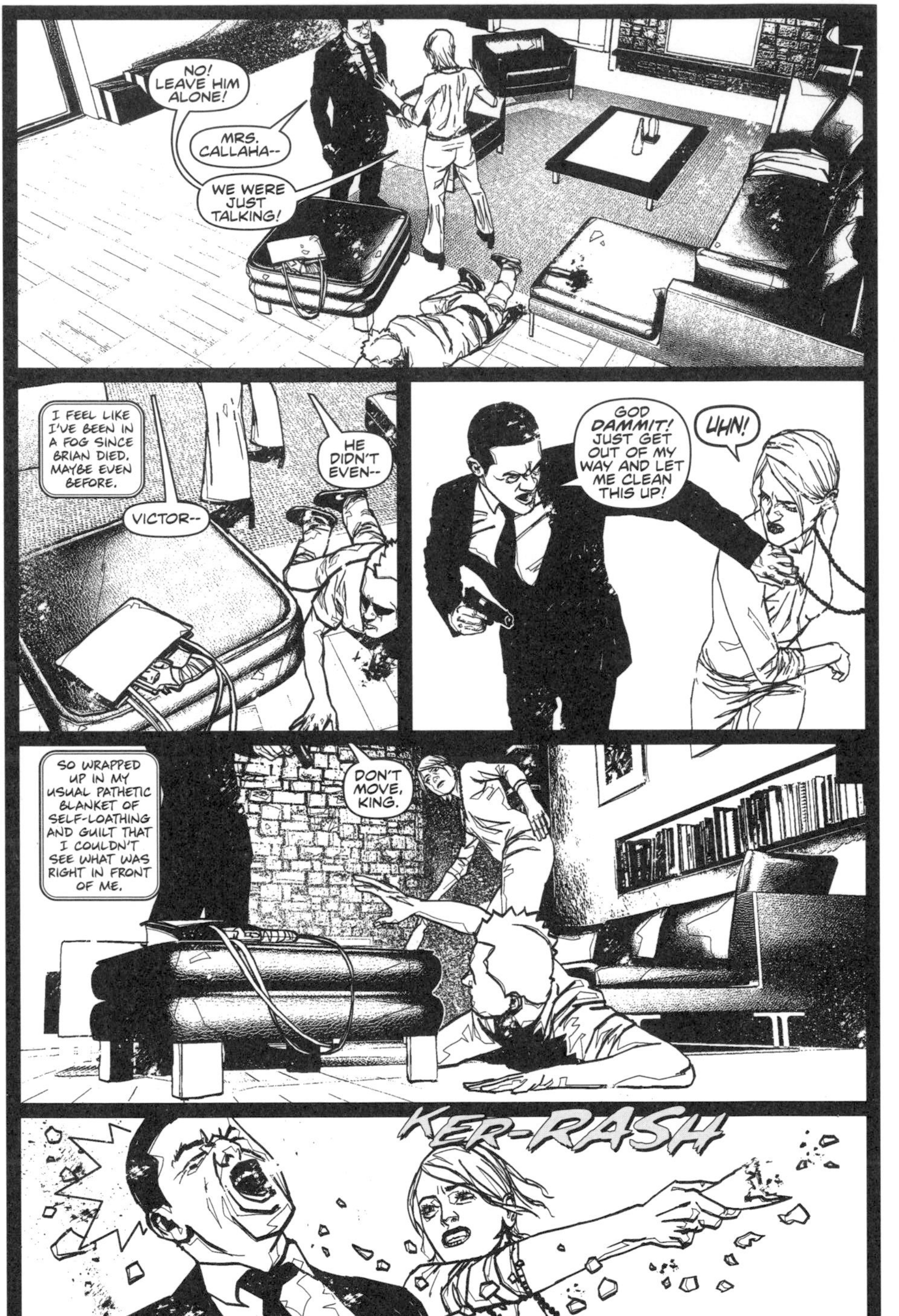
NO! LEAVE HIM ALONE!
MRS. CALLAHA--
WE WERE JUST TALKING!
I FEEL LIKE I'VE BEEN IN A FOG SINCE BRIAN DIED. MAYBE EVEN BEFORE.
HE DIDN'T EVEN--
VICTOR--
GOD DAMMIT! JUST GET OUT OF MY WAY AND LET ME CLEAN THIS UP!
UHN!
SO WRAPPED UP IN MY USUAL PATHETIC BLANKET OF SELF-LOATHING AND GUILT THAT I COULDN'T SEE WHAT WAS RIGHT IN FRONT OF ME.
DON'T MOVE, KING.
KER-RASH

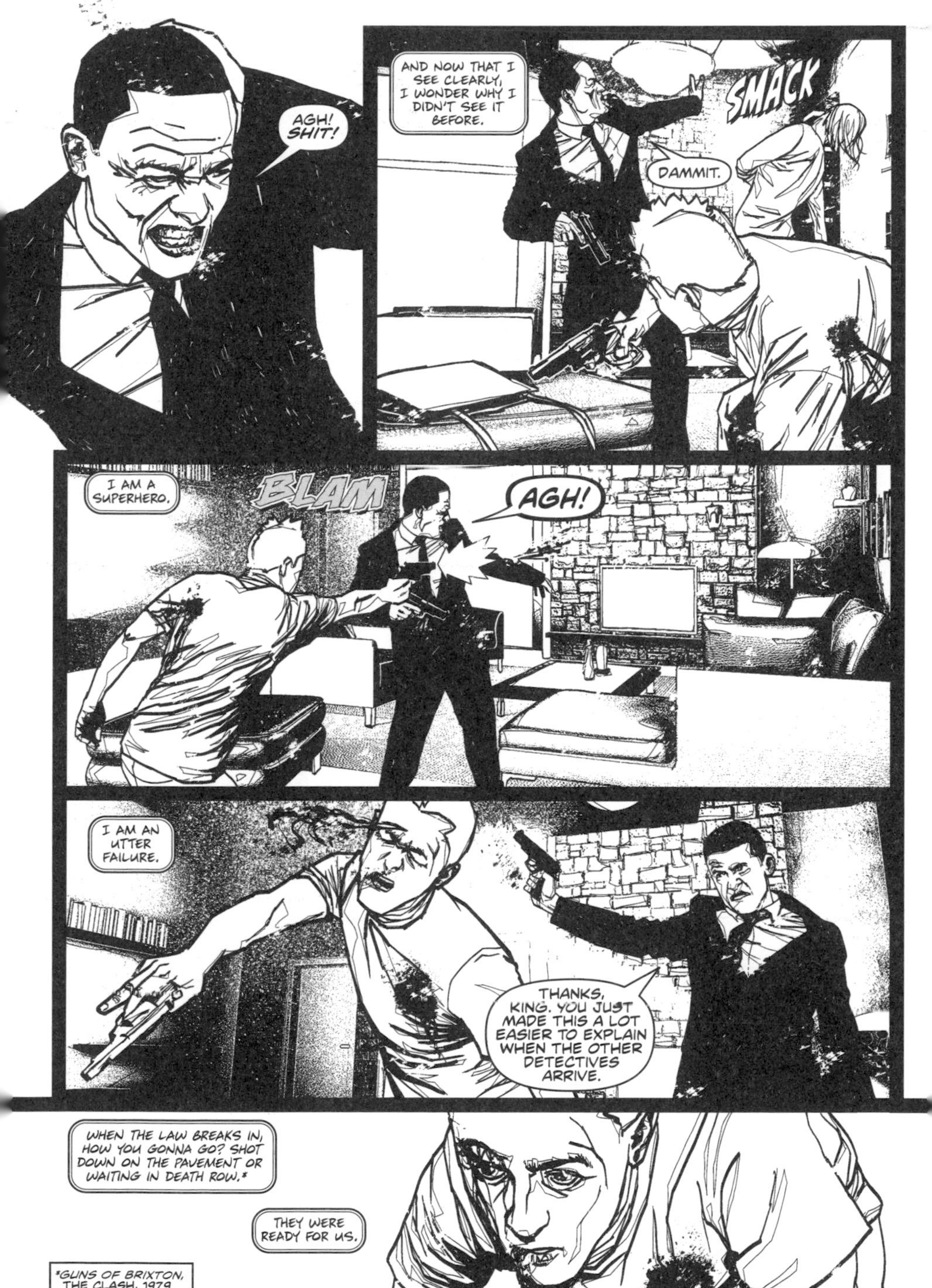
AGH! SHIT!
AND NOW THAT I SEE CLEARLY, I WONDER WHY I DIDN'T SEE IT BEFORE.
SMACK
DAMMIT.
I AM A SUPERHERO.
BLAM
AGH!
I AM AN UTTER FAILURE.
THANKS, KING. YOU JUST MADE THIS A LOT EASIER TO EXPLAIN WHEN THE OTHER DETECTIVES ARRIVE.
WHEN THE LAW BREAKS IN, HOW YOU GONNA GO? SHOT DOWN ON THE PAVEMENT OR WAITING IN DEATH ROW.*
THEY WERE READY FOR US.
*GUNS OF BRIXTON, THE CLASH, 1979

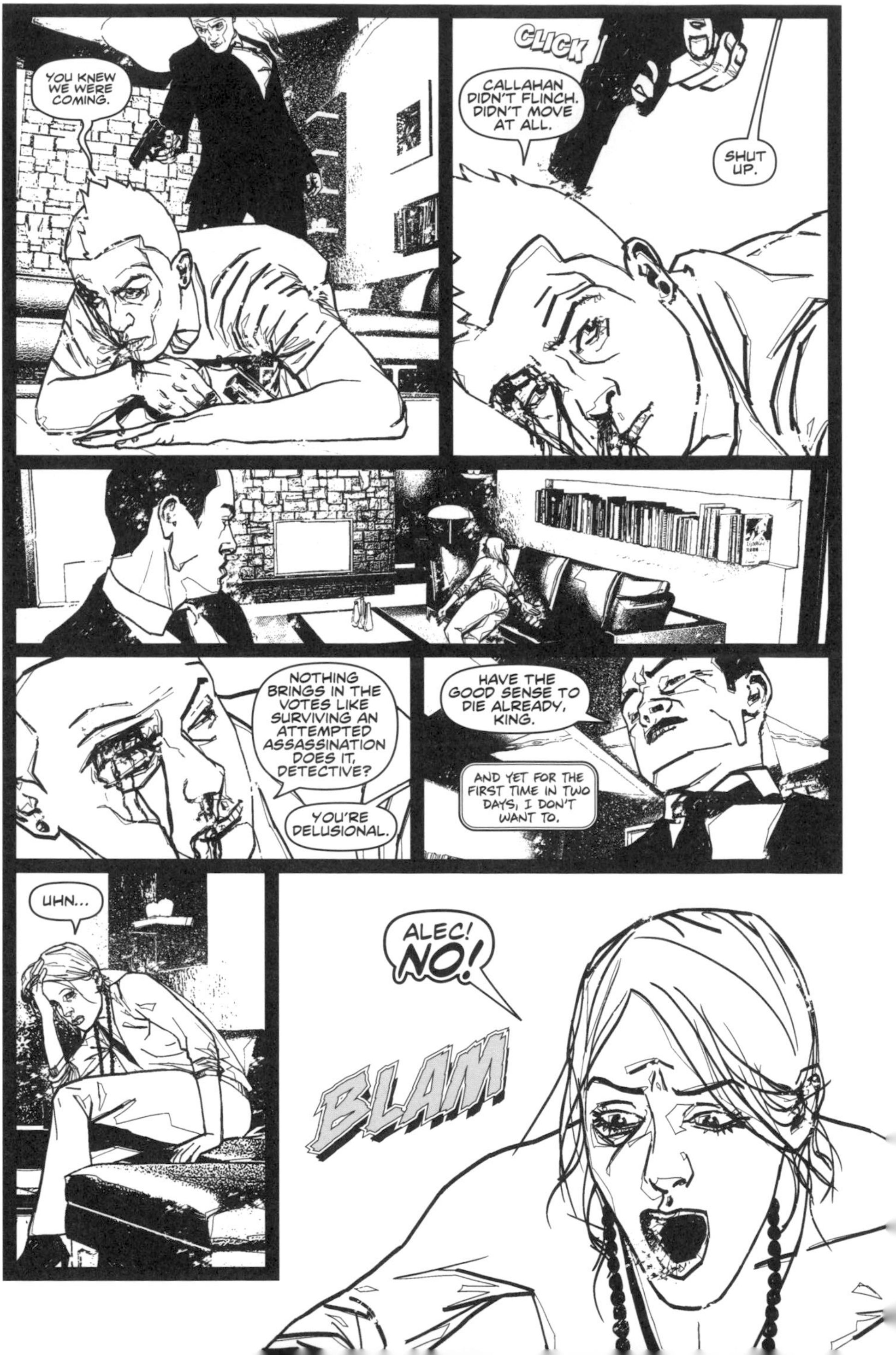
YOU KNEW WE WERE COMING.
CLICK
CALLAHAN DIDN'T FLINCH. DIDN'T MOVE AT ALL.
SHUT UP.
NOTHING BRINGS IN THE VOTES LIKE SURVIVING AN ATTEMPTED ASSASSINATION DOES IT, DETECTIVE?
YOU'RE DELUSIONAL.
HAVE THE GOOD SENSE TO DIE ALREADY, KING.
AND YET FOR THE FIRST TIME IN TWO DAYS, I DON'T WANT TO.
UHN...
ALEC! NO!
BLAM

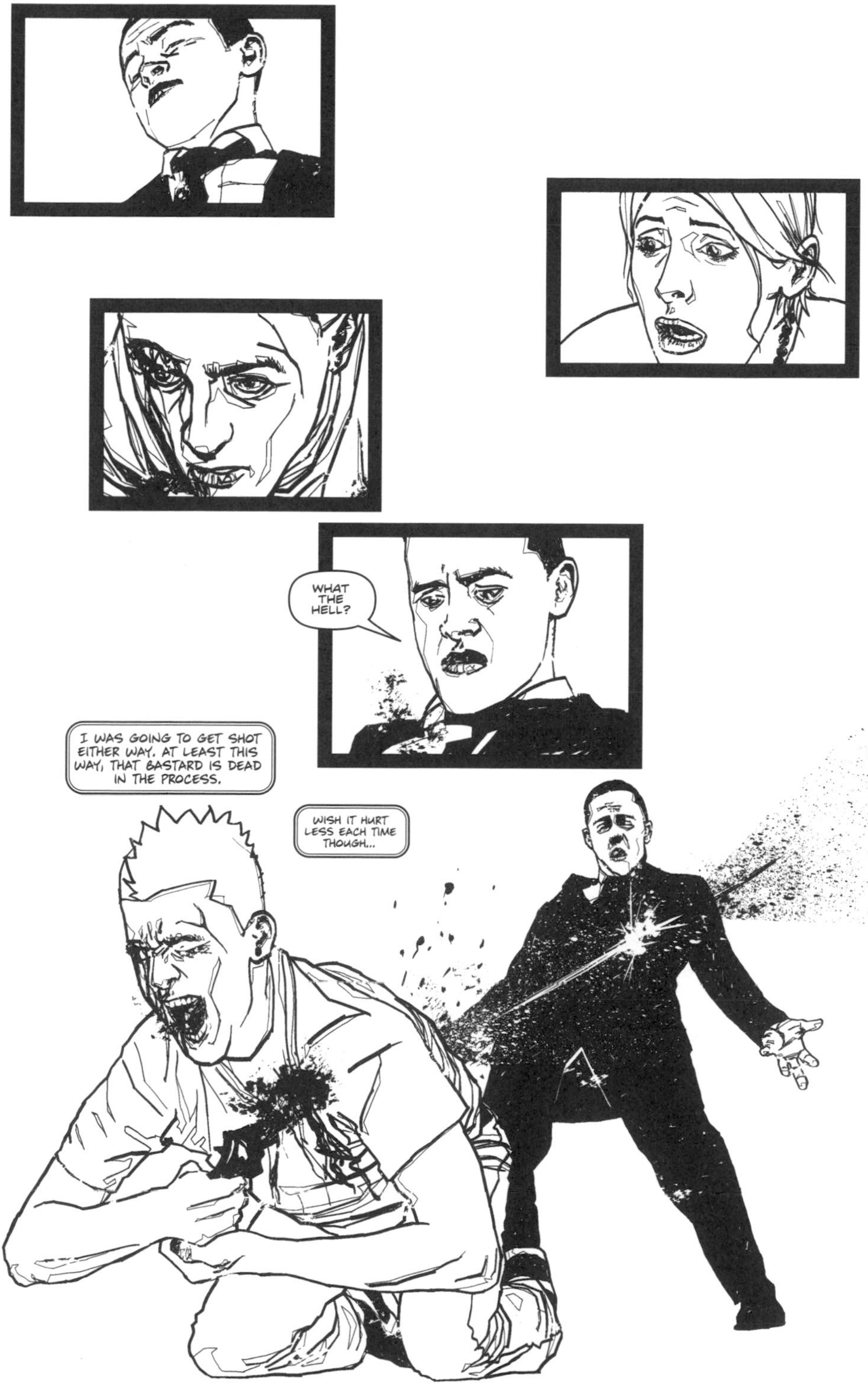
WHAT THE HELL?
I WAS GOING TO GET SHOT EITHER WAY. AT LEAST THIS WAY, THAT BASTARD IS DEAD IN THE PROCESS.
WISH IT HURT LESS EACH TIME THOUGH...

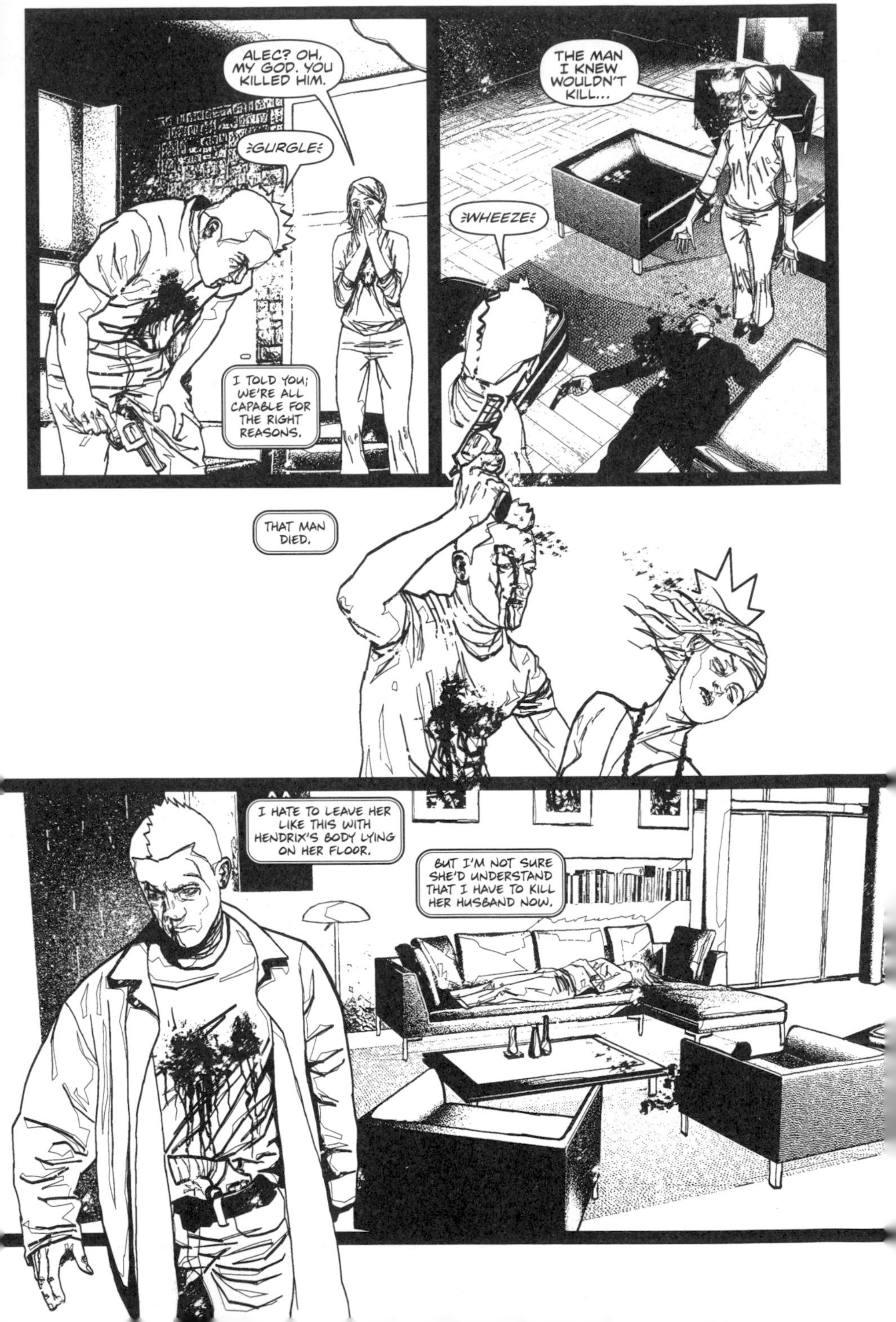
ALEC? OH, MY GOD. YOU KILLED HIM.
GURGLE
I TOLD YOU; WE'RE ALL CAPABLE FOR THE RIGHT REASONS.
THE MAN I KNEW WOULDN'T KILL...
WHEEZE
THAT MAN DIED.
I HATE TO LEAVE HER LIKE THIS WITH HENDRIX'S BODY LYING ON HER FLOOR.
BUT I'M NOT SURE SHE'D UNDERSTAND THAT I HAVE TO KILL HER HUSBAND NOW.

LAST MORTAL

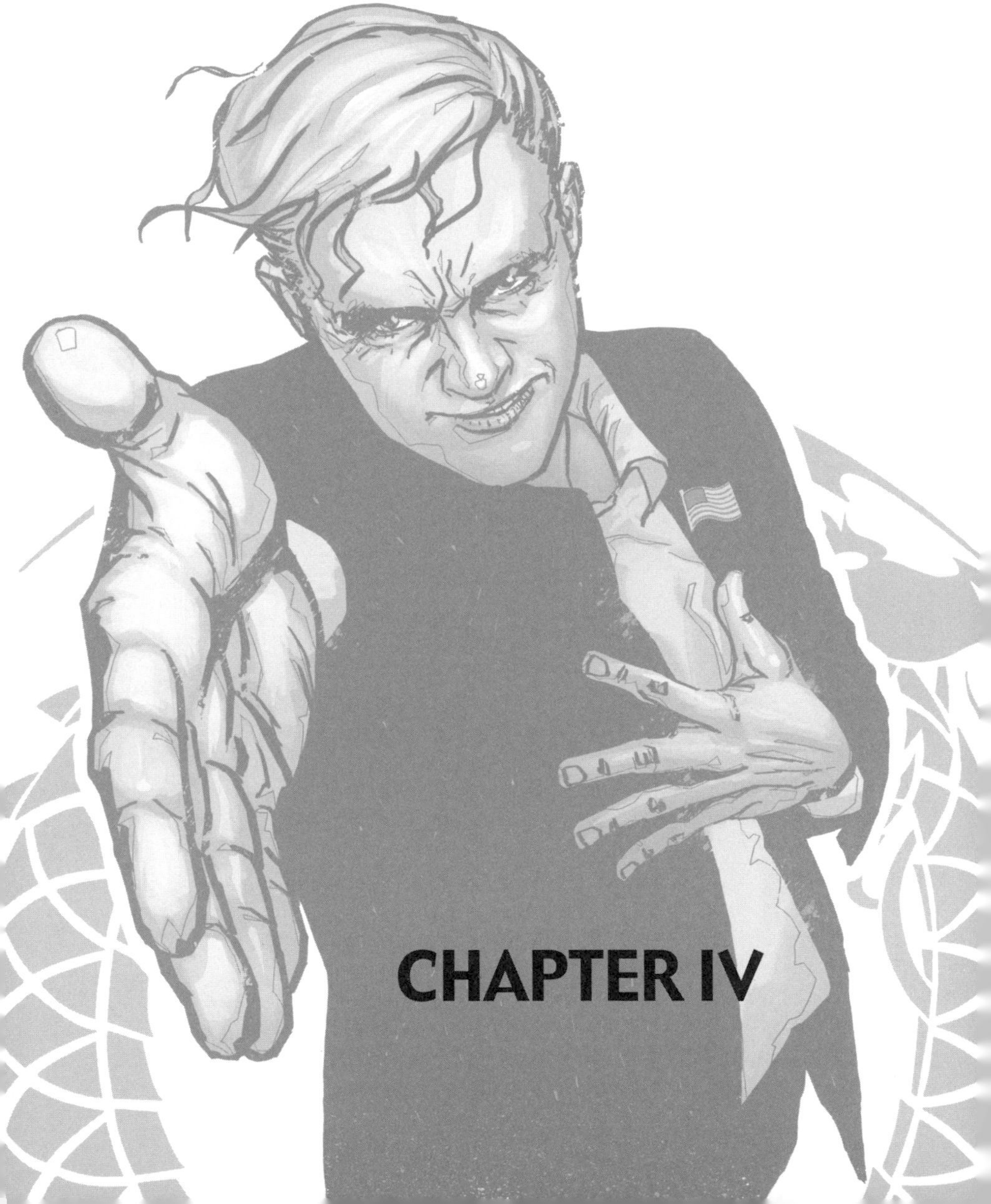

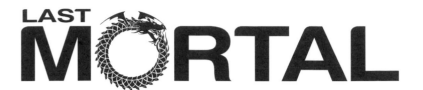

CHAPTER IV

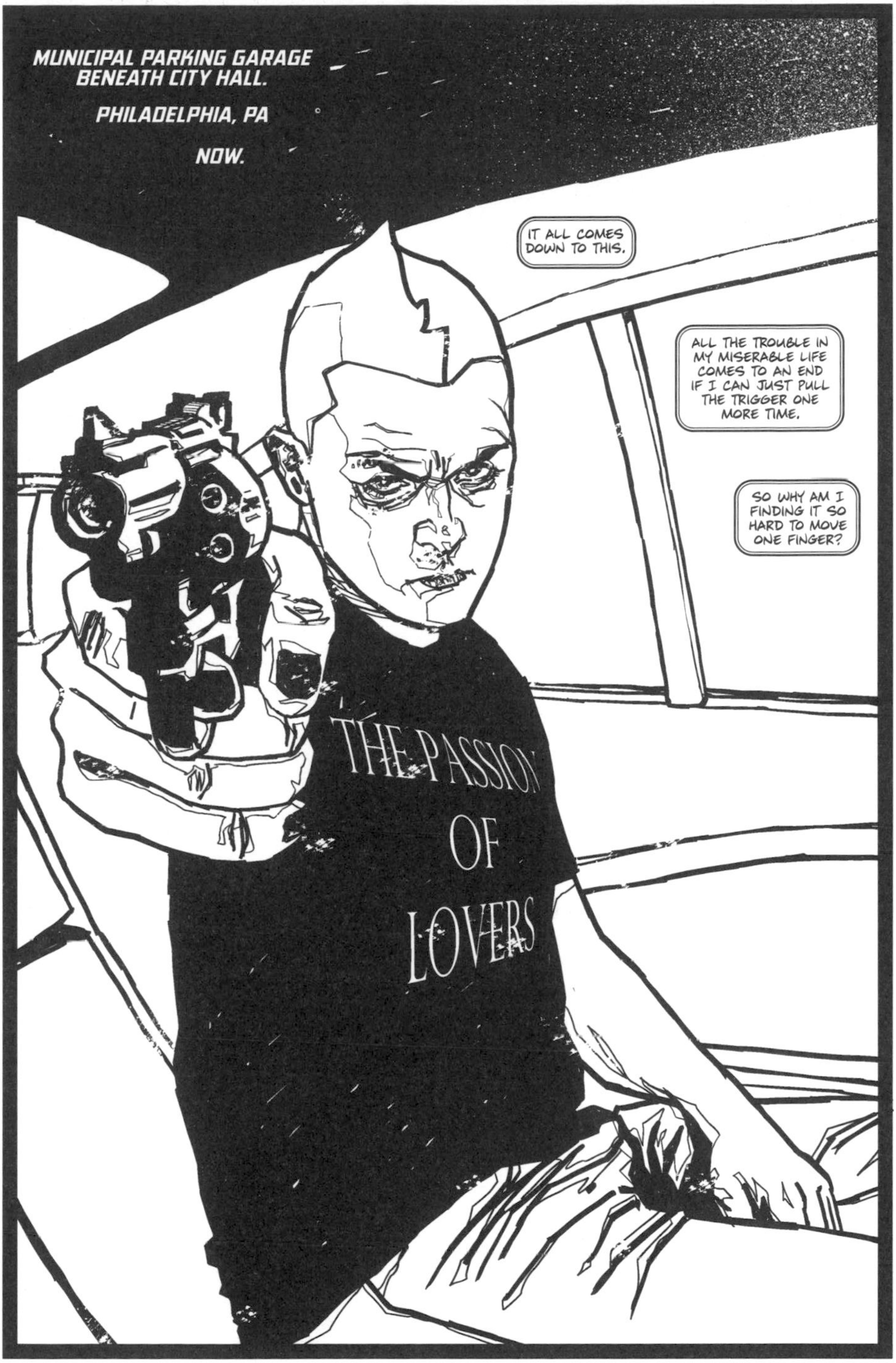
MUNICIPAL PARKING GARAGE BENEATH CITY HALL.
PHILADELPHIA, PA
NOW.
IT ALL COMES DOWN TO THIS.
ALL THE TROUBLE IN MY MISERABLE LIFE COMES TO AN END IF I CAN JUST PULL THE TRIGGER ONE MORE TIME.
SO WHY AM I FINDING IT SO HARD TO MOVE ONE FINGER?
THE PASSION OF LOVERS

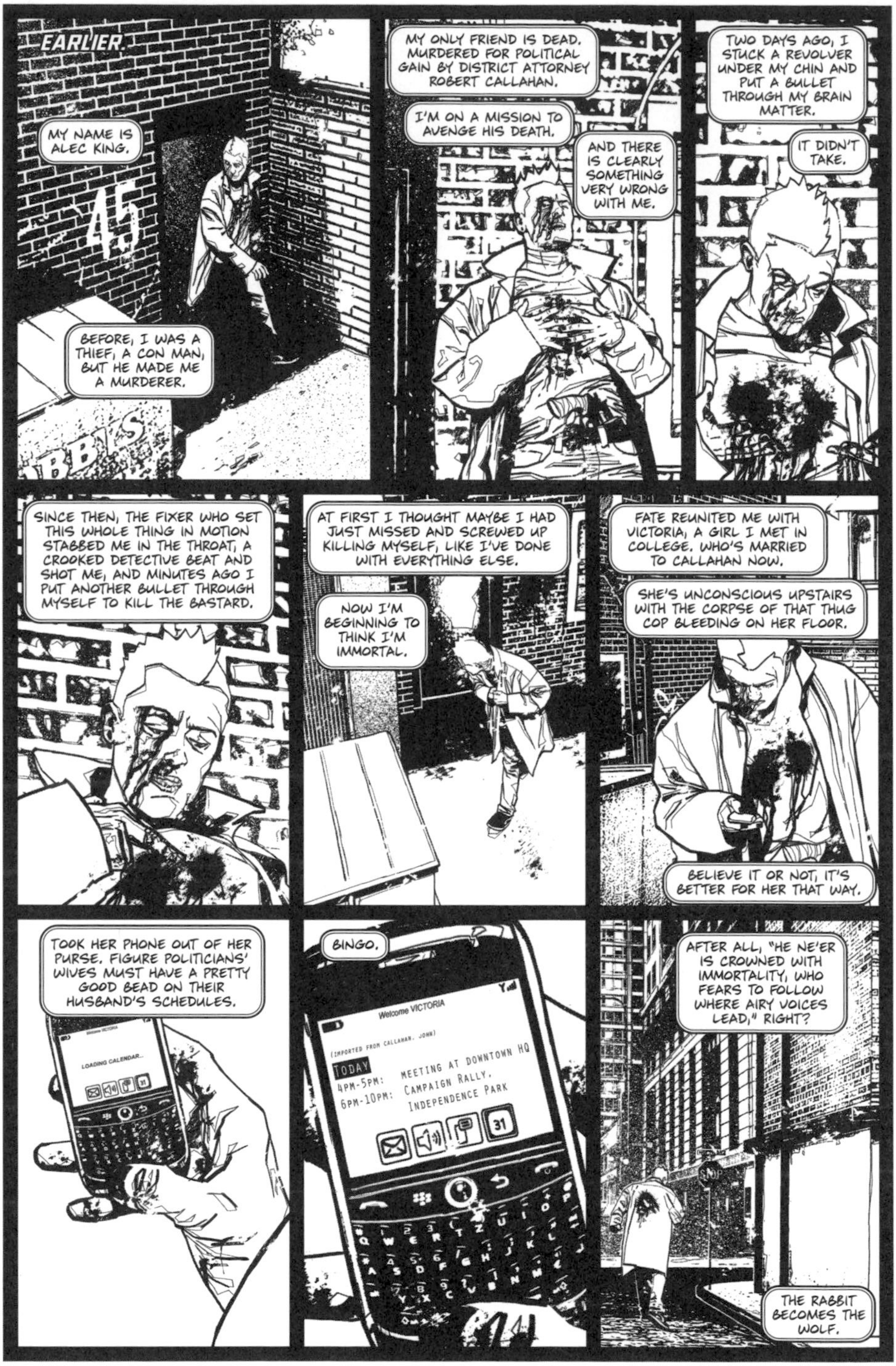
EARLIER.
MY NAME IS ALEC KING.
BEFORE, I WAS A THIEF, A CON MAN, BUT HE MADE ME A MURDERER.
MY ONLY FRIEND IS DEAD. MURDERED FOR POLITICAL GAIN BY DISTRICT ATTORNEY ROBERT CALLAHAN.
I'M ON A MISSION TO AVENGE HIS DEATH.
AND THERE IS CLEARLY SOMETHING VERY WRONG WITH ME.
TWO DAYS AGO, I STUCK A REVOLVER UNDER MY CHIN AND PUT A BULLET THROUGH MY BRAIN MATTER.
IT DIDN'T TAKE.
SINCE THEN, THE FIXER WHO SET THIS WHOLE THING IN MOTION STABBED ME IN THE THROAT, A CROOKED DETECTIVE BEAT AND SHOT ME, AND MINUTES AGO I PUT ANOTHER BULLET THROUGH MYSELF TO KILL THE BASTARD.
AT FIRST I THOUGHT MAYBE I HAD JUST MISSED AND SCREWED UP KILLING MYSELF, LIKE I'VE DONE WITH EVERYTHING ELSE.
NOW I'M BEGINNING TO THINK I'M IMMORTAL.
FATE REUNITED ME WITH VICTORIA, A GIRL I MET IN COLLEGE. WHO'S MARRIED TO CALLAHAN NOW.
SHE'S UNCONSCIOUS UPSTAIRS WITH THE CORPSE OF THAT THUG COP BLEEDING ON HER FLOOR.
BELIEVE IT OR NOT, IT'S BETTER FOR HER THAT WAY.
TOOK HER PHONE OUT OF HER PURSE. FIGURE POLITICIANS' WIVES MUST HAVE A PRETTY GOOD BEAD ON THEIR HUSBAND'S SCHEDULES.
LOADING CALENDAR...
BINGO.
Welcome VICTORIA
(IMPORTED FROM CALLAHAN, JOHN)
TODAY
4PM-5PM: MEETING AT DOWNTOWN HQ
6PM-10PM: CAMPAIGN RALLY, INDEPENDENCE PARK
AFTER ALL, "HE NE'ER IS CROWNED WITH IMMORTALITY, WHO FEARS TO FOLLOW WHERE AIRY VOICES LEAD," RIGHT?
THE RABBIT BECOMES THE WOLF.

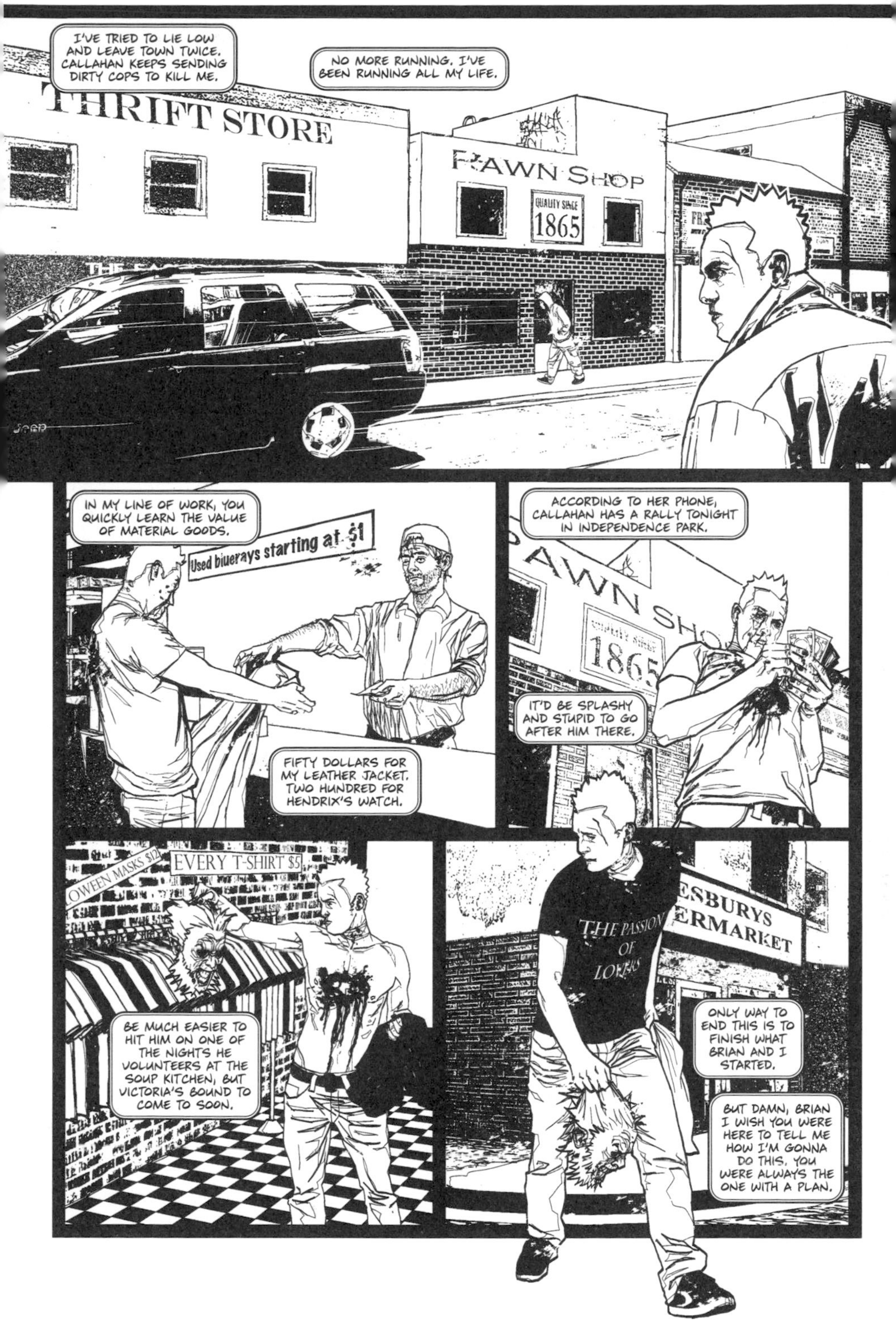
I'VE TRIED TO LIE LOW AND LEAVE TOWN TWICE. CALLAHAN KEEPS SENDING DIRTY COPS TO KILL ME.
NO MORE RUNNING. I'VE BEEN RUNNING ALL MY LIFE.
THRIFT STORE
PAWN SHOP
QUALITY SINCE 1865
IN MY LINE OF WORK, YOU QUICKLY LEARN THE VALUE OF MATERIAL GOODS.
Used biuerays starting at $1
FIFTY DOLLARS FOR MY LEATHER JACKET. TWO HUNDRED FOR HENDRIX'S WATCH.
ACCORDING TO HER PHONE, CALLAHAN HAS A RALLY TONIGHT IN INDEPENDENCE PARK.
IT'D BE SPLASHY AND STUPID TO GO AFTER HIM THERE.
OWEEN MASKS $12
EVERY T-SHIRT $5
BE MUCH EASIER TO HIT HIM ON ONE OF THE NIGHTS HE VOLUNTEERS AT THE SOUP KITCHEN, BUT VICTORIA'S BOUND TO COME TO SOON.
THE PASSION OF LOVERS
ESBURYS ERMARKET
ONLY WAY TO END THIS IS TO FINISH WHAT BRIAN AND I STARTED.
BUT DAMN, BRIAN I WISH YOU WERE HERE TO TELL ME HOW I'M GONNA DO THIS. YOU WERE ALWAYS THE ONE WITH A PLAN.

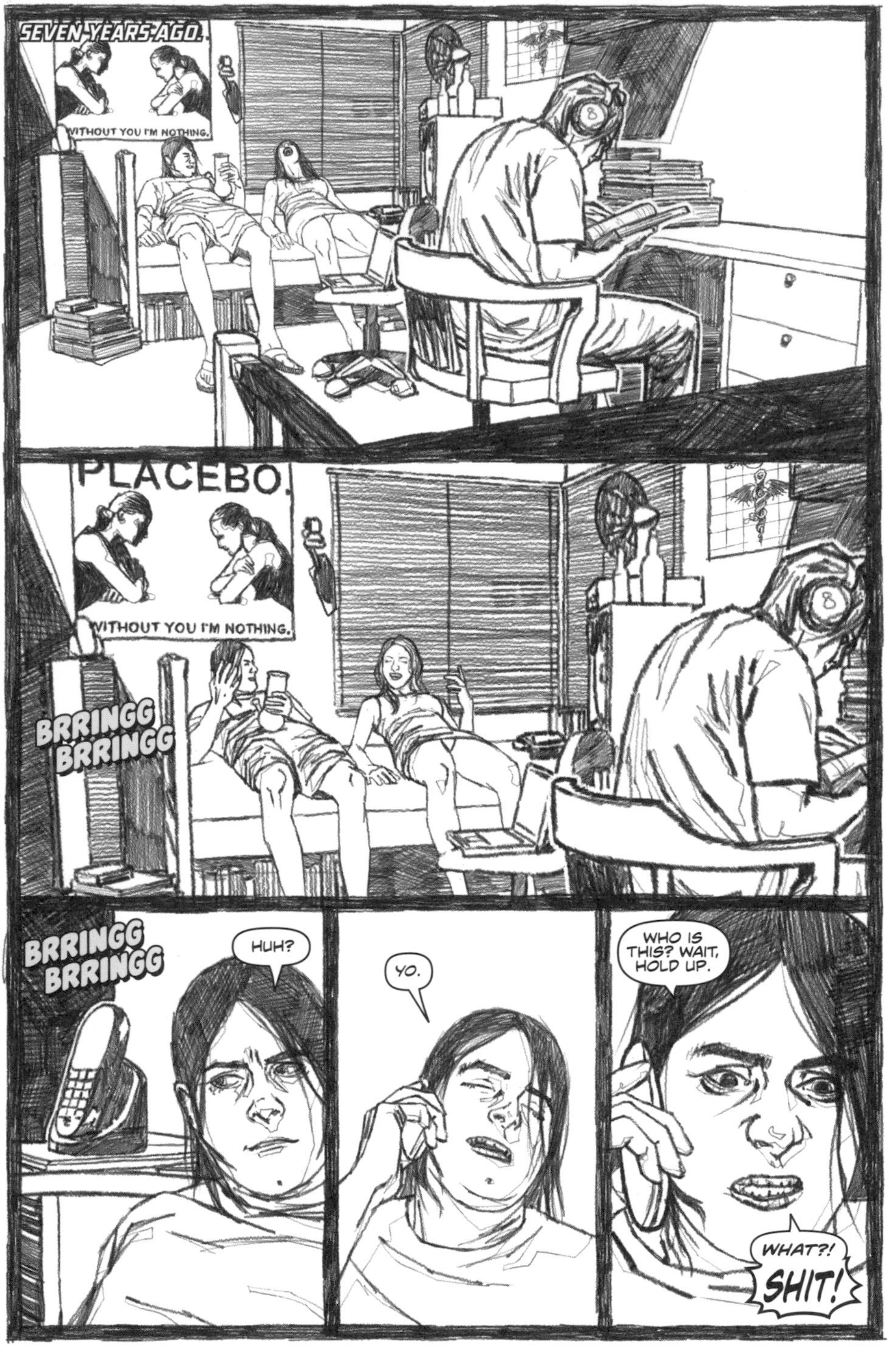
SEVEN YEARS AGO.
WITHOUT YOU I'M NOTHING.
PLACEBO.
WITHOUT YOU I'M NOTHING.
BRRINGG BRRINGG
BRRINGG BRRINGG
HUH?
YO.
WHO IS THIS? WAIT, HOLD UP.
WHAT?! SHIT!

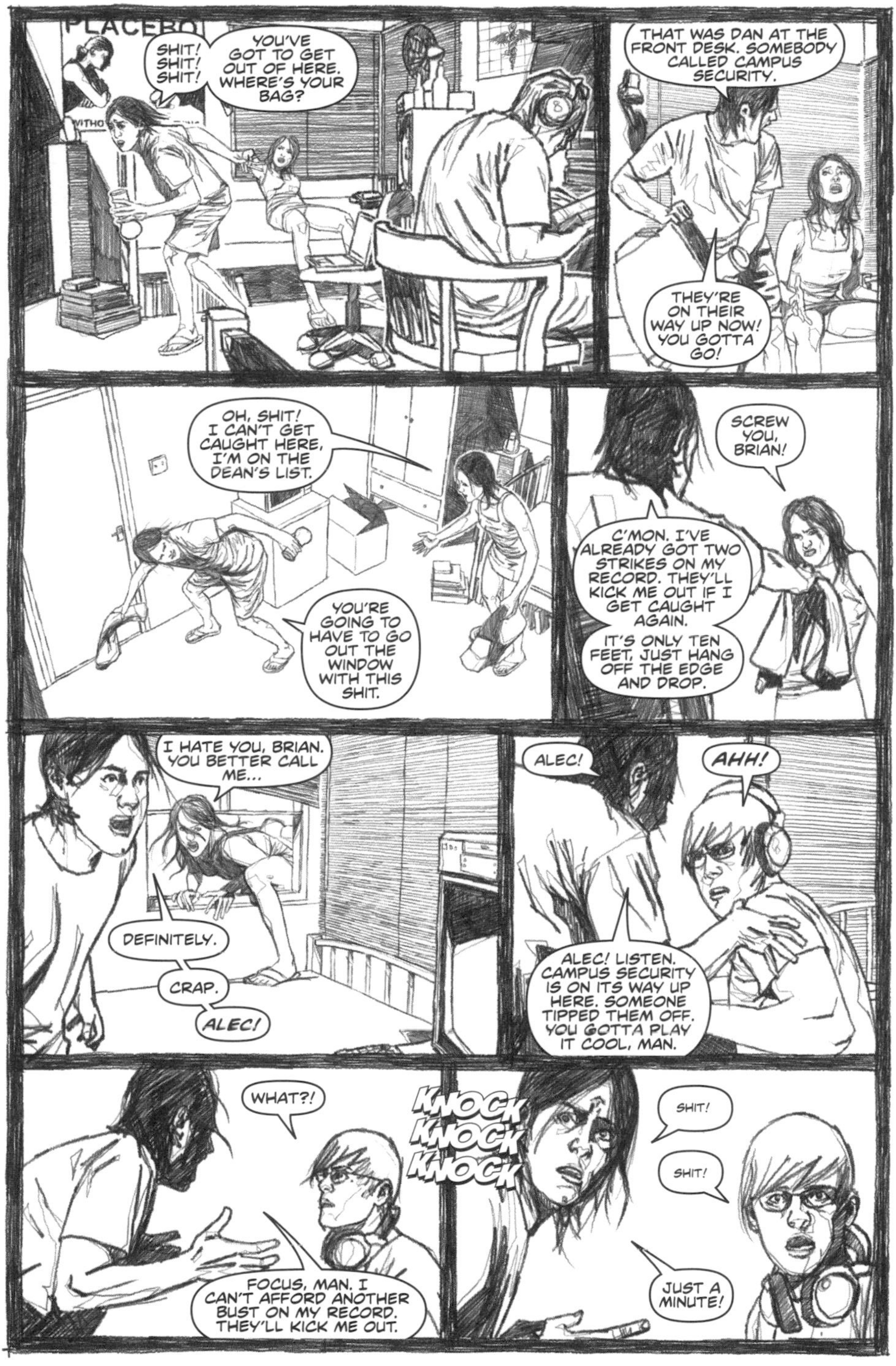
PLACEBO
WITHO
SHIT! SHIT! SHIT!
YOU'VE GOT TO GET OUT OF HERE. WHERE'S YOUR BAG?
THAT WAS DAN AT THE FRONT DESK. SOMEBODY CALLED CAMPUS SECURITY.
THEY'RE ON THEIR WAY UP NOW! YOU GOTTA GO!
OH, SHIT! I CAN'T GET CAUGHT HERE, I'M ON THE DEAN'S LIST.
YOU'RE GOING TO HAVE TO GO OUT THE WINDOW WITH THIS SHIT.
SCREW YOU, BRIAN!
C'MON. I'VE ALREADY GOT TWO STRIKES ON MY RECORD. THEY'LL KICK ME OUT IF I GET CAUGHT AGAIN.
IT'S ONLY TEN FEET, JUST HANG OFF THE EDGE AND DROP.
I HATE YOU, BRIAN. YOU BETTER CALL ME...
DEFINITELY.
CRAP.
ALEC!
ALEC!
AHH!
ALEC! LISTEN. CAMPUS SECURITY IS ON ITS WAY UP HERE. SOMEONE TIPPED THEM OFF. YOU GOTTA PLAY IT COOL, MAN.
WHAT?!
FOCUS, MAN. I CAN'T AFFORD ANOTHER BUST ON MY RECORD. THEY'LL KICK ME OUT.
KNOCK KNOCK KNOCK
SHIT!
SHIT!
JUST A MINUTE!

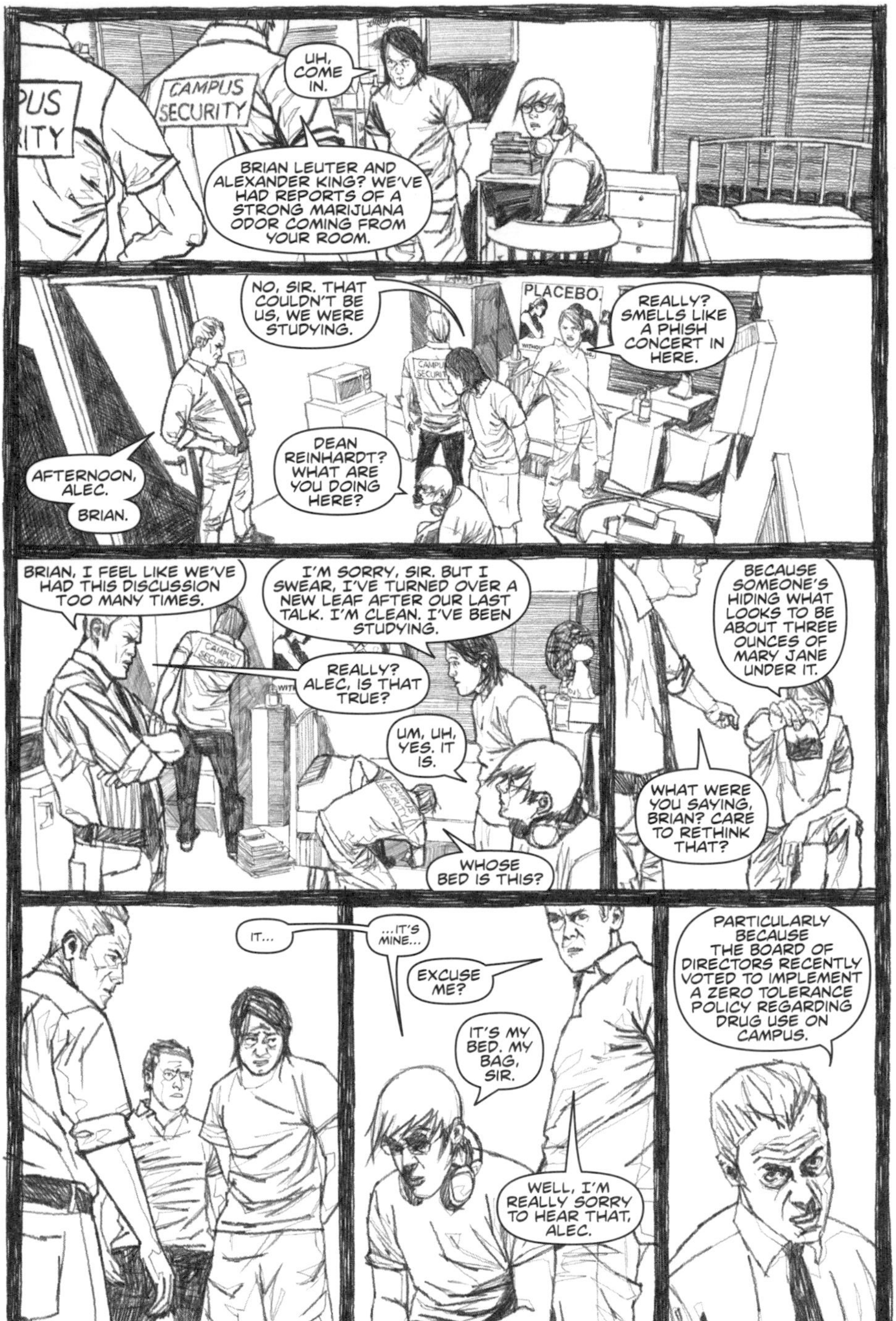

CAMPUS SECURITY
UH, COME IN.
BRIAN LEUTER AND ALEXANDER KING? WE'VE HAD REPORTS OF A STRONG MARIJUANA ODOR COMING FROM YOUR ROOM.
NO, SIR. THAT COULDN'T BE US, WE WERE STUDYING.
PLACEBO.
REALLY? SMELLS LIKE A PHISH CONCERT IN HERE.
AFTERNOON, ALEC.
BRIAN.
DEAN REINHARDT? WHAT ARE YOU DOING HERE?
BRIAN, I FEEL LIKE WE'VE HAD THIS DISCUSSION TOO MANY TIMES.
I'M SORRY, SIR. BUT I SWEAR, I'VE TURNED OVER A NEW LEAF AFTER OUR LAST TALK. I'M CLEAN. I'VE BEEN STUDYING.
REALLY? ALEC, IS THAT TRUE?
UM, UH, YES. IT IS.
WHOSE BED IS THIS?
BECAUSE SOMEONE'S HIDING WHAT LOOKS TO BE ABOUT THREE OUNCES OF MARY JANE UNDER IT.
WHAT WERE YOU SAYING, BRIAN? CARE TO RETHINK THAT?
IT...
...IT'S MINE...
EXCUSE ME?
IT'S MY BED. MY BAG, SIR.
WELL, I'M REALLY SORRY TO HEAR THAT, ALEC.
PARTICULARLY BECAUSE THE BOARD OF DIRECTORS RECENTLY VOTED TO IMPLEMENT A ZERO TOLERANCE POLICY REGARDING DRUG USE ON CAMPUS.

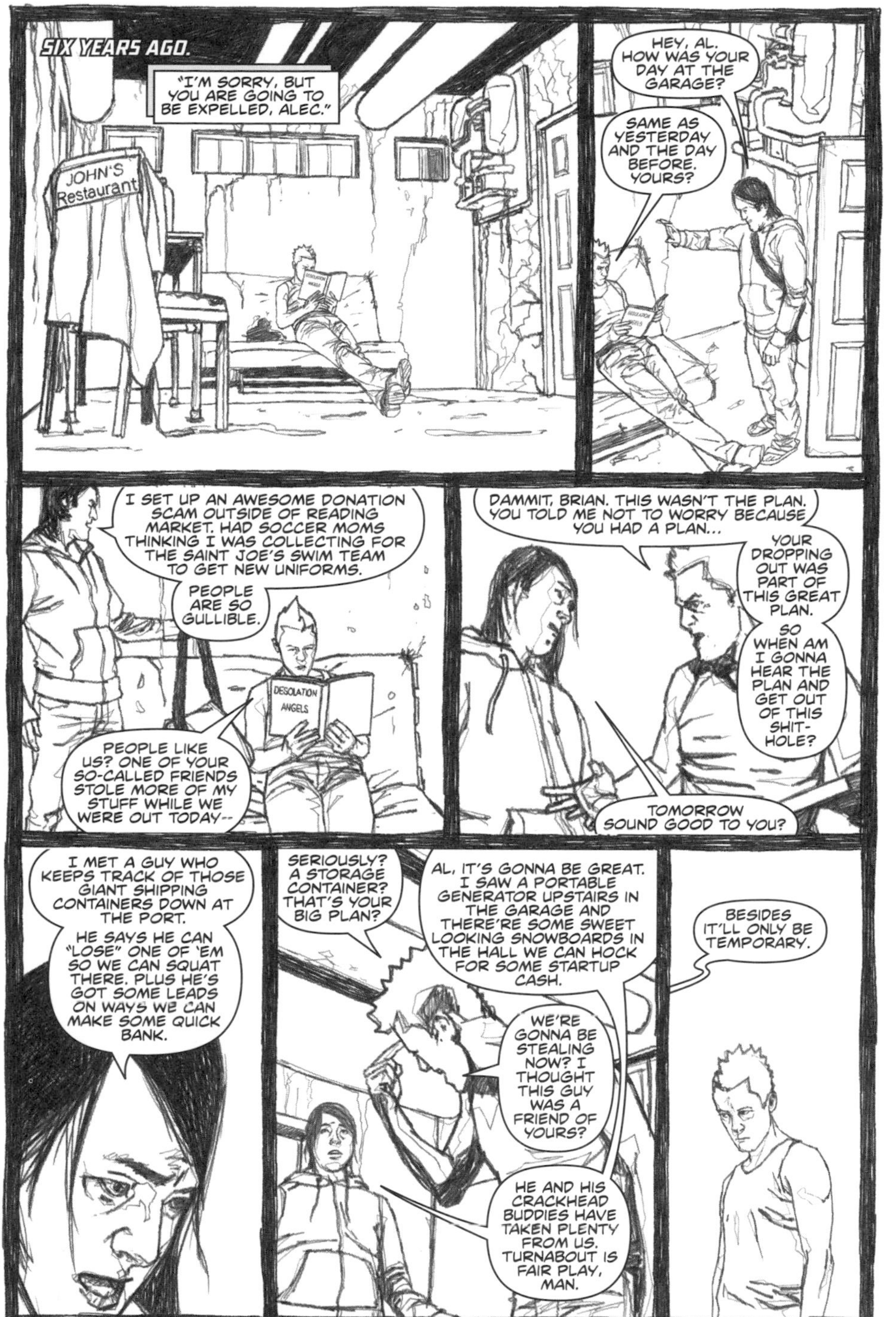
SIX YEARS AGO.
"I'M SORRY, BUT YOU ARE GOING TO BE EXPELLED, ALEC."
JOHN'S Restaurant
HEY, AL. HOW WAS YOUR DAY AT THE GARAGE?
SAME AS YESTERDAY AND THE DAY BEFORE. YOURS?
I SET UP AN AWESOME DONATION SCAM OUTSIDE OF READING MARKET. HAD SOCCER MOMS THINKING I WAS COLLECTING FOR THE SAINT JOE'S SWIM TEAM TO GET NEW UNIFORMS.
PEOPLE ARE SO GULLIBLE.
DESOLATION ANGELS
PEOPLE LIKE US? ONE OF YOUR SO-CALLED FRIENDS STOLE MORE OF MY STUFF WHILE WE WERE OUT TODAY--
DAMMIT, BRIAN. THIS WASN'T THE PLAN. YOU TOLD ME NOT TO WORRY BECAUSE YOU HAD A PLAN...
YOUR DROPPING OUT WAS PART OF THIS GREAT PLAN.
SO WHEN AM I GONNA HEAR THE PLAN AND GET OUT OF THIS SHIT-HOLE?
TOMORROW SOUND GOOD TO YOU?
I MET A GUY WHO KEEPS TRACK OF THOSE GIANT SHIPPING CONTAINERS DOWN AT THE PORT.
HE SAYS HE CAN "LOSE" ONE OF 'EM SO WE CAN SQUAT THERE. PLUS HE'S GOT SOME LEADS ON WAYS WE CAN MAKE SOME QUICK BANK.
SERIOUSLY? A STORAGE CONTAINER? THAT'S YOUR BIG PLAN?
AL, IT'S GONNA BE GREAT. I SAW A PORTABLE GENERATOR UPSTAIRS IN THE GARAGE AND THERE'RE SOME SWEET LOOKING SNOWBOARDS IN THE HALL WE CAN HOCK FOR SOME STARTUP CASH.
WE'RE GONNA BE STEALING NOW? I THOUGHT THIS GUY WAS A FRIEND OF YOURS?
HE AND HIS CRACKHEAD BUDDIES HAVE TAKEN PLENTY FROM US. TURNABOUT IS FAIR PLAY, MAN.
BESIDES IT'LL ONLY BE TEMPORARY.

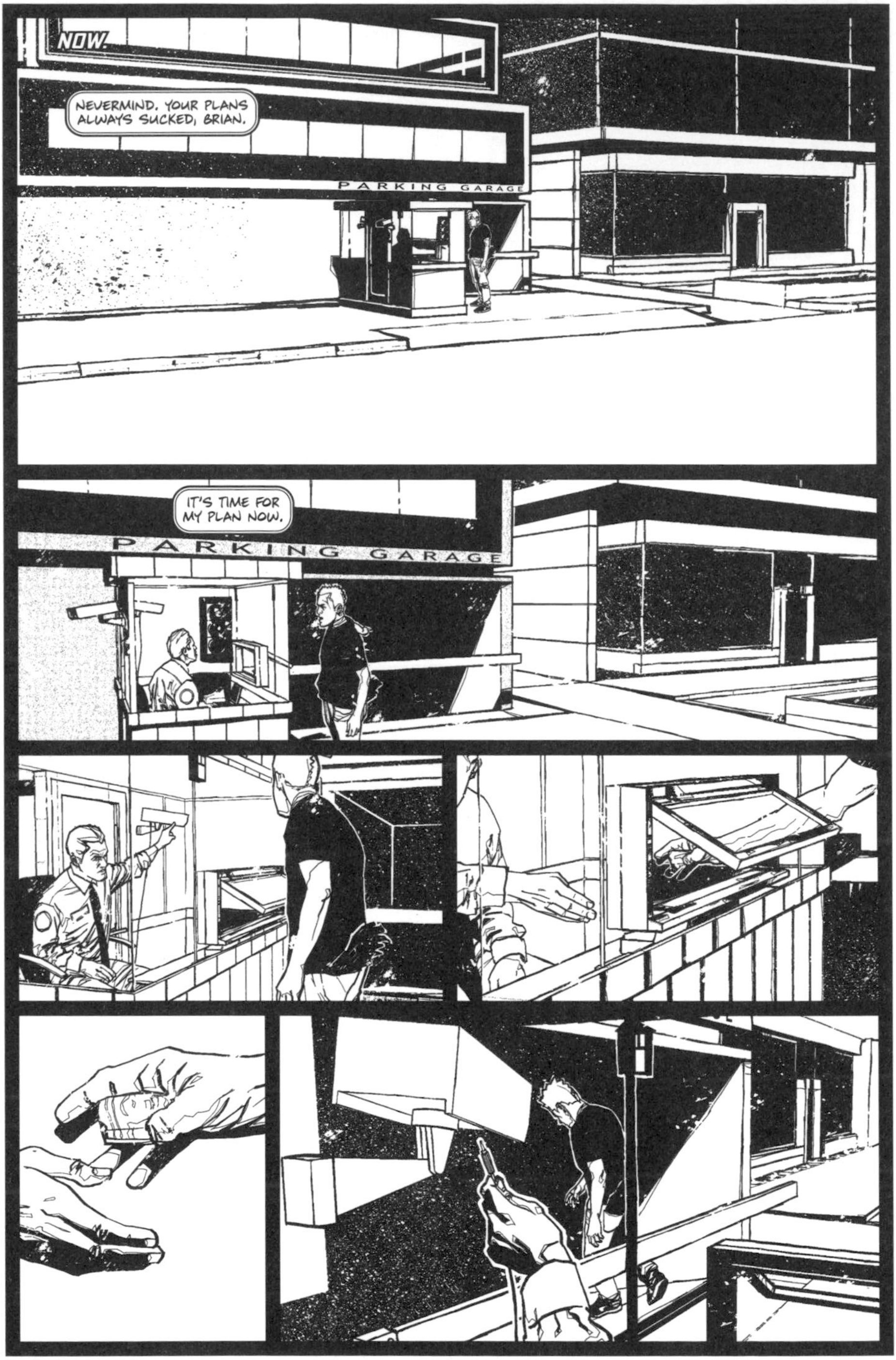
NOW.
NEVERMIND. YOUR PLANS ALWAYS SUCKED, BRIAN.
PARKING GARAGE
PARKING GARAGE
IT'S TIME FOR MY PLAN NOW.

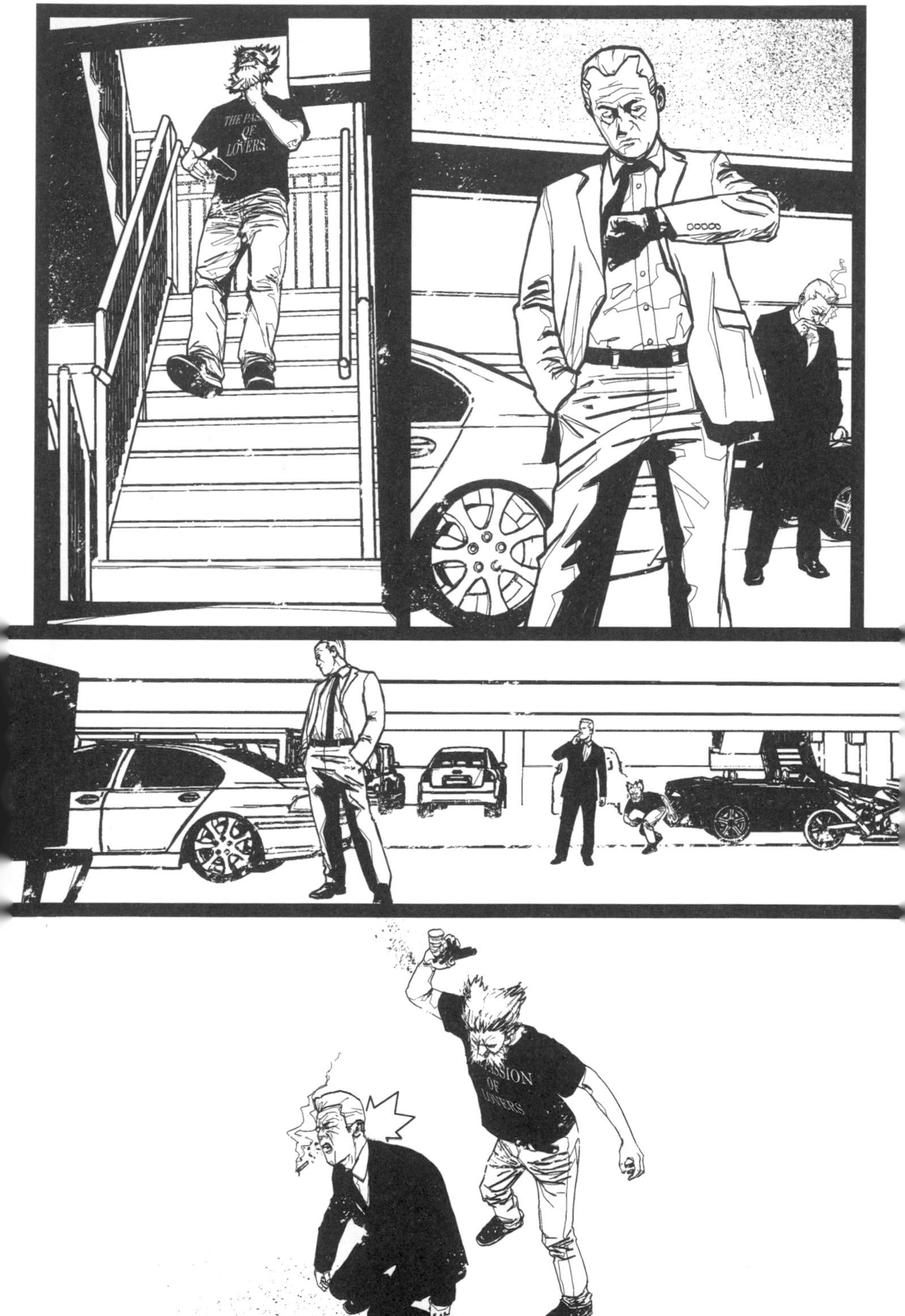
THE PAS
OF
LOVERS.
ASSION
OF
LOVERS

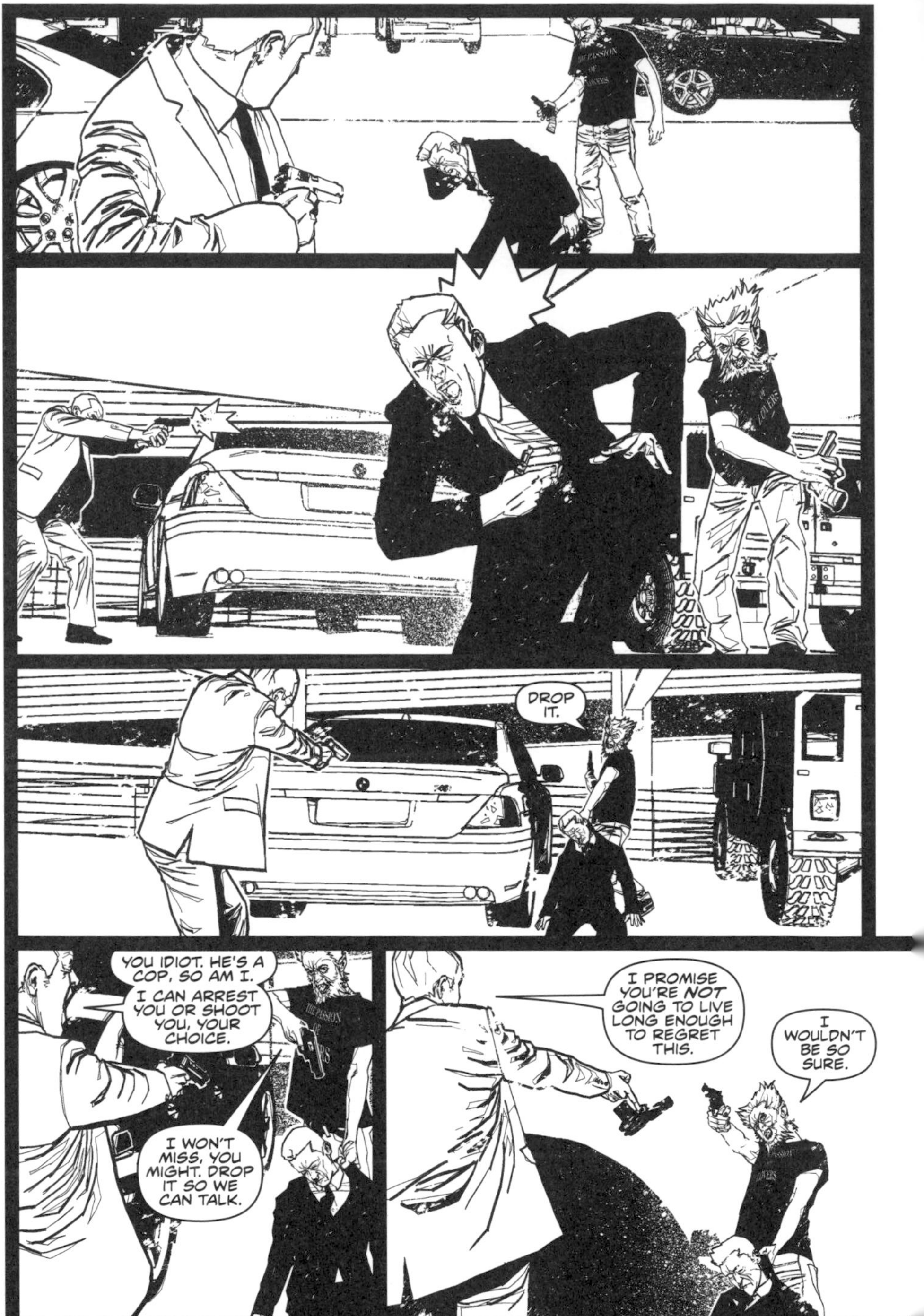
DROP IT.
YOU IDIOT. HE'S A COP, SO AM I.
I CAN ARREST YOU OR SHOOT YOU, YOUR CHOICE.
I WON'T MISS, YOU MIGHT. DROP IT SO WE CAN TALK.
I PROMISE YOU'RE NOT GOING TO LIVE LONG ENOUGH TO REGRET THIS.
I WOULDN'T BE SO SURE.

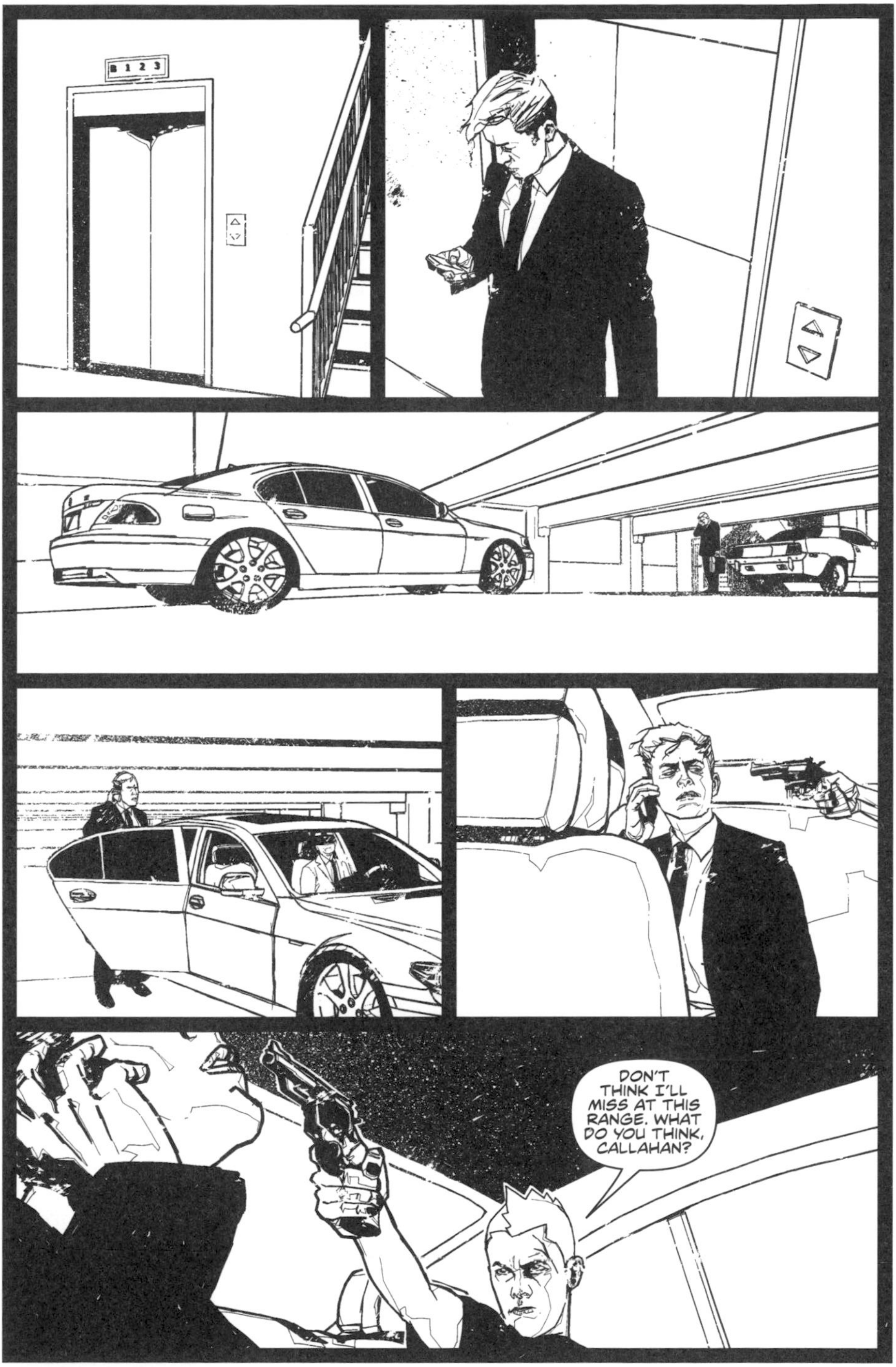
B 1 2 3
DON'T THINK I'LL MISS AT THIS RANGE. WHAT DO YOU THINK, CALLAHAN?

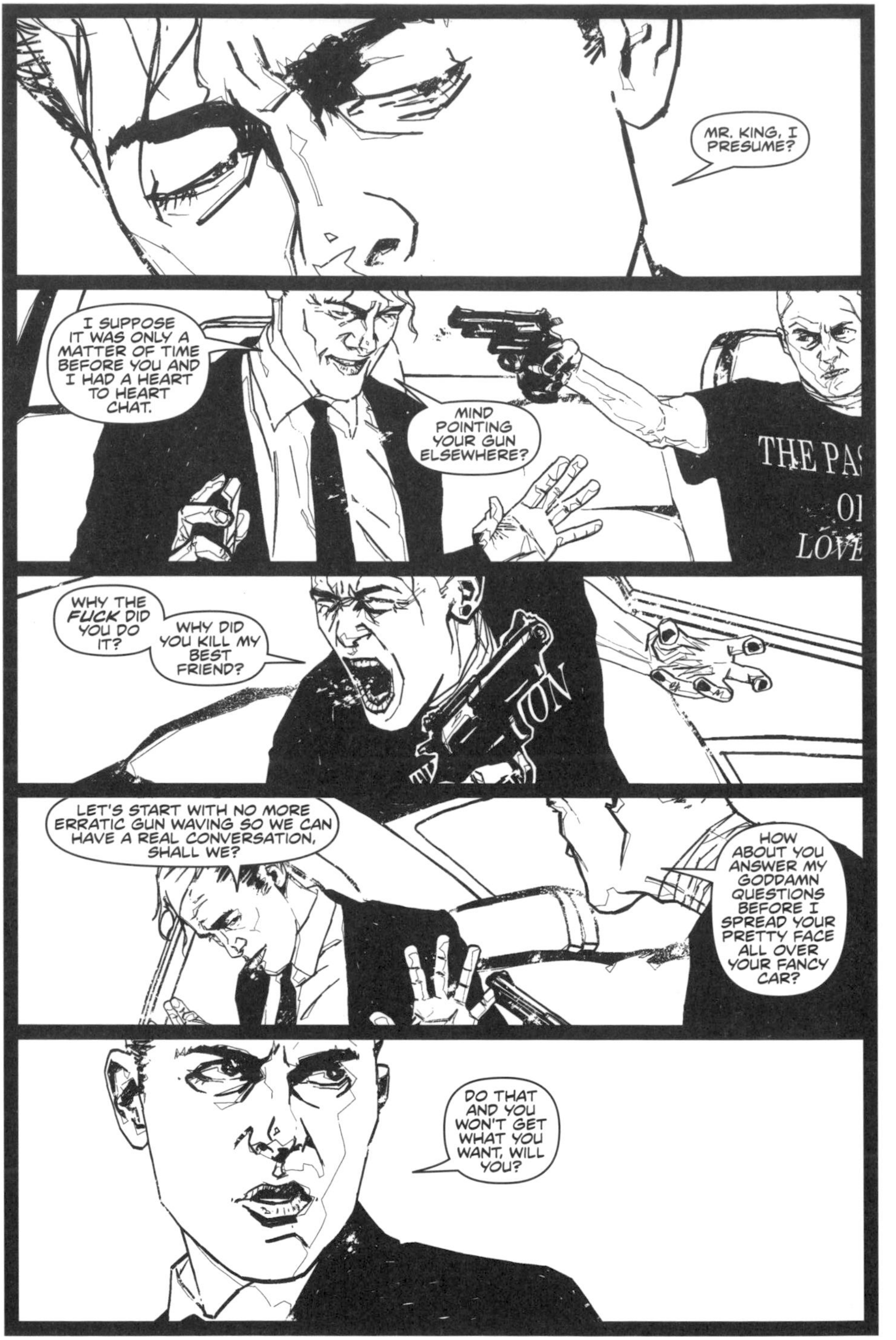

MR. KING, I PRESUME?
I SUPPOSE IT WAS ONLY A MATTER OF TIME BEFORE YOU AND I HAD A HEART TO HEART CHAT.
MIND POINTING YOUR GUN ELSEWHERE?
THE PAS
OI
LOVE
WHY THE FUCK DID YOU DO IT?
WHY DID YOU KILL MY BEST FRIEND?
LET'S START WITH NO MORE ERRATIC GUN WAVING SO WE CAN HAVE A REAL CONVERSATION, SHALL WE?
HOW ABOUT YOU ANSWER MY GODDAMN QUESTIONS BEFORE I SPREAD YOUR PRETTY FACE ALL OVER YOUR FANCY CAR?
DO THAT AND YOU WON'T GET WHAT YOU WANT, WILL YOU?

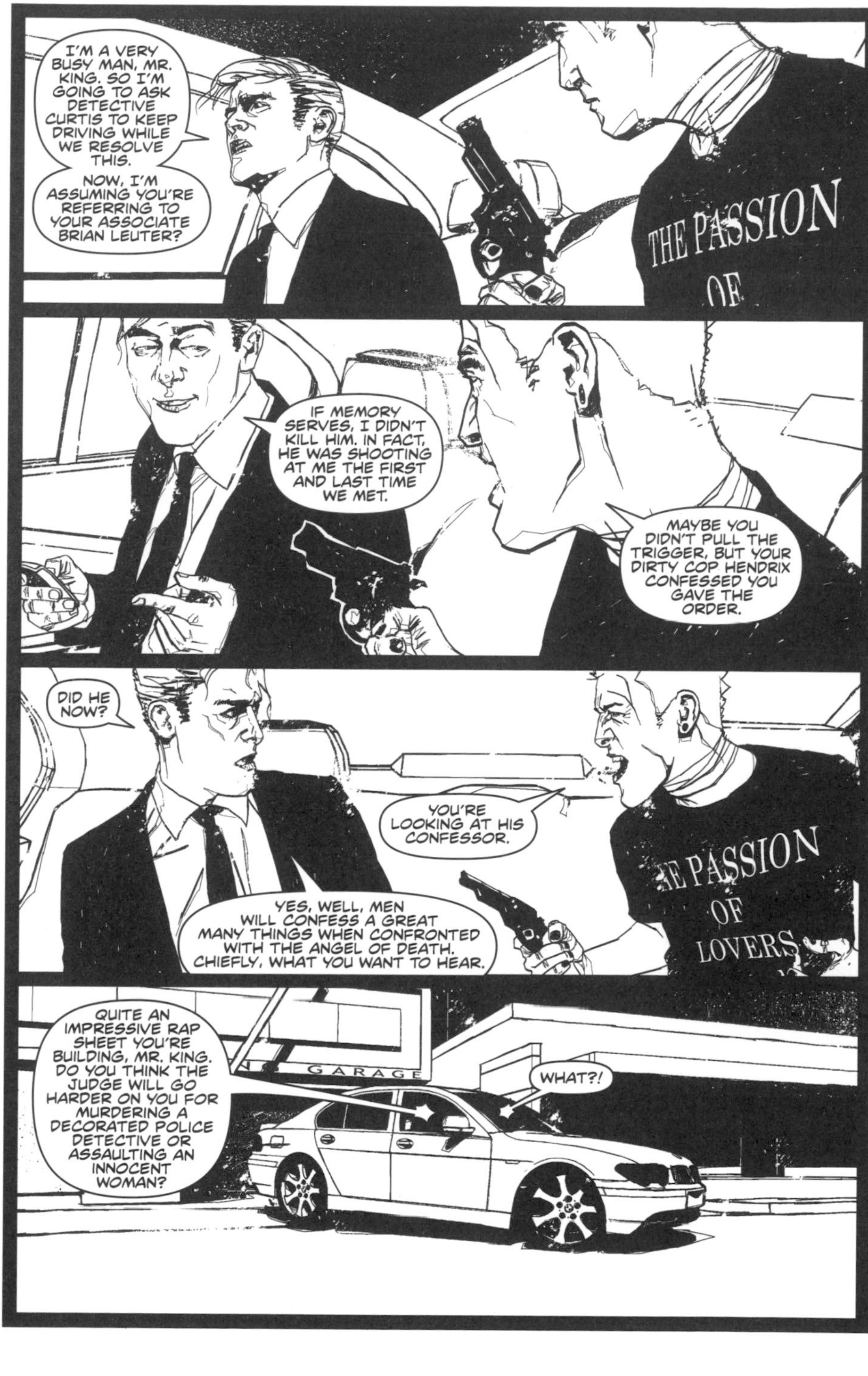
I'M A VERY BUSY MAN, MR. KING. SO I'M GOING TO ASK DETECTIVE CURTIS TO KEEP DRIVING WHILE WE RESOLVE THIS.
NOW, I'M ASSUMING YOU'RE REFERRING TO YOUR ASSOCIATE BRIAN LEUTER?
THE PASSION OF
IF MEMORY SERVES, I DIDN'T KILL HIM. IN FACT, HE WAS SHOOTING AT ME THE FIRST AND LAST TIME WE MET.
MAYBE YOU DIDN'T PULL THE TRIGGER, BUT YOUR DIRTY COP HENDRIX CONFESSED YOU GAVE THE ORDER.
DID HE NOW?
YOU'RE LOOKING AT HIS CONFESSOR.
YES, WELL, MEN WILL CONFESS A GREAT MANY THINGS WHEN CONFRONTED WITH THE ANGEL OF DEATH. CHIEFLY, WHAT YOU WANT TO HEAR.
PASSION OF LOVERS
QUITE AN IMPRESSIVE RAP SHEET YOU'RE BUILDING, MR. KING. DO YOU THINK THE JUDGE WILL GO HARDER ON YOU FOR MURDERING A DECORATED POLICE DETECTIVE OR ASSAULTING AN INNOCENT WOMAN?
GARAGE
WHAT?!

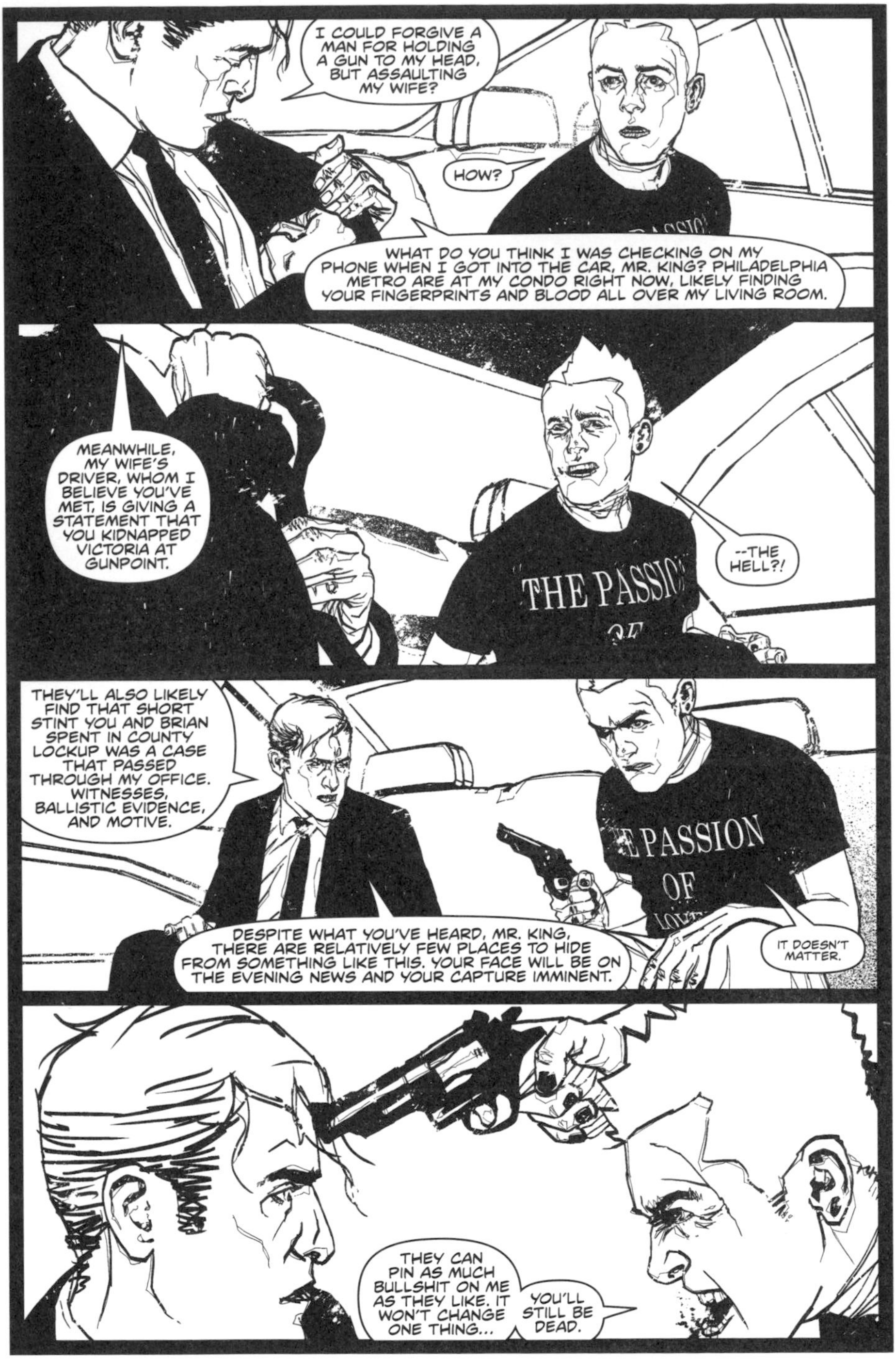
I COULD FORGIVE A MAN FOR HOLDING A GUN TO MY HEAD, BUT ASSAULTING MY WIFE?
HOW?
WHAT DO YOU THINK I WAS CHECKING ON MY PHONE WHEN I GOT INTO THE CAR, MR. KING? PHILADELPHIA METRO ARE AT MY CONDO RIGHT NOW, LIKELY FINDING YOUR FINGERPRINTS AND BLOOD ALL OVER MY LIVING ROOM.
MEANWHILE, MY WIFE'S DRIVER, WHOM I BELIEVE YOU'VE MET, IS GIVING A STATEMENT THAT YOU KIDNAPPED VICTORIA AT GUNPOINT.
--THE HELL?!
THE PASSION
THEY'LL ALSO LIKELY FIND THAT SHORT STINT YOU AND BRIAN SPENT IN COUNTY LOCKUP WAS A CASE THAT PASSED THROUGH MY OFFICE. WITNESSES, BALLISTIC EVIDENCE, AND MOTIVE.
PASSION OF
DESPITE WHAT YOU'VE HEARD, MR. KING, THERE ARE RELATIVELY FEW PLACES TO HIDE FROM SOMETHING LIKE THIS. YOUR FACE WILL BE ON THE EVENING NEWS AND YOUR CAPTURE IMMINENT.
IT DOESN'T MATTER.
THEY CAN PIN AS MUCH BULLSHIT ON ME AS THEY LIKE. IT WON'T CHANGE ONE THING...
YOU'LL STILL BE DEAD.

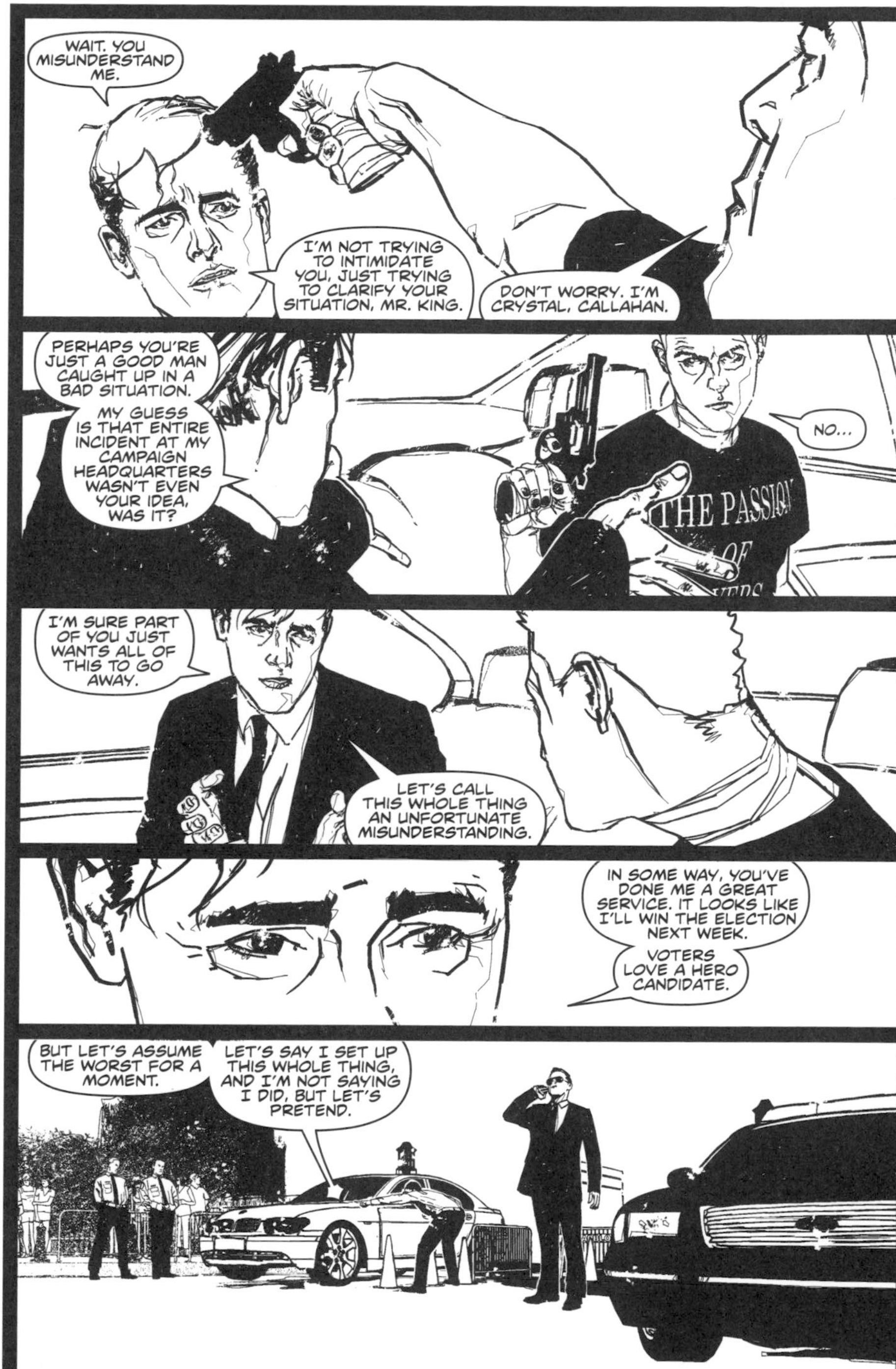
WAIT. YOU MISUNDERSTAND ME.
I'M NOT TRYING TO INTIMIDATE YOU, JUST TRYING TO CLARIFY YOUR SITUATION, MR. KING.
DON'T WORRY. I'M CRYSTAL, CALLAHAN.
PERHAPS YOU'RE JUST A GOOD MAN CAUGHT UP IN A BAD SITUATION.
MY GUESS IS THAT ENTIRE INCIDENT AT MY CAMPAIGN HEADQUARTERS WASN'T EVEN YOUR IDEA, WAS IT?
NO...
THE PASSION OF
I'M SURE PART OF YOU JUST WANTS ALL OF THIS TO GO AWAY.
LET'S CALL THIS WHOLE THING AN UNFORTUNATE MISUNDERSTANDING.
IN SOME WAY, YOU'VE DONE ME A GREAT SERVICE. IT LOOKS LIKE I'LL WIN THE ELECTION NEXT WEEK.
VOTERS LOVE A HERO CANDIDATE.
BUT LET'S ASSUME THE WORST FOR A MOMENT.
LET'S SAY I SET UP THIS WHOLE THING, AND I'M NOT SAYING I DID, BUT LET'S PRETEND.

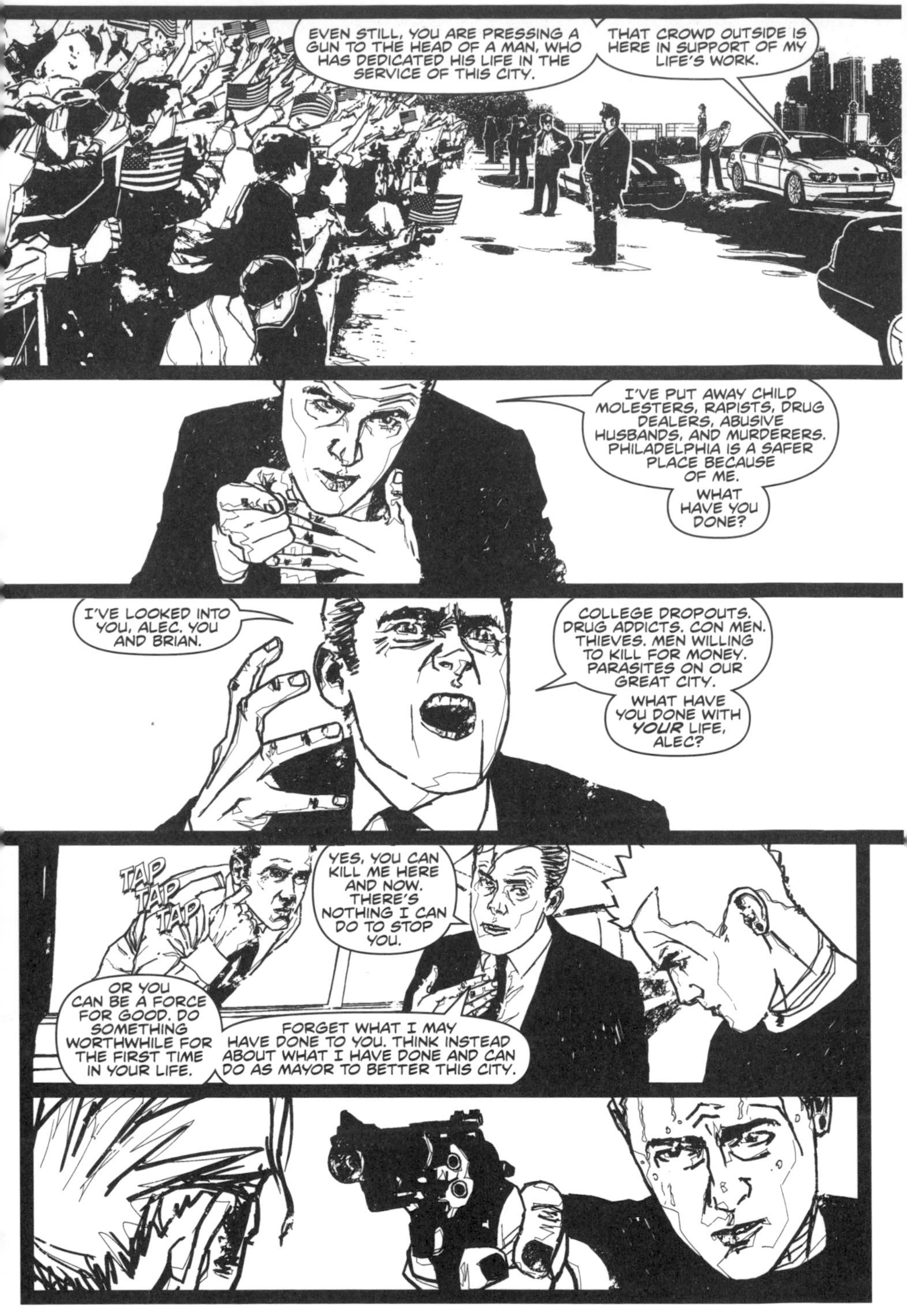
EVEN STILL, YOU ARE PRESSING A GUN TO THE HEAD OF A MAN, WHO HAS DEDICATED HIS LIFE IN THE SERVICE OF THIS CITY.
THAT CROWD OUTSIDE IS HERE IN SUPPORT OF MY LIFE'S WORK.
I'VE PUT AWAY CHILD MOLESTERS, RAPISTS, DRUG DEALERS, ABUSIVE HUSBANDS, AND MURDERERS. PHILADELPHIA IS A SAFER PLACE BECAUSE OF ME.
WHAT HAVE YOU DONE?
I'VE LOOKED INTO YOU, ALEC. YOU AND BRIAN.
COLLEGE DROPOUTS. DRUG ADDICTS. CON MEN. THIEVES. MEN WILLING TO KILL FOR MONEY. PARASITES ON OUR GREAT CITY.
WHAT HAVE YOU DONE WITH *YOUR* LIFE, ALEC?
TAP TAP TAP
YES, YOU CAN KILL ME HERE AND NOW. THERE'S NOTHING I CAN DO TO STOP YOU.
OR YOU CAN BE A FORCE FOR GOOD. DO SOMETHING WORTHWHILE FOR THE FIRST TIME IN YOUR LIFE.
FORGET WHAT I MAY HAVE DONE TO YOU. THINK INSTEAD ABOUT WHAT I HAVE DONE AND CAN DO AS MAYOR TO BETTER THIS CITY.

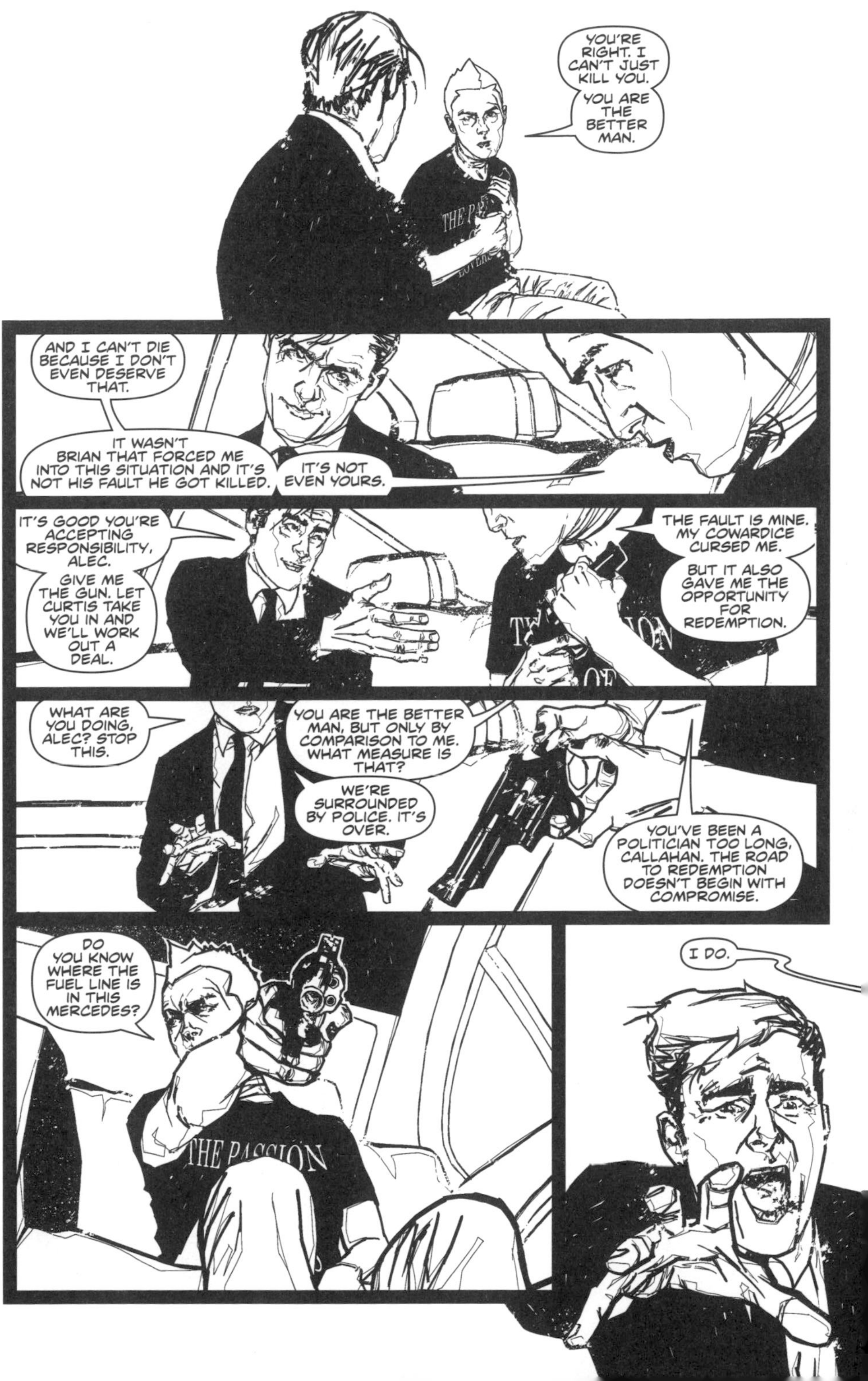
YOU'RE RIGHT. I CAN'T JUST KILL YOU.
YOU ARE THE BETTER MAN.
AND I CAN'T DIE BECAUSE I DON'T EVEN DESERVE THAT.
IT WASN'T BRIAN THAT FORCED ME INTO THIS SITUATION AND IT'S NOT HIS FAULT HE GOT KILLED.
IT'S NOT EVEN YOURS.
IT'S GOOD YOU'RE ACCEPTING RESPONSIBILITY, ALEC.
GIVE ME THE GUN. LET CURTIS TAKE YOU IN AND WE'LL WORK OUT A DEAL.
THE FAULT IS MINE. MY COWARDICE CURSED ME.
BUT IT ALSO GAVE ME THE OPPORTUNITY FOR REDEMPTION.
WHAT ARE YOU DOING, ALEC? STOP THIS.
YOU ARE THE BETTER MAN, BUT ONLY BY COMPARISON TO ME. WHAT MEASURE IS THAT?
WE'RE SURROUNDED BY POLICE. IT'S OVER.
YOU'VE BEEN A POLITICIAN TOO LONG, CALLAHAN. THE ROAD TO REDEMPTION DOESN'T BEGIN WITH COMPROMISE.
DO YOU KNOW WHERE THE FUEL LINE IS IN THIS MERCEDES?
I DO.

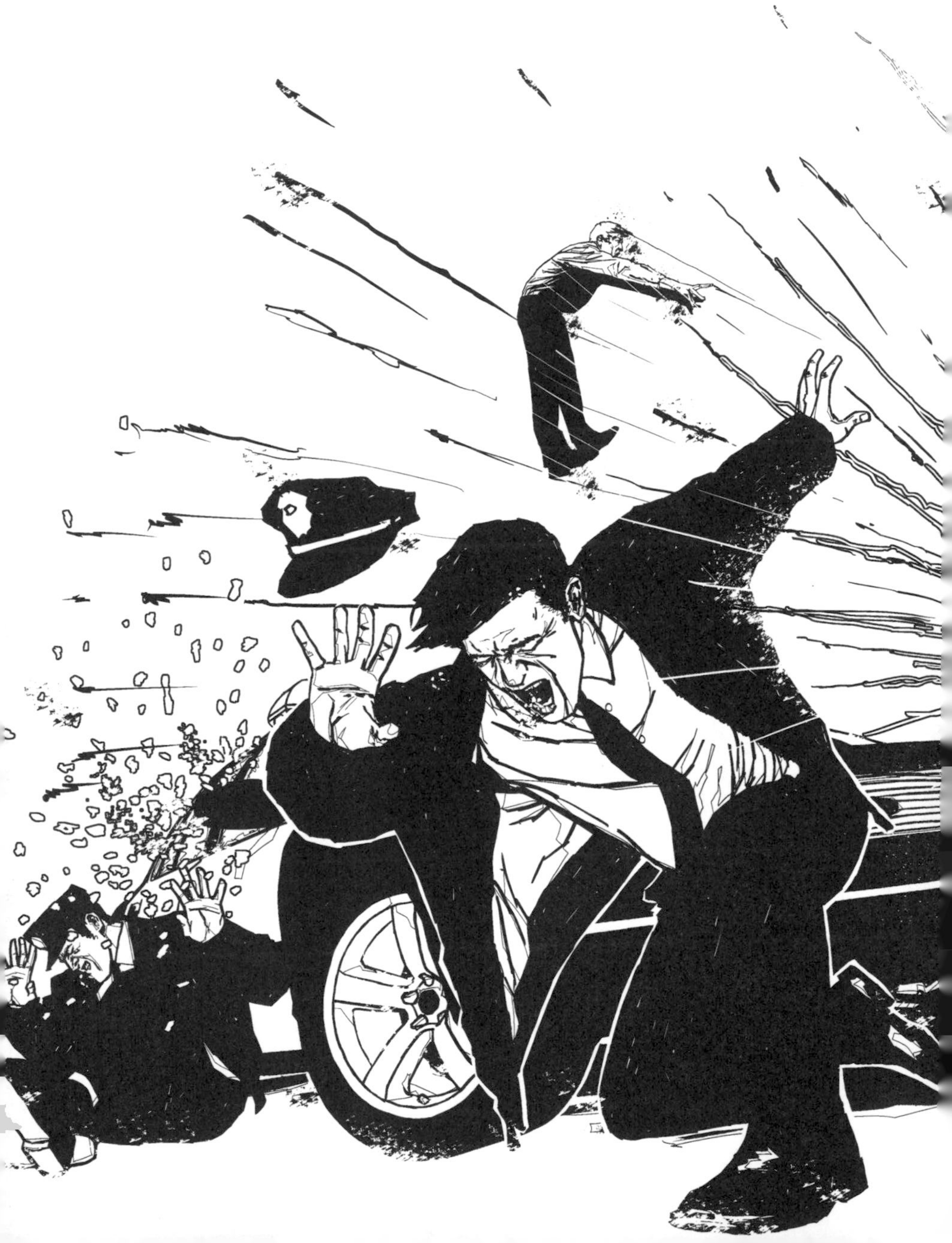

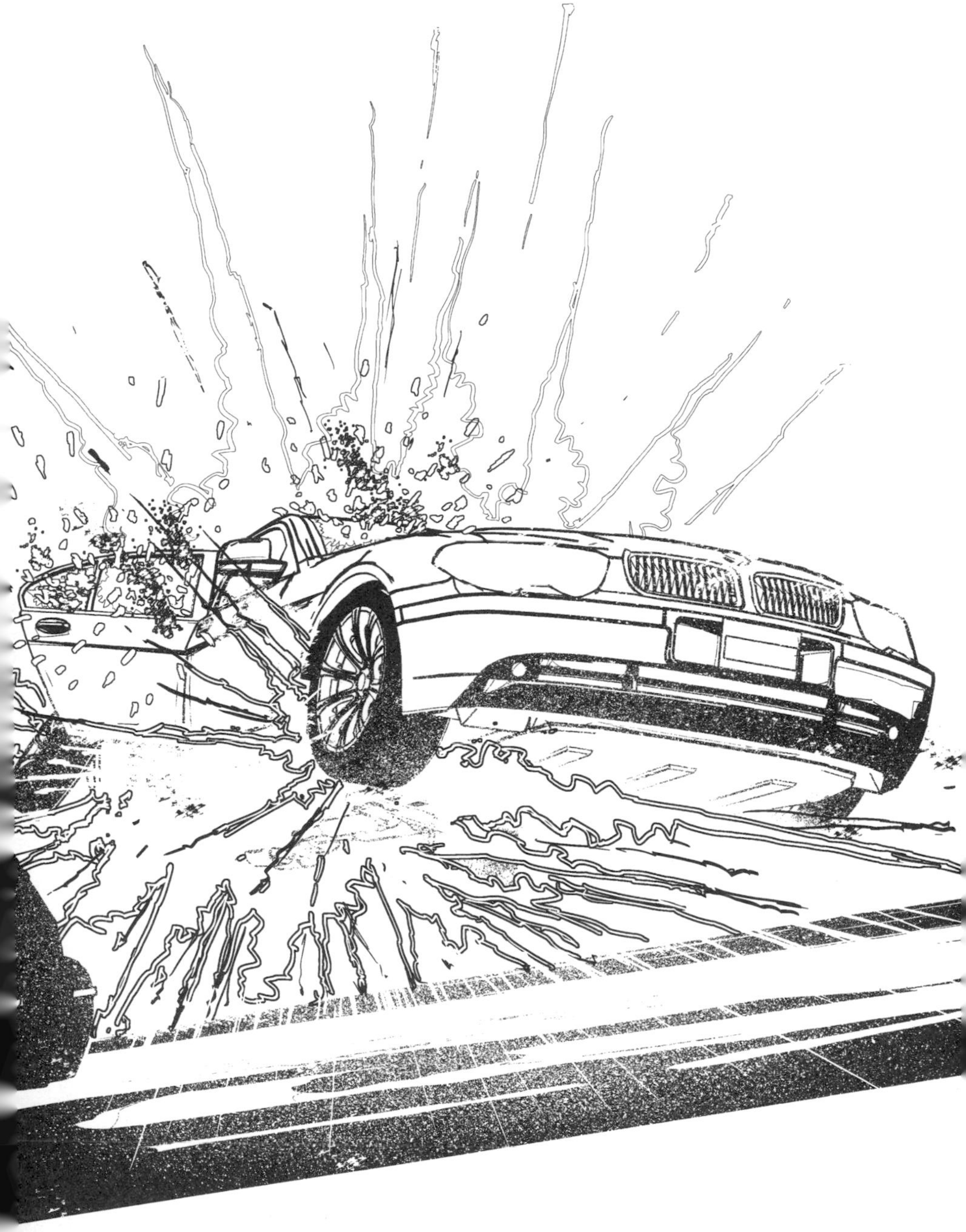

IT DIDN'T WORK, OF COURSE.

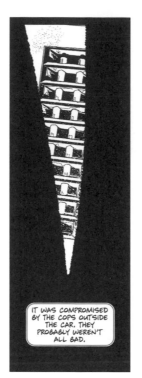

IT WAS COMPROMISED BY THE COPS OUTSIDE THE CAR. THEY PROBABLY WEREN'T ALL BAD.

BUT IT'S A START. TWO FEWER CORRUPT EXCUSES FOR MEN ARE WALKING THE STREETS.

BUT A LIFETIME OF MISTAKES IS NOT ABSOLVED IN A SINGLE ACT.

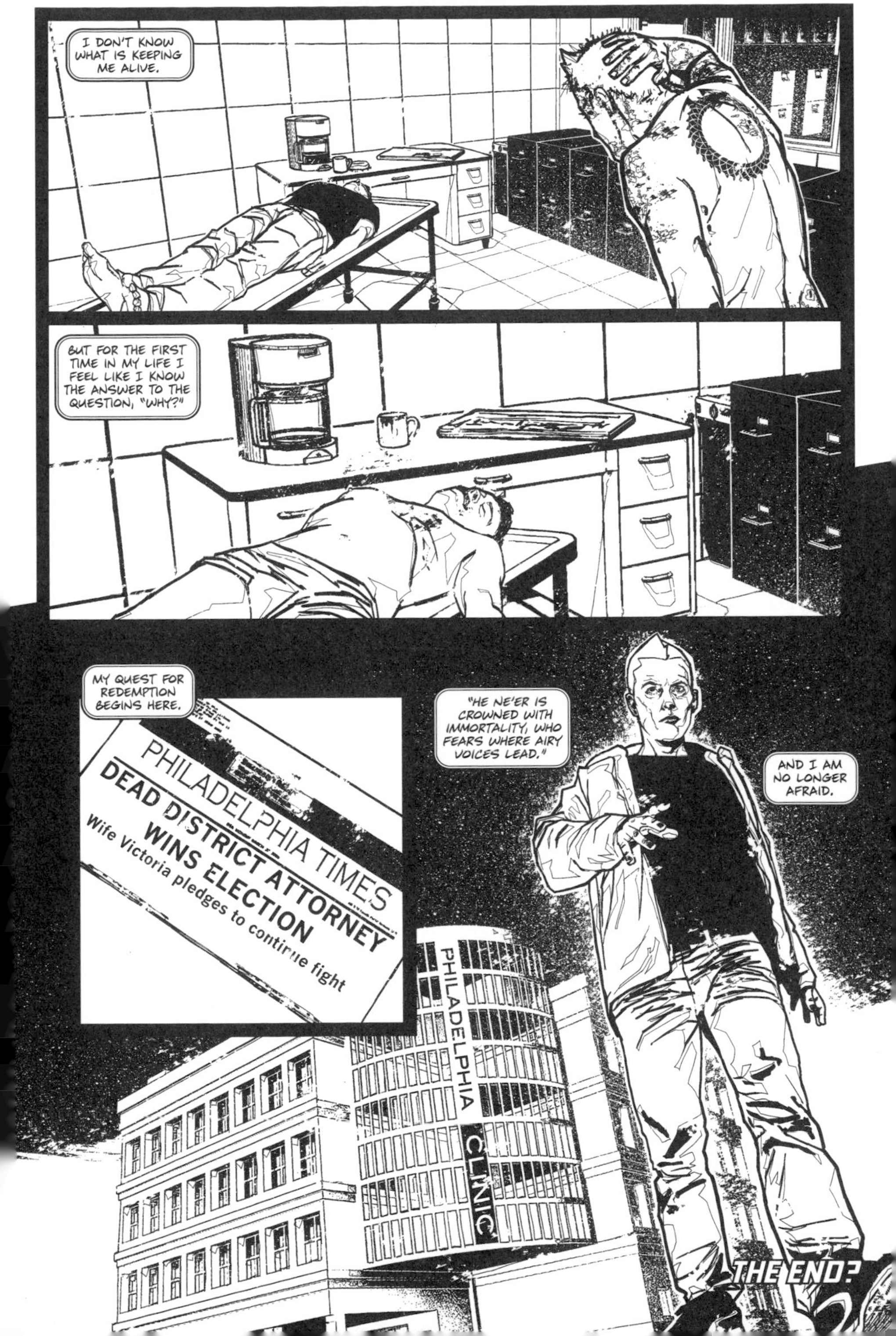
I DON'T KNOW WHAT IS KEEPING ME ALIVE.
BUT FOR THE FIRST TIME IN MY LIFE I FEEL LIKE I KNOW THE ANSWER TO THE QUESTION, "WHY?"
MY QUEST FOR REDEMPTION BEGINS HERE.
PHILADELPHIA TIMES
DEAD DISTRICT ATTORNEY WINS ELECTION
Wife Victoria pledges to continue fight
"HE NE'ER IS CROWNED WITH IMMORTALITY, WHO FEARS WHERE AIRY VOICES LEAD."
AND I AM NO LONGER AFRAID.
PHILADELPHIA
CLINIC
THE END?

LAST MORTAL

Last Mortal is a project that has its genesis over fifteen years ago, when middle school friends John and Filip first began to create comics together. The journey to bring the project to print went through many incarnations and evolutions. In the following pages, we offer a glimpse at the pitch that was eventually approved for production at Minotaur Press.

BONUS FEATURES

FOREVER MAN
Initial Pitch
Created by: Filip Sablik & John Mahoney

Staring down the infinite blackness within the barrel of his Beretta 9mm, Alec couldn't help but watch his life flash before his eyes. In the cold, quiet, emptiness of that storage unit he had to admit – his life was hardly worth the effort. His hands trembled as he adjusted the pistol between his teeth. He took a deep breath, closed his eyes, and thought about the look on Brian's face. "I'm sorry", Alec whispered as he pulled the trigger. The beginning.

Beginning at the moment he recognized his own mortality, life everlasting, Immortality, has been the sweetest dream of man. It eclipses the pursuit of wealth and power. Immortality is the most elusive prize; unless of course, the one thing you yearn for is death. That is the story of Alec King, the Forever Man, the suicidal immortal.

Alec is a loser, a nobody living at the bottom of society. He is a drug addict from the suburbs who failed out of college and is now living a dirty life in Charm City- Baltimore. Alec is a petty criminal who has seemingly never succeeded at anything in life. The only thing that has kept him from completely giving up is his best friend & partner in crime, Brian. At the outset of the story, Brian has just landed the two friends a chance at a big time hit contract, one which will pay well and lead to bigger and brighter criminal enterprises. During the course of this job, Brian is killed, the direct result of Alec's incompetence. Alec places the blame firmly on himself and, sitting alone in the storage unit the two rented for their rendezvous point, places a gun in his mouth and ends his life. It is at this moment that Alec discovers he cannot die. He is immortal. Thus begins the true story, as Alec must discover something, anything, which will make his life worth living.

The Forever Man is envisioned as an ongoing series or maxi-series. The initial story arc would follow Alec as he uses his new found ability to take revenge upon the people directly responsible for Brian's death.

FOREVER MAN
Outline of First Story Arc
By: John Mahoney and Filip Sablik

Issue One

Opens on the Baltimore, MD Harbor with our protagonist slumped on the floor of an almost empty industrial storage unit. Through voiceover we learn he is ALEC KING and that he has killed his best friend. As he sits up, he displays a pistol, which he intends to turn upon himself. As he apologizes to his missing friend, Alec lifts the gun to his head and pulls the trigger.

Cut to two days earlier when Alec is happier and killing an afternoon while citizens are at work. Meanwhile, via interlude, a group of shadowy figures are discussing hiring hit men to kill a certain mayoral candidate.

We return to Alec and find him at the harbor passing a group of storage units. He enters one just as a man in a sleazy suit (FIXER) walks out. BRIAN, the previously mentioned best-friend, is inside and is very excited. He tells Alec that he has just secured a job for them as hit men for the mob. They have been hired to kill the previously mentioned Candidate. Their conversation reveals three things; Alec is against transitioning from petty criminal to murderer, is generally a pessimist, and is easily manipulated by Brian (who is scary persuasive). In the end, Alec acquiesces because there is no alternative, either they do the job or the mob kills THEM. Brian explains that the Candidate has headquarters downtown, and the two may hit him by posing as window washers, thanks to a permit given to them by the Fixer.

Later: Alec and Brian at the building setting up their window-washing operation. As they work their way down the building it is clear Alec is petrified. When they reach the correct floor they peer inside the window and see the Candidate and his two BODYGUARDS. Alec and Brian take their guns from inside their jumpsuits. Brian fires through the window, just missing the Candidate. Alec fumbles with his gun and, as he struggles to get a grip, ducks below the window, accidentally jarring the release handle on the platform. Gunfire from the Bodyguards explodes through the window, barely missing them as the platform plummets the street below. Alec is able to stop the fall, but in the process jars Brian off the platform. The fall breaks Brian's jaw and shoulder and leaves him semi-conscious.

Alec leaps from the platform from about a story up and begins dragging Brain towards their get-away vehicle. But, just as the pair begins their escape, the Bodyguards, who have burst through an emergency exit into the alley, shoot Brian. Alec panics and immediately leaps out of the alley and into the middle of the busy city street. Angry drivers keep the Bodyguards from following. Instead they slide their guns into their jackets and follows Alec from the sidewalk. After about a block, a city bus barrels between the guards and Alec. By the time it has passed, Alec is gone.

Later: Back to the beginning of the issue: Alec in the storage unit and committing suicide. Everything goes black. Slowly light begins to creep into the frame as Alec opens his eyes and finds himself staring at the ceiling. He thinks perhaps he botched the attempt, but there is a massive pool of dried blood underneath him and he can feel a new scar on his head. Alec is left with the possibility he cannot die.

Issue Two

Alec is sitting in a crappy city diner, a cup of coffee and a newspaper in front of him. A week and a half has passed since he shot himself. Absent-mindedly he rubs the scar on his head while contemplating what is happening to him. On the front page of the paper is news indicating that the Candidate's popularity has surged since the assassination attempt. He is now leading his opponents by a healthy margin. Alec flashes back to Brian and the first job they worked together. After the flashback, Alec leaves the diner, set with the new purpose of getting revenge for his dead friend. Meanwhile an old man in the diner calls someone on a cell and says that the guy they are looking for just left the diner.

Alec is walking down a crummy street trying to figure out where to start. He concludes that he needs to go after the guy who hired them. As he is deep in thought, a black sedan glides down the street behind him. Alec turns around just as the car hits him. He goes flipping over the top and lands hard on the other side. Alec stumbles back to his feet, obviously injured, and limps down an alley. The car pulls up to the entrance of the alley revealing two things; the driver is the Bodyguard who killed Brian and this is a Police Cruiser. He gets out and stalks Alec down the alley. Alec throws a couple weak punches, which the Bodyguard easily parries and then retaliates with some brutal hooks and kicks. As Alec hits the alley wall and slides to the pavement, the Bodyguard pulls out a hand cannon. The reader gets a clear view of the Bodyguard's police badge as he plugs Alec several times in the gut. The Bodyguard then calls someone on his cell phone and reports that the job is done. He reassures the voice on the line that he understands how bad it could be if Alec were to survive.
Alec waits until the Bodyguard is gone before opening his eyes and struggling to his knees. He crawls off, wondering why the mob bodyguard has a police badge, just before more cops show up.
Alec makes it back to the storage unit. He is discovering something about his new found ability, he can't die, but he can still get hurt. He collapses in a corner and takes a swig of Jack before passing out. He is bleeding heavily on the floor. Alec is brought back to consciousness by the sound of someone talking near him. He opens his eyes a crack and sees the Fixer who originally hired he and Brian. The Fixer says into his cell that Alec is dead. As he bends over to check Alec's breathing, Alec swings the Jack bottle and shatters it over the guy's head. Alec then pulls the gun from his pocket and shoots the guy in the shin. The Fixer falls over screaming, clutching his leg and dropping the still open cell phone. Alec drags himself over to the guy and puts the gun to the goodfella's head. He starts interrogating the guy, who, despite the pain, is acting tough. He only drops hints to the larger picture. The main reveal is that the Fixer is actually a cop, not a goodfella. As Alec is taken aback by his comments, the Fixer pulls a knife from his belt and stabs Alec, aiming for his heart. The sudden pain causes Alec to pull the trigger and he shoots the guy through the chest. Alec is briefly stunned from his first actual kill, even if it was accidental. When he recovers he searches the man, finding a wallet and a business card from a local restaurant in Little Italy. He begins to take the man's outer clothes (jacket, hat, etc.) and uses them to disguise himself, but not before using the man's shirt to bandage himself up. The dropped cell phone on the floor goes dead... the other side has heard enough.

Issue Three

Alec is diving behind a knocked over table as a group of MAFIA THUGS open fire on him. The voiceover comments how this seemed like a good idea at the time… Flashback to Alec standing outside a quiet Little Italy restaurant in the outfit he borrowed from the dead FIXER. He's steeling himself to go in. With a deep breath he enters the restaurant, keeping his jacket collar high and his hat low. Imitating the Fixer's voice he throws out a "he in?" at the concierge, who confirms and points toward the back. Alec walks into the back room of the establishment, where a group of DIRTY COPS are sitting around a table. The table is spread with cash and confiscated baggies of drugs. They greet Alec thinking he's the Fixer. Alec stutters something and then pulls his and the Fixer's guns from his jacket. Leveling them at the dirty cops, he begins demanding answers. Almost immediately the cops realize Alec is bluffing and draw their guns. Meanwhile, the Bodyguard walks into the restaurant. He asks the concierge some questions, looking for the Fixer. Just as the concierge is indicating he has just come in, the back door flies opens and Alec backs out, guns drawn. The Bodyguard shouts at Alec, who turns his head, and at that moment the cops open fire through the doorway. Alec curses and dives under a table as patrons go scrambling. He knocks the table over and hides behind it. The Bodyguard moves through the restaurant as the crowd scatters, drawing his gun. Alec fires some wild shots over the table and misses all of the cops. The Bodyguard gets clear of the crowd and opens fire on Alec too, putting him in a deadly crossfire. Alec pivots the table, and looking around in a panic, spots an open cognac bottle. He throws it in the direction of the Bodyguard and fires at the bottle. It explodes in front of the Bodyguard causing him to dive back. Meanwhile, Alec lifts the table and uses it as shield, rushing the cops. As he makes impact with two of them, driving them back and knocking them off balance, they fire their guns into the air. The stray bullets strike the gas line above the grills in the open kitchen and ignite. Alec ducks down as the larger explosion rocks the cops forward. Moments later he crawls over to one of the cops who is prone but still alive and begins to interrogate him. The cop stammers that they didn't really expect Alec and Brian to be successful before perishing. As Alec pauses to think about this, he feels cold steel pressed up to the back of his head and the unmistakable click of a gun cocking. The Bodyguard has recovered. The two have a tense exchange as Alec discretely pulls one of the guns from his coat and palms it in front of him. The Bodyguard tells Alec to make peace with his maker and Alec closes his eyes and grits his teeth. There is a gun shot and gun smoke from Alec's back. The Bodyguard is shocked as he looks down at the bullet hole in his abdomen; Alec has shot him through his own torso. The Bodyguard collapses and Alec slowly drags up. He proceeds to search the cops and the Bodyguard.

Alec goes into the back room and roughly dresses his wounds, takes an obscene amount of pills from the cops' stash, then ransacks the room, finding some paperwork revealing the name of the owner of the restaurant. Later, Alec breaks into the Bodyguard's apartment, where he finds clues that connect the dirty cops to Candidate Callahan. As Alec puts the pieces together he realizes the Candidate was expecting them. He moved before Brian fired. It finally dawns on Alec that the mafia is not involved at all and the most likely suspect for orchestrating this whole fiasco is the Candidate himself.

Alec is violently throwing a small appliance at the viewer and screaming in rage. Alec proceeds to throw stuff around inside the Bodyguard's apartment in frustration, basically turning the place upside down. When Alec is done ranting, he collects himself and analyzes his options. He resolves that the candidate will have to pay for killing Brian. He collects his guns and the Bodyguard's ID and security card. As Alec turns to leave it's apparent that his gun shot wounds are healing, but he is still heavily injured.

Meanwhile, Candidate Callahan is at his campaign headquarters making a number of phones calls. These phone calls reveal that he is working to keep Internal Affairs away form his lackeys, the dirty cops who set up the assassination attempt. The Candidate is livid as he finds out about the firefight in the restaurant. His Chief of Staff comes into the room and the two argue briefly about a pressing engagement. The Candidate finally concedes that appearances must be maintained and the two leave the office.

The Candidate and his Chief of Staff come down into a parking garage and walk over to a basic black sedan. In the back seat of the sedan Alec is hiding, breathing heavy and holding one of the guns close to him. They get in the car and continue their conversation as they exit the parking garage. As the car pulls out onto the street, Alec pops up in the back seat and levels a gun at both the Candidate and his Chief of Staff. A tense conversation ensues between the three people in the car. In the conversation the Candidate reveals his plan to Alec. He knew that he was behind in the polls. He had the Fixer hire two small timers who were guaranteed to fail and dumb enough not to question why they got the job offer in the first place. The Bodyguard was supposed to have killed both of them. He hadn't counted on Alec being so persistent.

Alec is so incensed and upset that he doesn't notice where the Candidate has been driving. The car stops and Alec looks around in confusion and panic. A police officer comes to the driver's side window, which the Candidate lowers. Alec quickly hides his guns inside his jacket. The officer welcomes the Candidate and says they are ready for him. He mentions how proud the police department is of the Candidate's bravery and that he has his support. The Candidate thanks him graciously and the officer opens his door as other cops open up the back door and the passenger door. Alec gets out with the others in confusion and is herded with the Candidate towards a stage. They have arrived at the final political rally before the election. The Candidate climbs up to the stage and comes to the podium. He gives a very inspiring and polished speech. During the speech he brings Alec, who is prodded by the Chief of Staff, up to the podium, and tells the crowd that Alec is one of the thousands of hard working citizens of Baltimore who lost their jobs under the last administration. He pledges to help get those people their jobs back and make their neighborhoods safer. The crowd applauds loudly.

The Candidate and his entourage step down from the stage. Alec grabs the Candidate roughly by the arm and whispers angrily in his ear, threatening him. The Candidate turns and smiles at Alec, telling him that he is not touchable by the likes of him. As Alec moves to respond to the Candidate, reporters swarm the area and begin peppering the Candidate with question. The Candidate takes a moment to smile and look Alec coldly in the eyes, before turning to address the reporters. Alec slowly fades into the background and disappears into the crowd.

LAST MORTAL #1 COVER LAYOUT VERSION A

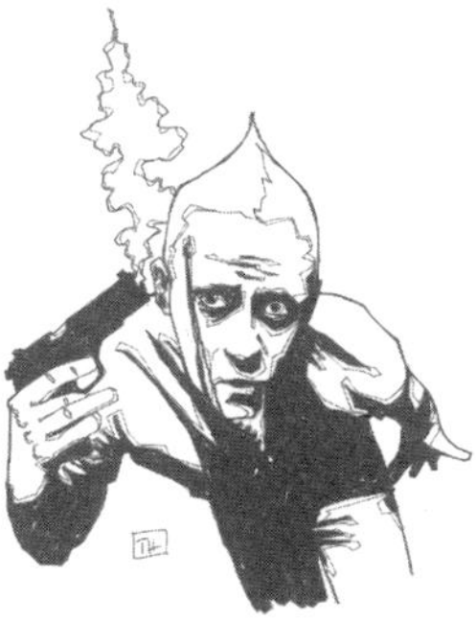

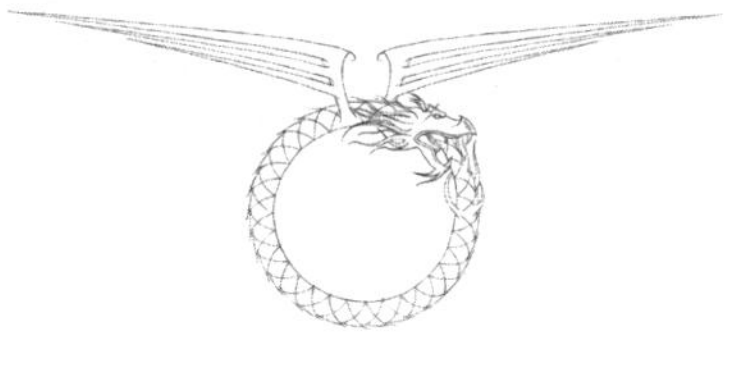

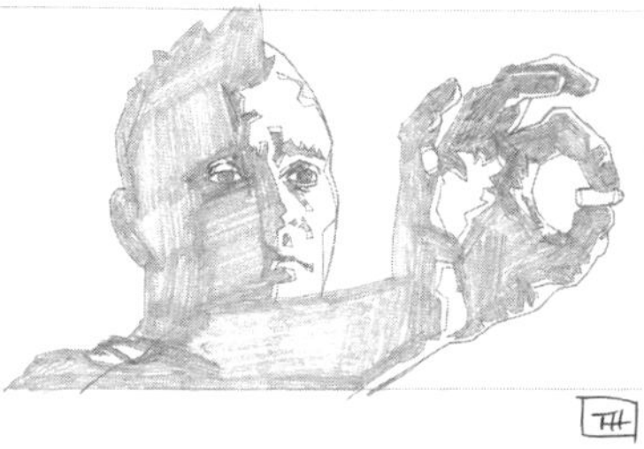

LAST MORTAL #1 COVER VERSION B

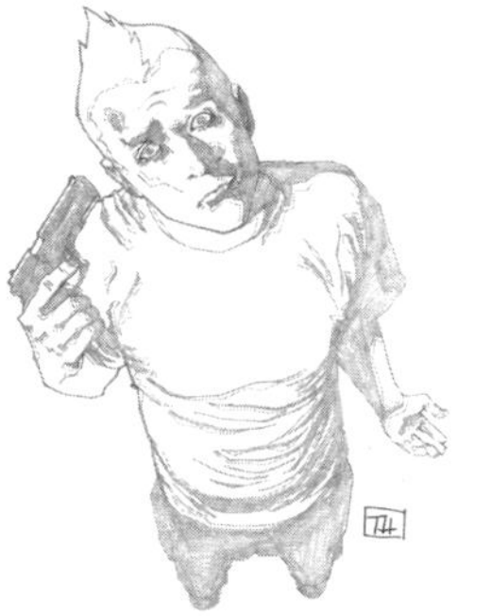

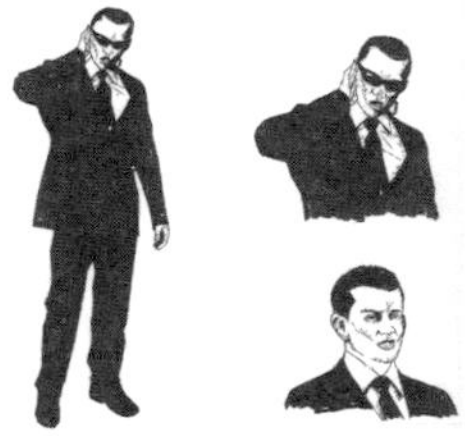

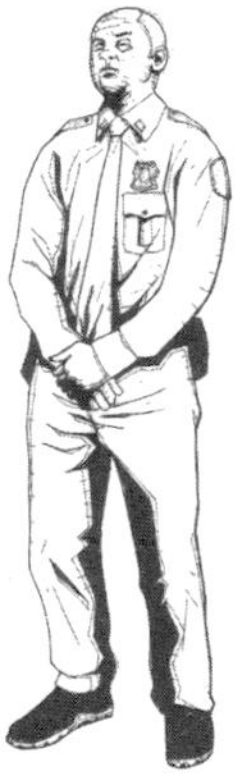

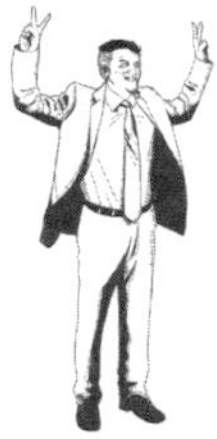

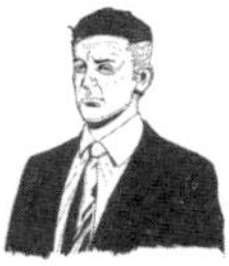

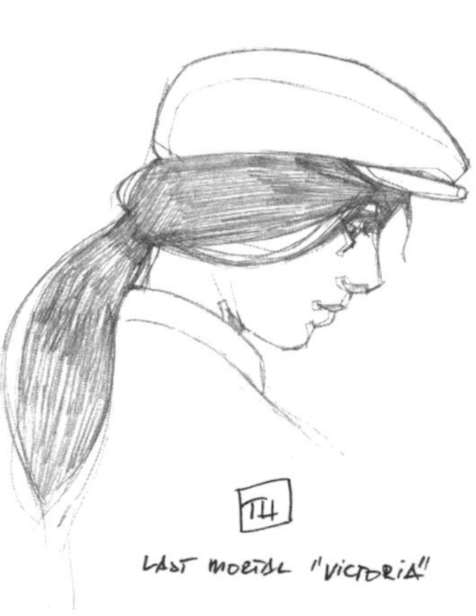

LAST MORTAL "VICTORIA"

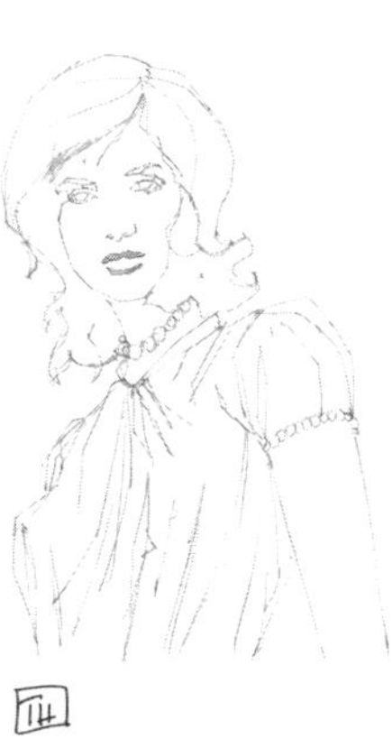

LAST MORTAL "VICTORIA"

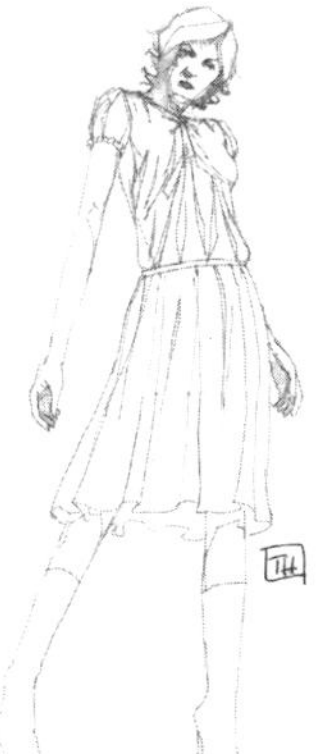

LAST MORTAL "VICTORIA"

Character Design:
ALEC

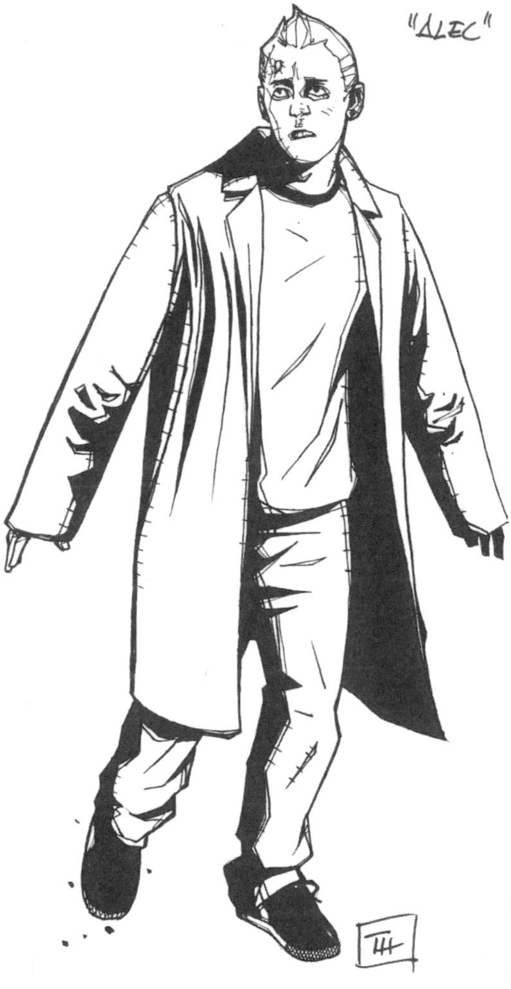
"ALEC"
TH

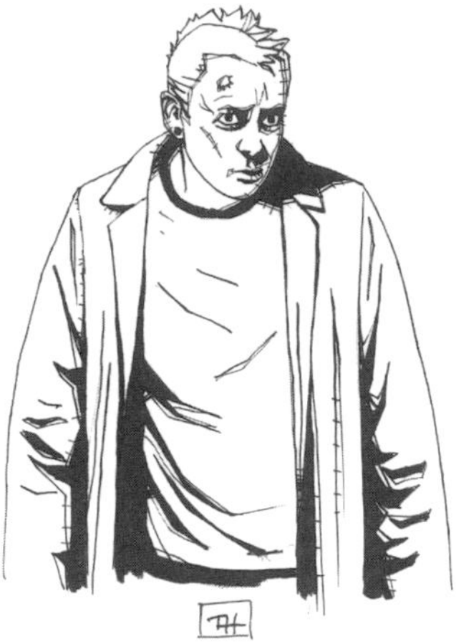
TH

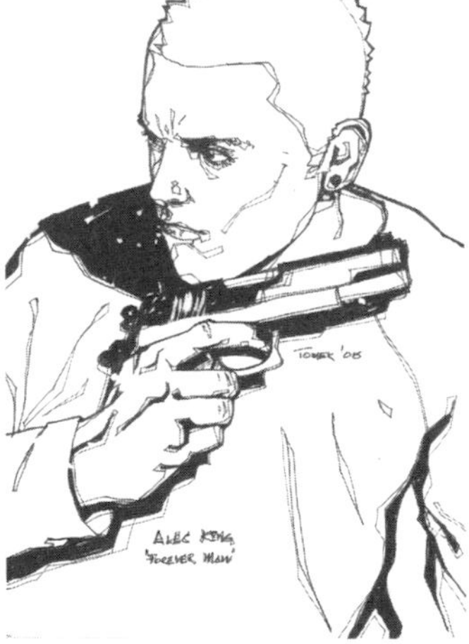
TOMER '05
ALEC KING
'FOREVER MAN'

Character Design:
BRIAN

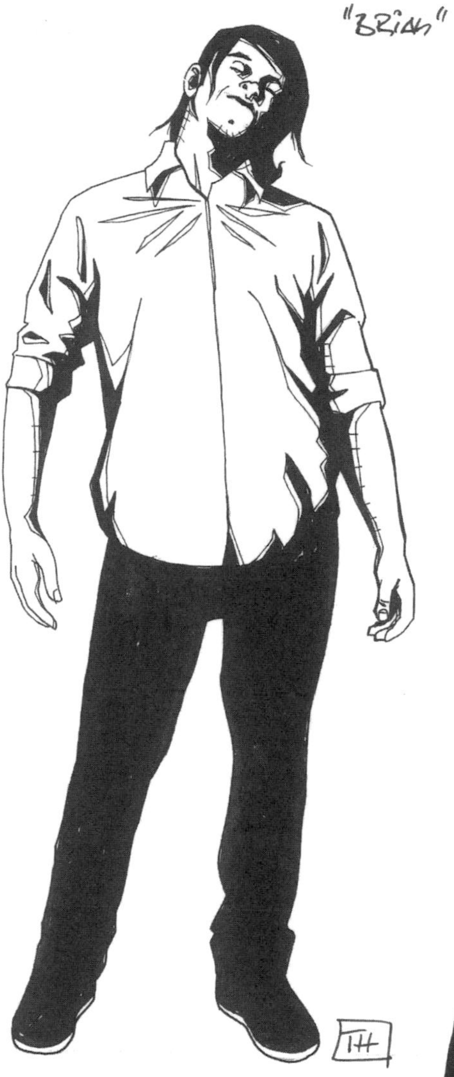
"BRIAN"

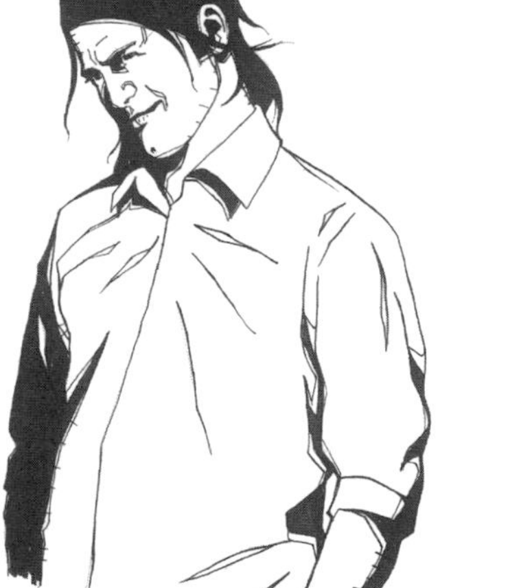

LAST MORTAL

As previously mentioned, John and Filip first conceived of the character of Alec, the suicidal immortal, while they were in middle school in the mid-nineties. Originally developed as a series called "Forever Man," with John writing and Filip drawing, the pair have pulled some key items from their archives to illustrate how far the series has come.

THE FOREVER MAN issue #1   John Mahoney
Full Script/17 pages
"Nothing To Fear..."   Roanoke, VA 24018
Third Draft/June 16, 1995

PAGE ONE/SPLASH

MEDIUM SHOT, EARLY EVENING

NEW YORK CITY

ALEC DUPREE is walking down the sidewalk of a dirty New York
city neighborhood. The buildings surrounding him are in disrepair
and most of the streetlights are broken. ALEC is walking with head
down and his hands in his pockets. He is wearing a brown
trenchcoat, a grungy tanktop, black combat boots, and beat-up black
jeans. He's in his late twenties, unshaven, and generally looks
like he hasn't slept in a week.

1 CAPTION   New York City

2 CAPTION   Thursday, April 14, 1995. 7:12 p.m.

4 ALEC   (thought balloon)...almost got caught that time. What's
             wrong with me?! Every time I get a good thing going I
             wimp out. It's like somethings' holding me back.

FOREVER MAN/Nothing To Fear.../Mahoney

PAGE TWO

PANEL ONE MEDIUM SIDE SHOT As he muses, ALEC turns a corner and passes an electronics store. In the front window of the shop are a variety of televisions, many of which are tuned into the evening news. The ANCHOR-PERSON is an hispanic female in her early twenties, behind her is a photograph of ROBERT WASHINGTON, candidate for mayor.

1 T.V. (electronic blurb) ...and in other news, the Independent candidate for mayor, Robert Washington, paid a visit to an area day-care center today to draw attention to his new health care proposal...

PANEL TWO MEDIUM SIDE SHOT ALEC has continued walking and is now passing a boarded-up alley. Pasted to the boards are a variety of posters, including several "Washington For Mayor" posters with George Washington's picture (from the one-dollar bill) on them.

2 ALEC (thought balloon) I just wish I could got over this fear of gettin' caught. This damn fear has crippled me, kept me from ever making anything of my worthless life.

PANEL THREE INSET PANEL ALEC is opening the door of a rather run-down looking red brick warehouse. A sign above his head reads "Titan Movers" and has a silhouette of a caped superhero flying, carrying a moving van above his head.

3 ALEC (thought balloon) I've got more skill then anyone else in this hell-hole. But I'm too afraid to use it.

PANEL FOUR DOWN SHOT the inside of a shadowy warehouse. Boxes are piled everywhere. ALEC is coming through a door at one side of the room and in the center is a round table with two men, BRIAN FIELDING (ALEC's partner in crime) and JASON PARKER (a "big time hood from Jersey")

4 & 5

1 BRIAN (yelling around the boxes) Alec! Over here!

2 ALEC (thought bubble) I guess this is it...

PANEL ONE   MEDIUM SHOT, ALEC sits down at the table, obviously nervous. BRIAN is sitting a bit to his left, barely able to contain his enthusiasm. BRIAN is a wiry little guy in his late twenties and is wearing a faded LED ZEPPELIN t-shirt and jeans. JASON is a robust man in his mid-thirties and is wearing a black pin-stripe Armani suit. He's leaning back in his chair smoking a cigarette.

1 BRIAN   (enthusiastically) Alec, it's about time you got here. This is Mr. Parker, he says he's got a job requiring our particular troubleshooting abilities...

2 ALEC   um...okay, I'm all ears.

PANEL TWO   MEDIUM CLOSE-UP of JASON, who's leaning forward with his elbows on the table, fingers interlocked, looking mysterious and supremely confident.

3 JASON   Okay you two, here's tha' deal. I heard from...a reliable source, that you two are pretty quick. I also heard that business has been...a little slow. So I'm hear to offer you two a business proposal.

4 BRIAN   (off panel) um-hm

PANEL THREE   MEDIUM CLOSE-UP SIDE SHOT of all three men

5 JASON   It has recently come to my attention that the independent candidate for mayor, one Robert Washington, may cause my...associates and I considerable...discomfort...if elected. I want the two of you to make sure this possibility does not occur.

6 ALEC   (visibly shaken) You mean...kill him?!..I don't know about this Brian. I...this is a little too heavy.

7 BRIAN   (smiling widely, cutting ALEC off) Shut up Alec. (to Parker) We're in.

PANEL FOUR   CLOSE UP of JASON, who throws two bundles of money on to the table.

8 JASON   You two are a real cute couple. Here's ten grand in advance, consider it incentive. If you get him, then I'll meet you back here for the rest. Understood?

(CONTINUED)

PAGE THREE CONTINUED

PANEL FIVE MEDIUM CLOSE-UP ALEC is leaning on the table with his face in his hands, mumbling incoherently. BRIAN is standing with one hand on ALEC's back and the other shaking JASON's hand (also standing)

9 BRIAN   (enthusiastically) Consider it done.

10 JASON   (with just a hint of sarcasm) I hope so, 'cause I'd hate ta have to kill a couple a nice boys like you two.

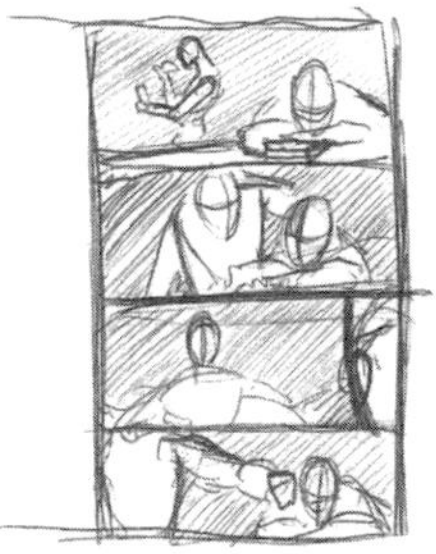

FOREVER MAN/Nothing to Fear.../Mahoney

PAGE FOUR

PANEL ONE MEDIUM SHOT JASON has left. The partners are alone. BRIAN is pacing around the table excitedly with a wad of money clutched in his hand, while ALEC leans on the table with his arms folded under his head, his money remains untouched.

1 BRIAN This is great! This is our chance to make it big time! Just call me Brian Dillinger. Bitchin'

PANEL TWO BRIAN has finally noticed that ALEC isn't quite as enthused as he is about this and has stopped walking, he is now leaning on the other end of the table directly across from ALEC, whom is leaning back in his chair.

2 BRIAN What's wrong with you? You look kinda green...

3 ALEC There's a big difference between burglary and murder, Bri.

PANEL THREE BRIAN has thrown his gaze towards the heavens and is flailing his arms wildly. ALEC has raised his head and is now staring at him.

4 BRIAN (angry) You've got some nerve, man. You don't care about Washington, you don't even care about the money! You're just afraid of gettin' caught, you friggin pansy!

5 ALEC Come on Brian, you know I...look, I just need some time to think, okay?

PANEL FOUR MEDIUM SHOT BRIAN has walked over to ALEC and has put his hand on his shoulder.

6 BRIAN Sure, man, I understand. Look, meet me tomorrow at the Empire State Building, that's where Washington's campaign headquarters are. We'll take him out then and get it over with. Quick and easy, cool?

7 ALEC Cool...and um, Brian, thanks.

8 BRIAN Sure man, anytime.

FOREVER MAN/Nothing To Fear.../Mahoney

PAGE FIVE

PANEL ONE EXTREME LONG-SHOT the New York City skyline centered on
the EMPIRE STATE BUILDING.

1 CAPTION   Friday, April 15, 1995. 9:30 a.m.

PANEL TWO LONG-SHOT the front of the Empire State Building. A dark
spot can be seen about 1/4 of the way up the building.

PANEL THREE MEDIUM SHOT ALEC and BRIAN are standing on a window
washing platform. They are wearing white overalls and have wipers
in their hands, buckets sit at their feet.

2 ALEC   (sarcastically) Gee, Brian, what a great idea. Now
             instead of just worrying about being arrested or
             shot...we get to worry about taking a swan-dive into the
             pavement. Joy.

3 BRIAN   (smiling) Bite me, man.

4 BRIAN   See...you've really gotta control that fear of yours,
             Alec. It's gonna be the death of you...(laugh)

PANEL FOUR MEDIUM SHOT ALEC is actually attempting to clean a
window and BRIAN is turned toward him smiling.

4 BRIAN   Don't sweat it man! Look, we know Washington's in
             his morning staff meeting on the 95th floor. All we have
             to do is move up a few levels and I'll take care of
             him...all you have to do is cover me, okay?

5 ALEC   Have I ever let you down?

PANEL FIVE MEDIUM CLOSE-UP ALEC and BRIAN interlock their fingers
in an arm-wrestling-like handshake, both have huge smiles on their
faces.

7 BRIAN   No, Al. Never.

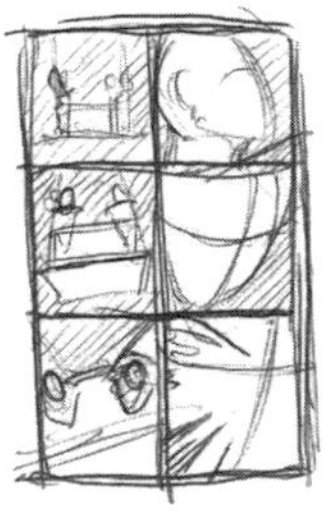

FOREVER MAN/Nothing to Fear.../Mahoney

PAGE SIX

PANEL ONE MEDIUM CLOSE-UP The partners begin pulling themselves up level by level.

1 CAPTION The 92nd Floor

PANEL TWO CLOSE-UP of ALEC's face which is beginning to sweat.

PANEL THREE MEDIUM CLOSE-UP The partners pull themselves up another level.

2 CAPTION The 93rd Floor

PANEL FOUR CLOSE-UP of ALEC's face, he is sweating more and now looks really scared.

PANEL FIVE MEDIUM CLOSE-UP the partners have ascended another level

3 CAPTION The 94th Floor

PANEL SIX CLOSE-UP of ALEC's face. He is now shivering, and quietly gasping for breath.

4 ALEC (whisper)...can't breath...

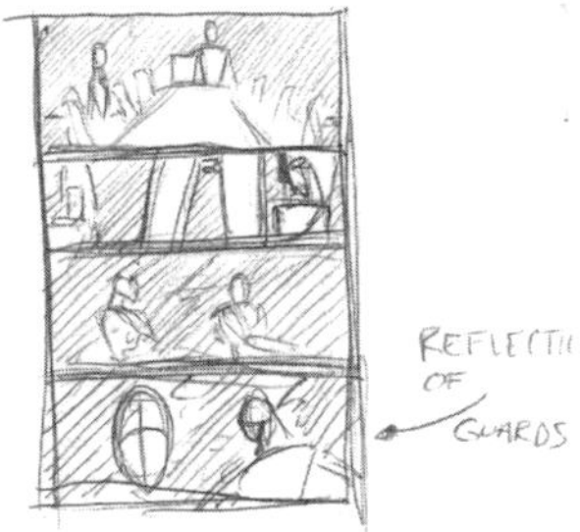
REFLECTI
OF
GUARDS

PAGE SEVEN

PANEL ONE MEDIUM SHOT inside of ROBERT WASHINGTON's conference room, which is expensive looking and "Washington for Mayor" posters with George Washington's picture (from the one-dollar bill) are everywhere. ROBERT WASHINGTON is a tall, well-built Greek god of a man looking to be in his late twenties. He sits at the head of an oval table facing the windows which ALEC and BRIAN are outside washing. There are six other seats, all filled with businessmen and women in expensive suits. At the rear left corner of the room is a door. The business woman sitting at the far-left "corner" of the table is standing, addressing WASHINGTON.

1 WOMAN ...so, what I'm really trying to say here is, to have any real chance at a victory, sir, you've to do something drastic, and soon.

PANEL TWO CLOSE-UP outside the office. We are behind ALEC and BRIAN and on the level of their pails. We see the arm of each man reaching into his pail and pulling out an uzi.

2 BRIAN (above panel) NOW!

PANEL THREE ALEC's shivers have become more violent and are now full blown convulsions. As he leans back (reaching for a support rope) he drops his weapon. BRIAN is turned towards him, a confused look on his face. In the background (inside the office) we see the business people leaping out of their seats and diving for cover.

3 ALEC (whispers) uhnn...B-B-rian...c-c-an't...b-breath!

4 BRIAN Alec?!

PANEL FOUR Still outside. Through the glass we see two guards (one shorter with greased hair and mustache, the second larger with long flowing locks) charge through the door at the back of the room, looking surprised and pulling out small handguns. ALEC is looking through the window with a look of absolute horror on his face. BRIAN is looking over the back of the platform at ALEC's falling gun.

5 BRIAN NO!

PAGE EIGHT

PANEL ONE MEDIUM SHOT FROM BEHIND. The window explodes in a rain of bullets, BRIAN is hit several times and is flung backwards off the platform. ALEC dives to the platform reaching for him, narrowly avoiding being shot.

1 ALEC   BRIAN!!!!

PANEL TWO FROM A FEW FEET ABOVE THE PLATFORM We see ALEC's back and his arm reaching down towards BRIAN, who is a few hundred feet below, bullets still flying above Alec's head.

2 ALEC   Brian! don't leave me here alone!

PANEL THREE same as PANEL TWO except BRIAN has hit the protective net outside the 10th floor and bullets fly straight through the left window-washing platform rope.

PANEL FOUR same angle as PANEL THREE except the platform is swinging downwards. ALEC is clutching it for dear life, tears rolling down his face.

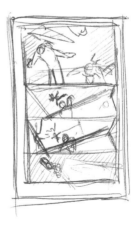

PAGE NINE

PANEL ONE FROM INSIDE THE BUILDING (LARGE PANEL). ALEC comes crashing through the window of a presently empty office head-first with his arms crossed like an "X" to protect his face, taking a set of venician blinds with him. The room is dark and shadowy. The only light in the room comes from the hole in the window (the rest is blocked out by blinds)

PANEL TWO ABOVE SHOT FROM THE POV OF THE WINDOW (LARGE PANEL) ALEC is sprawled across the floor in a circle of light, shattered glass is scattered chaotically around him.

PANEL THREE ALEC has pushed himself up and is now hobbling towards a door at the front of the room. Small puddles of blood remain at his landing spot, along with pieces of bloody glass.

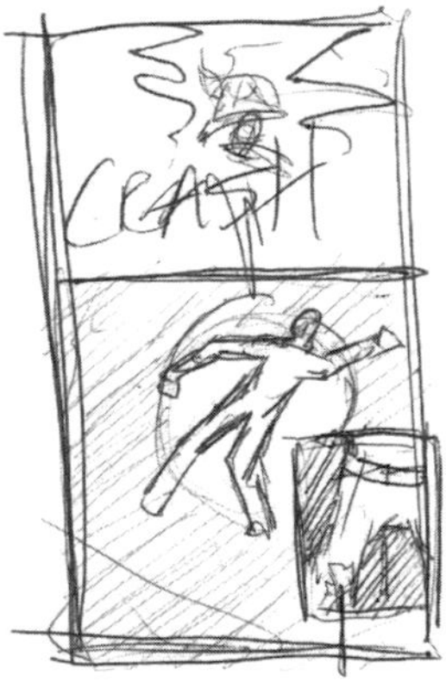
CRASH

PAGE TEN

PANEL ONE WASHINGTON's office. WASHINGTON is standing beside the table pointing towards the door, one guard is looking out the window (hole?) as he pushes two business people aside. The other guard is standing near WASHINGTON in a protective stance. The other four business people are running out the door.

1 GUARD (the one by the window) Only one of them fell, sir, the other went through the window of the empty offices downstairs!

PANEL TWO The two guards (We'll call them GERALDO and FABIO) run out of the office and into an elevator

PANEL THREE FROM INSIDE THE ELEVATOR we see the guards waiting impatiently for the door to open.

PANEL FOUR same as PANEL THREE but with doors open and ALEC standing outside. He is bleeding from multiple wounds and basically looks like hell. A look of utter horror on his face.

PANEL FIVE MEDIUM SHOT with ALEC running toward the reader with bullets arcing over his head. In the background the guards are firing at him.

3 FABIO Get him! Washington'll kill us if he gets away!

PANEL SIX FROM INSIDE OF THE STAIRWELL ALEC slams through the door to the stairs.

4 ALEC Holy...!

PANEL SEVEN DOWN SHOT The GUARDS (Fabio & Geraldo) are leaning over the railing of the stairs firing at ALEC as he dives through a door two floors below.

PANEL ONE MEDIUM SHOT   ALEC is leaning against the door to the stairs. The sign on the door reads "FLOOR 92"

1 ALEC   (huff) (huff) (huff)

PANEL TWO   ALEC dives to the side as a volley of bullets tear through the doors.

2 ALEC   damn

PANEL THREE MEDIUM CLOSE-UP   ALEC scrambles down the hallway towards the reader. Behind him we see the GUARDS slam through the door, knocking it down as they do. The hallway has a few bystanders who have been pushed to the walls by ALEC who's sweating profusely and looks like he's going to topple over in exhaustion any second now.

PANEL FOUR   ALEC dives into an elevator just as its door are closing, knocking a businessman out into the hall as bullets whiz by. The elevator next to it is just opening, a group of surprised business people standing awestruck inside.

PANEL FIVE   the GUARDS push everyone out of the second elevator and climb in, then push the LOBBY button.

3 GERALDO   He's not getting away that easy...

PANEL SIX FULL SHOT OF EMPIRE STATE BUILDING LOBBY   ALEC is running out of the elevator towards the front doors. The doors to the second elevator are just beginning to open.

PANEL SEVEN   ALEC dives out the front doors as the GUARDS open fire on him. He escapes unscathed, but the front windows are completely destroyed.

PAGE TWELVE

PANEL ONE   FULL SHOT of the "Titan Movers" warehouse. Night. ALEC
is walking towards the building in the same posture as during the
opening. A homeless man stands between him and the warehouse.

1 CAPTION   The warehouse district. Saturday, April 16, 10:15 p.m.

2 BUM   Hey man...spare a buck?

PANEL TWO MEDIUM SHOT through the eyes of the bum, we see Alec with
wallet in hand pulling out a dollar and looking at it deep in
thought.

3 ALEC   (thought bubble) ...a dollar...

PANEL THREE same shot as above but ALEC is turned towards the BUM
and is handing him the wallet, from the right corner of the panel
an arm reaches out to accept the gift.

4 ALEC   Here, you deserve this more than I do.

5 BUM   What? Friggin neighborly of you bud. Much
             appreciated.

PANEL FOUR LONG SHOT from the other side of the street as ALEC
enters the warehouse and the BUM begins walking in the opposite
direction.

PAGE THIRTEEN

PANEL ONE OVERHEAD LONG SHOT of ALEC sitting in the fetal position in the dim light of a window high overhead. The only other light in the warehouse comes from a lamp over the table the partners had been planning at earlier in the story. ALEC's wad of money still lies, untouched on the table.

PANEL TWO OVERHEAD MEDIUM SHOT We can see that ALEC has obviously been crying. He is still wearing the overalls from the day before, coated with blood and torn in many places. He is sitting with his left arm hugging his knees and his right rests on the floor with a small pistol in hand.

1 ALEC   (thought balloon) How could I do it? He died...I let him
          die. My best friend...I let him die!

PANEL THREE CLOSE-UP OF ALEC'S FACE he has begun crying again.

2 ALEC   (whispering)...I dropped the gun...It should of been
          me.

MAY BE
THIS
SHOULD BE
TWO PANELS?

3 ALEC   (screaming) IT SHOULD OF BEEN ME. I'M THE WORTHLESS
          ONE!!!

PANEL FOUR MEDIUM SHOT ALEC. He's raised his head and is talking heavenward.

4 ALEC   Brian, I'm so sorry I let you down, man. I...I lost it,
          but I owe you more than lame excuses, a lot more...

PAGE FOURTEEN

PANEL ONE CLOSE-UP OF ALEC'S HEAD he has the gun up to his head, tears streaming down his cheeks and a look of utter hopelessness on his face.

1 ALEC   (whispering) I hope I make it up there with you...

NOTE: In the gutter between PANELS ONE and TWO is a gun shot

2 CAPTION   BOOM

PANEL THREE MEDIUM SHOT (LARGE PANEL) ALEC's left arm and leg have fallen limply to the side. His right arm is stretched away from his body and the gun has been thrown a few feet to his right. The wall behind him, as well as the floor, are both thoroughly coated with blood.

3   PANEL FOUR CLOSE-UP OF THE GUN (barrel facing the reader, ALEC in the background)

4   PANEL FIVE EXTREME CLOSE-UP OF THE GUN (barrel facing the reader)

5   PANEL SIX   COMPLETE BLACKNESS

6   PANEL SEVEN DARKNESS CRACKED WITH SMALL STREAMS OF LIGHT CREEPING IN.

FOREVER MAN/Nothing To Fear.../Mahoney

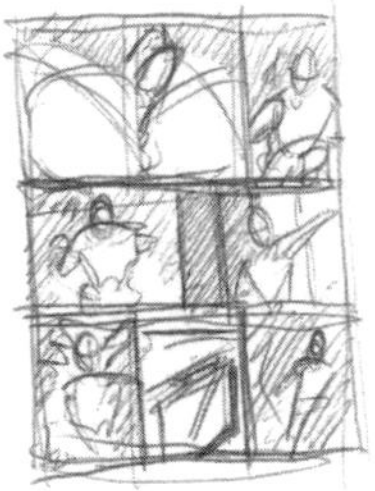

PAGE FIFTEEN

PANEL ONE CLOSE-UP OF ALEC'S HEAD which is completely fine except for a scar over the right temple. His eyes are open and he looks completely confused. The room is bathed in the light of early morning.

PANEL TWO ALEC gingerly reaches up and touches the scar, a look a slight pain on his face.

1 ALEC Huh...what?...head hurts...

PANEL THREE ALEC leaps up and looks around, obviously remembering the fact that he's supposed to be dead. Dried blood stains are on and all around him.

2 ALEC Holy...!

PANEL FOUR ALEC runs to another corner of the room and prays to the porcelain goddess (or, in other words...pukes).

PANEL FIVE ALEC stands up and hobbles out the door. We can now see that his skin is cracked and he's very pale (looking severely mal-nourished)

3 ALEC (thought bubble)...I'm so hungry. How long have I been out?

PANEL SIX / ALEC is standing dumbstruck just outside of the warehouse. In front of him is a newspaper vending machine. The cover date of the paper is Saturday April 30, 1994 (fourteen days after he shot himself!)

ADD ONE MORE PANEL HERE →

PANEL SEVEN. ALEC backs into the warehouse, his eyes never leaving the vending machine.

PAGE SIXTEEN/SPLASH

ALEC flops down into a chair at the table in the center of the warehouse.

1 ALEC (yelling) <u>WHY CAN'T I END THIS!?</u>

PAGE SEVENTEEN

1 CAPTION "EPILOGUE"

PANEL ONE LONG-SHOT of a PRESS CONFERENCE on the steps of CITY
HALL. ROBERT WASHINGTON is standing behind a wooden lectern
addressing the audience, composed mostly of reporters with a few
civilians in the back. Two new guards are standing off to the
sides.

2 WASHINGTON   ...in addition, if elected I promise to do
                 everything in my power to eliminate organized
                 crime! Remember!...a vote for me...is a vote for
                 George! (Washington)

3 CIVILIANS   WA-SHING-TON!...WA-SHING-TON!...

4 WASHINGTON   I will now open the floor to questions...yes you in
                 front...

PANEL TWO MEDIUM SHOT, at the left is WASHINGTON and below him to
the right a reporter, who strongly resembles GERALDO RIVERA, stands
up with note pad in hand.

5 REPORTER   MR. Washington. What DO you have to say about the
                 recent rumors of an ATTEMPT on your life?

6 WASHINGTON   Ha...ha...ha what trash tabloid do you work for?!
                 Next question.

7 CIVILIANS   ha...ha...ha

PANEL THREE CLOSE-UP of the REPORTER, who has a nasty smirk on his
face.

8 REPORTER   Then what do you have to say about the two men, BOTH
                 of whom worked as your PERSONAL body-guards, who
                 were found DEAD in front of YOUR hotel this
                 morning!

PANEL FOUR CLOSE-UP WASHINGTON straightens his tie and no longer
looks so confident.

9 WASHINGTON   ahem...no comment...

PANEL FIVE MEDIUM SHOT of FABIO and GERALDO lying in body-bags in
the morgue. In the background we can also see the body of BRIAN
FIELDING.

10 BLURB BOX TO BE CONTINUED...

Forever man©

John H. Mahoney

Filip S. Sablik

A SPECIAL ASHCAN FOR HEROESCON '96

June 12, 1996

Greetings. What you hold in your hands is but a sample of a larger two year endeavor. It is intended to give the reader a broad overview of the epic of the Forever Man, Alec Dupree. Included is a summary of the concept of the Forever Man, an eight page full script of a sample story, as well as pencilled art which accompanies that story.

The intent of this ashcan is to find a home for the Forever Man. Hopefully, at your publishing company. We hope that at HeroesCon '96, we had an oppertunity to speak to you personally on behalf of our project.

Included in our book is a self-addressed stamped envelope. Even if you feel that our book does not meet your needs, we hope you will take the time to send us your comments. The reason this ashcan was given to you is because we respect your opinion, any criticism you could offer would be gratefully appreciated. Thank you for taking the time to listen to us and to look over our project.

Sincerely,

John H. Mahoney

Filip S. Sablik

John Mahoney
May 22, 1996

A SUMMARY OF THE FOREVER MAN

The Forever Man is the epic about the journey of the human spirit. The Forever Man is the title of the epic, not the name of the character. The main character is Alec Dupree. The Forever Man is the story of Alec's journey of self discovery and his growth as a man.

Alec Dupree is, to put it lightly, a mediocre man. It wouldn't be too much of a stretch to call him worthless. He is just another societal parasite preying off the careless and naive. He is a con man, a thief, a pick pocket, and (in the end) an assassin. A first year college drop-out who has no family and few friends. Alec is now in his late twenties, an unshaven, dirty man. His most noticeable feature is his wild, unkept hair which stands out even more due to its flaming orange tint. As well his eyes have permanent bags underneath and multiple rings adorn both ears. He wears torn, black jeans over combat boots; a t-shirt displaying the logo of an obscure 70's band which is partially hidden beneath a thin 70's style leather jacket.

Alec's life only becomes noteworthy after, on a misadventure with his partner, Brian Fielding, he discovers he is immortal. Now, immortality would be considered a gift to most human, yet for Alec it is a curse. He has lost his freewill, the ability to end his existence was what allowed Alec to continue living. For the first time in his life, he can't take the easy way out.

Here begins a journey of self-discovery. Alec must now find something, _anything_ to give his life meaning. Thus, at the conclusion of Alec's adventure to avenge his friend's death, he leaves New York and begins his journey of self-discovery. Alec is responding to the call to adventure after his life is metamorphosed through supernatural "aid". From this point the true tale of Alec's life begins. A cornerstone of this epic will be realism, aside from Alec there are no other "superhumans", and no storyline will ever break reality (though it might possibly _bend_ it).

This epic is a tale with a definite beginning and end, yet no length restrictions. The story should be told as a trilogy; the call to adventure, the search for identity, and metamorphosis, in a _minimum_ of three story block of no less than 155 pages each.

Because the root of Alec's inability to succeed is his fear of failure, any person who has ever experienced self-doubt will be able to appreciate and connect with the hero. We are all human after all. Read as a whole the epic will illustrate a spiritual as well as mental and physical growth within Alec and ourselves.

THE FOREVER MAN
Full Script/8 pages
"Ode to a Grecian Urn"
June 12, 1996

John Mahoney
3936 Skylark Circle
Roanoke, VA 24018
(540) 989-9171

PAGE ONE/SPLASH

MEDIUM UP-SHOT of ALEC DUPREE diving out through the window of a burning building. Glass is flying everywhere and flames erupt from behind. ALEC is wearing a seventies style black leather jacket, BAUHAUS t-shirt, black jeans and Doc Martin boots. As he comes through the window he has raised his left arm in front of his head to protect himself and beneath his right arm he clutches a rather beat up leather bound BOOK.

1 CAPTION   My life for a book

2 CAPTION   My life as a book

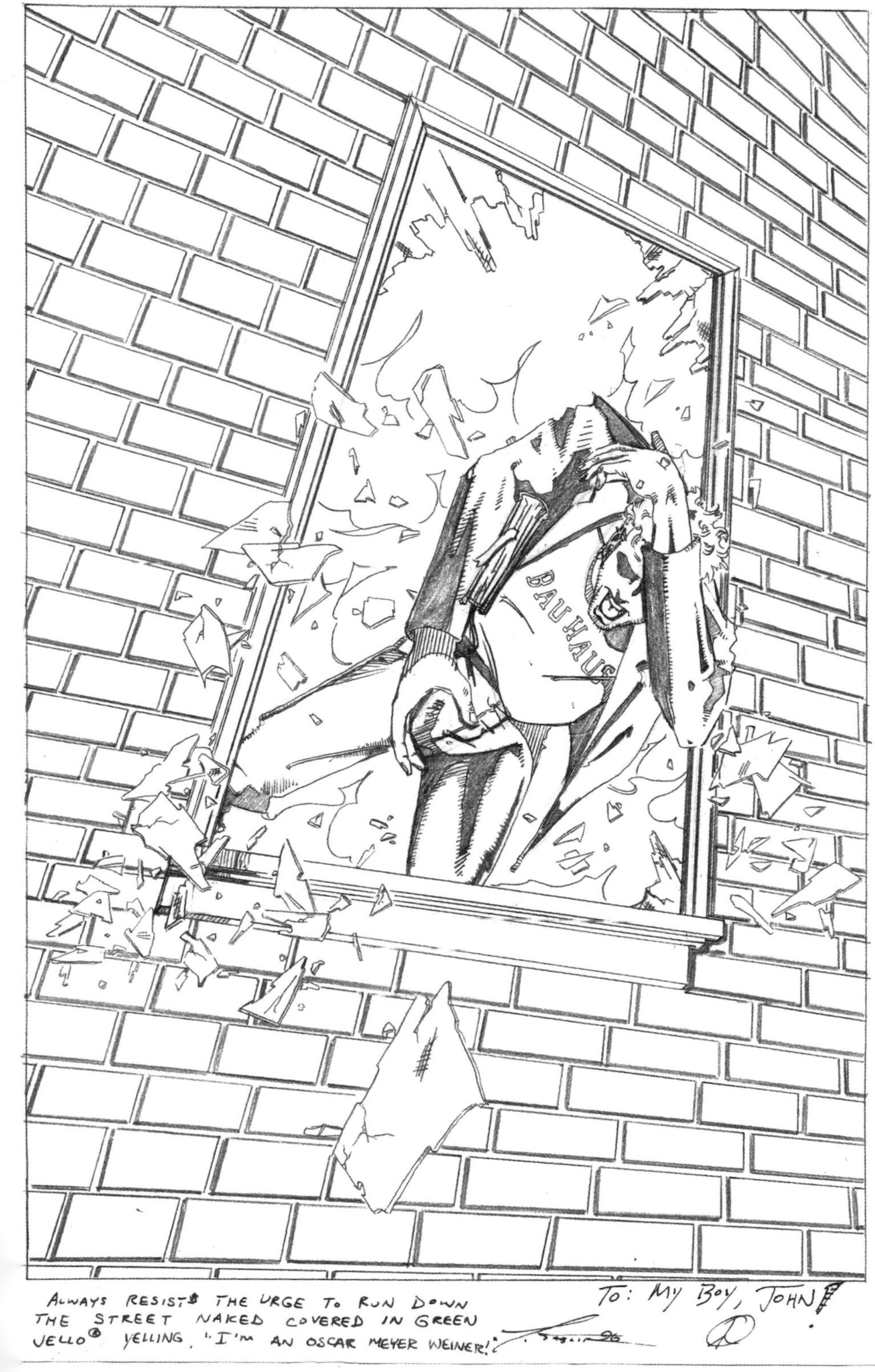
BAUHAUS

ALWAYS RESIST THE URGE TO RUN DOWN THE STREET NAKED COVERED IN GREEN JELLO® YELLING, "I'M AN OSCAR MEYER WEINER!"

To: My Boy, John!

PAGE TWO

PANEL ONE MEDIUM SHOT of ALEC as he runs down a deserted sidewalk away from the burning building. His jacket is smoldering and he is obviously in a great deal of pain. Every step is absolute agony.

1 CAPTION   I've changed greatly over the past few weeks. So much that I barely even recognize myself. The old me fades more daily, for better or worse I'm becoming a new man.

PANEL TWO MEDIUM SHOT ALEC has collapsed on the sidewalk, completely disregarding his own body. His only care is protecting the BOOK.

2 CAPTION   I've decided to keep a journal of this change because I've come to fear the past as much as the future.

PANEL THREE MEDIUM CLOSE-UP of ALEC's upper body as he pushes himself up from the pavement, charred flakes of leather falling from his shoulders. We can see in his face that he realizes he must get as far from the scene of the crime as possible before the police/fire department arrive. He's in great pain but he can't stop.

3 CAPTION   I do this not out of vanity, I do this so I won't forget.

PANEL FOUR CLOSE-UP of ALEC's boots as he begins running again. Charred jean-flakes falling from his ankles.

4 CAPTION   I do this so I won't be forgotten.

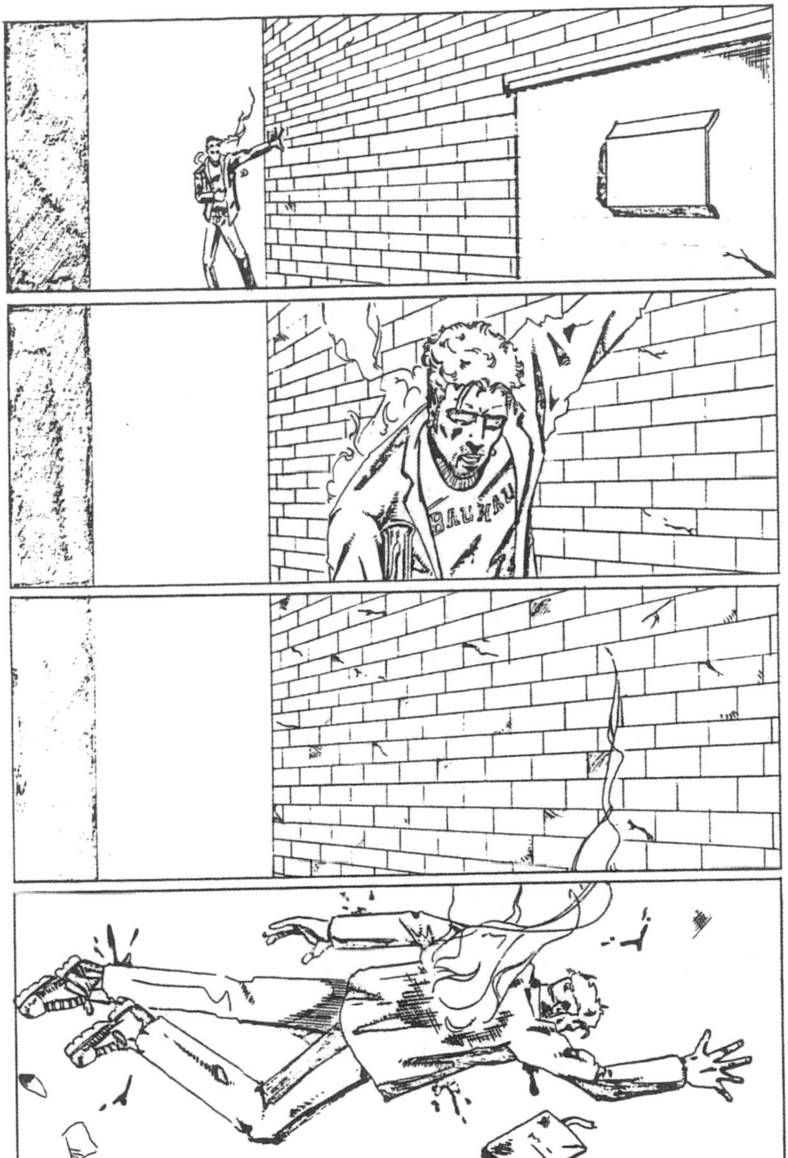
BAUHAU

PANEL ONE MEDIUM SHOT as ALEC rounds a corner into an alleyway. At
the end of the alley is a large trash bin on which he has fixed his
gaze. His jacket still smoldering, ALEC is on his last legs and is
forced to lean against the building for support. A moment's rest
before pushing forward.

1 CAPTION   I saw an advertisement in "the Times" today about an
                exhibit of Greek art at the museum downtown. Over
                the copy blurb was a picture of an urn with two
                lovers painted on it. Lovers not yet entwined

PANEL TWO CLOSE-UP from just below his shoulder to just above his
head. ALEC has managed to inch several feet forward but has now
reached his limit. He can go no further. This panel should catch
his last breath before death.

2 CAPTION   Twenty-four inch ceramic remembrances of the
                classical legacy.

PANEL THREE same as PANEL TWO but without ALEC. This is an empty
panel.

PANEL FOUR DOWN SHOT from directly above ALEC, who lies face down
on the pavement. Small pools of blood have begun to creep out from
beneath him and the BOOK, seeming to have been dropped, lies to his
right. The leather jacket continues to smolder.

3 CAPTION   Dancers gliding
                musicians piping
                fighters warring

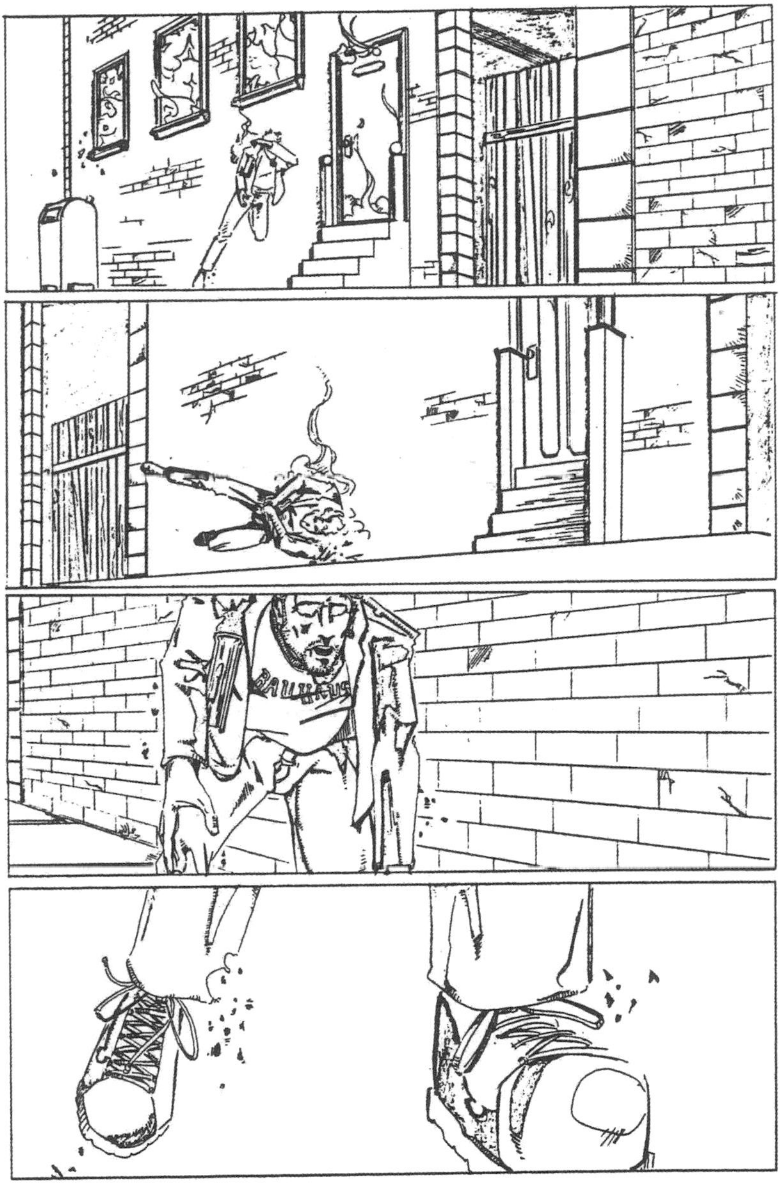
BAUHAUS

PANEL ONE (INSET) BIRD'S EYE VIEW of ALEC who is lying in the fetal position. Whatever curse has been keeping him from dying seems to have worked again and he is beginning to wake up. Just behind him is the earlier mentioned dumpster as well as a bunch of trash bags. ALEC has obviously moved rather significantly since he "died". As well the jacket is no longer smoldering. It should be obvious that a significant amount of time has passed.

PANEL TWO MEDIUM SHOT of ALEC as he pushes himself up from the pavement. He is rejuvenated and his thoughts once again turn to the BOOK.

1 CAPTION   conversations spun endlessly, emotionlessly for three thousand years. Yet the dance is interrupted at the first step, the song never even begun, the first blow left unthrown.

PANEL THREE CLOSE UP ALEC is now leaning against the wall of the alley and has begun reading the BOOK.

2 CAPTION   This picture reminds me of two things:

PANEL FOUR MEDIUM SHOT ALEC is now walking down the once again deserted sidewalk, completely enraptured in the book and oblivious to his surroundings.

3 CAPTION   the anticipation of great things which I always feel yet never experience

PANEL FIVE MEDIUM SHOT this is the same as PANEL FOUR except from behind. We can see a large burn mark in the center of ALEC's back. He remains oblivious.

4 CAPTION   and a book of poetry that I saw on Faustus's shelf behind the glass case.

PANEL SIX CLOSE UP of ALEC's upper body from the BOOK to just above his head. On the building in the background is a sign for CHEERS, est. 1896.

5 CAPTION   I.wish Faustus would have recognized the degree to which I needed to see his book.

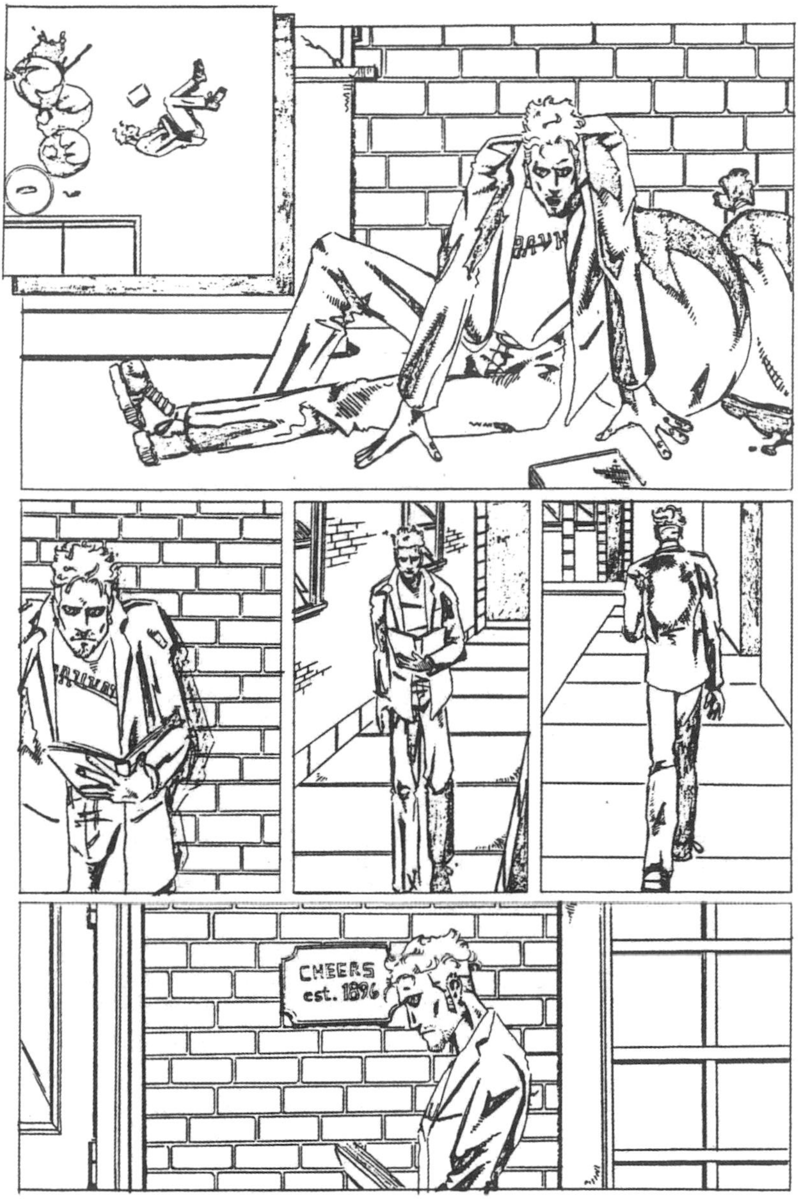
CHEERS
est. 1896

FOREVER MAN/Ode to a Grecian Urn/Mahoney

PAGE FIVE

PANEL ONE MEDIUM SHOT INTERIOR OF CHEERS BAR. Two men sit at the bar in high-backed stools. Behind the bar is a cabinet from which several glasses hang. Painted on the front facade of the cabinet is CHEERS. As he enters the bar Alec puts the book under his right arm and raises his left signaling the unseen bartender to order a beer.

1 CAPTION   He's dead now.

PANEL TWO MEDIUM CLOSE UP Alec has sat down at the bar, the BOOK open in front of him and a mug of beer sits to his right. His arms hang loosly by his sides and he is concentrating intently on what he is reading. Something he has just read has profoundly effected him.

2 CAPTION   It wasn't my fault.

PANEL THREE CLOSE UP OF ALEC's chin and the beer mug as he raises it to his lips to drink.

3 CAPTION   I swear.

PANEL FOUR CLOSE UP of ALEC's hand on the back of the book, covering up most of the letters on the cover, only the letters "--ATS" are visible.

4 CAPTION   Regardless, I have the book.

PANEL FIVE MEDIUM SHOT the BARTENDER and a PATRON are at the end of the bar talking in the foreground as ALEC sits meditating over his beer in the background. He is wrestling with inner demons of some sort.

5 CAPTION   The bindings are dried and cracked, the pages are brittle and worn. The book should be on a bookshelf behind a glass case, but I have to read it one last time before I put it away. Take one last glance onto the quill pen scratches on the paper put there by the poet himself untold ages ago.

PANEL SIX same as PANEL FIVE except without ALEC. The beer and BOOK remain on the table. The BARTENDER is looking back at the empty seat in surprise. ALEC left without paying. (CONTINUED)

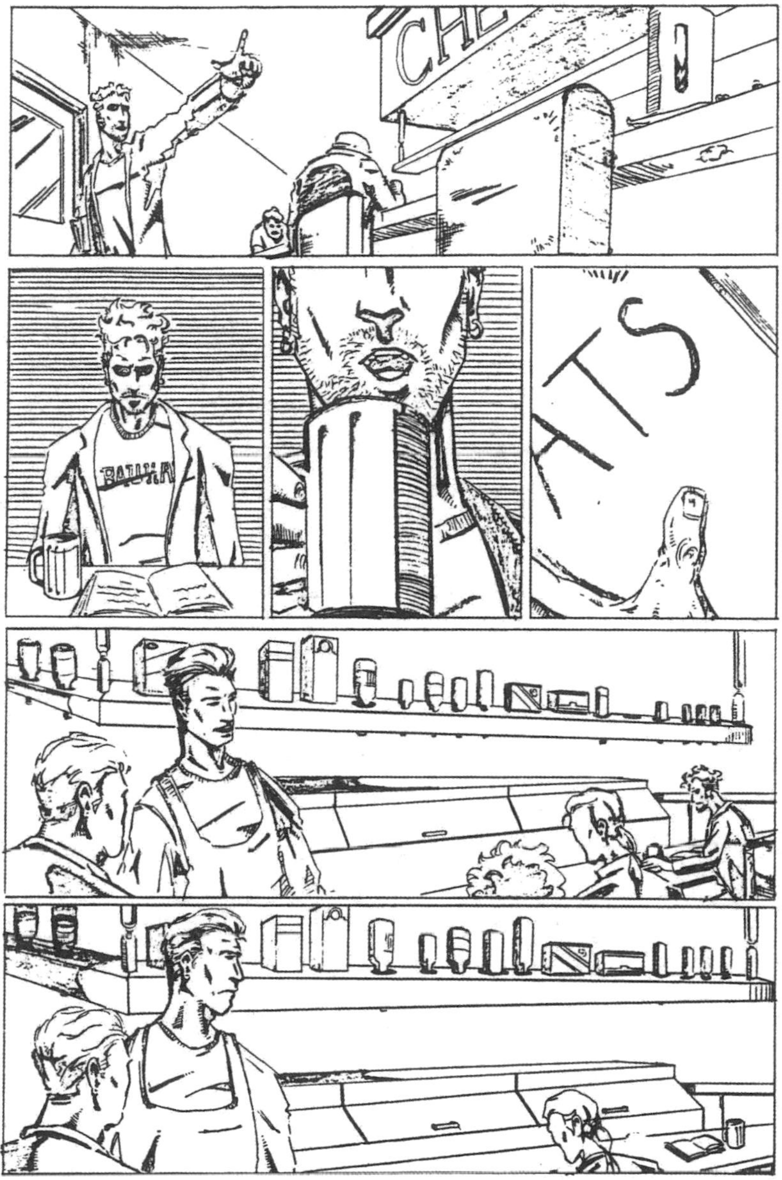
CHE
HTS

PAGE FIVE (CONTINUED)

6 CAPTION   With a copy the magic would have been lost. Only
               the original draft in the authors own hand would do.
               I would never have built up the nerve to do what I
               must without the original.

PAGE SIX

PANEL ONE MEDIUM SHOT of the bar as the BARTENDER walks down
towards ALEC's seat. He no longer seems angry, he's more interested
in the BOOK.

1 CAPTION   This book reminds me that Adam didn't eat the
               fruit of knowledge because Eve told him to.

PANEL TWO same as PANEL ONE except now the BARTENDER is standing
over the BOOK reading it. He seems genuinely interested in what it
has to say.

2 CAPTION   He did it to end his existence.

PANEL THREE CLOSE UP of the book, the BARTENDER's hand covering
most of the right page. We can see the remains of a page which has
been torn out. To the left is the beer which is still half-full.

3 CAPTION   In the Garden of Eden he was an animal. He lived an
               endless life of looking at trees which made good
               food and were beautiful to his sight, yet was forced
               to avert his gaze from the most beautiful.

PANEL FOUR EXTREME CLOSE UP of the BOOK, the remains of the page
now very clearly visible.

4 CAPTION   He was denied the gift most grand; knowledge of
               his own futility.

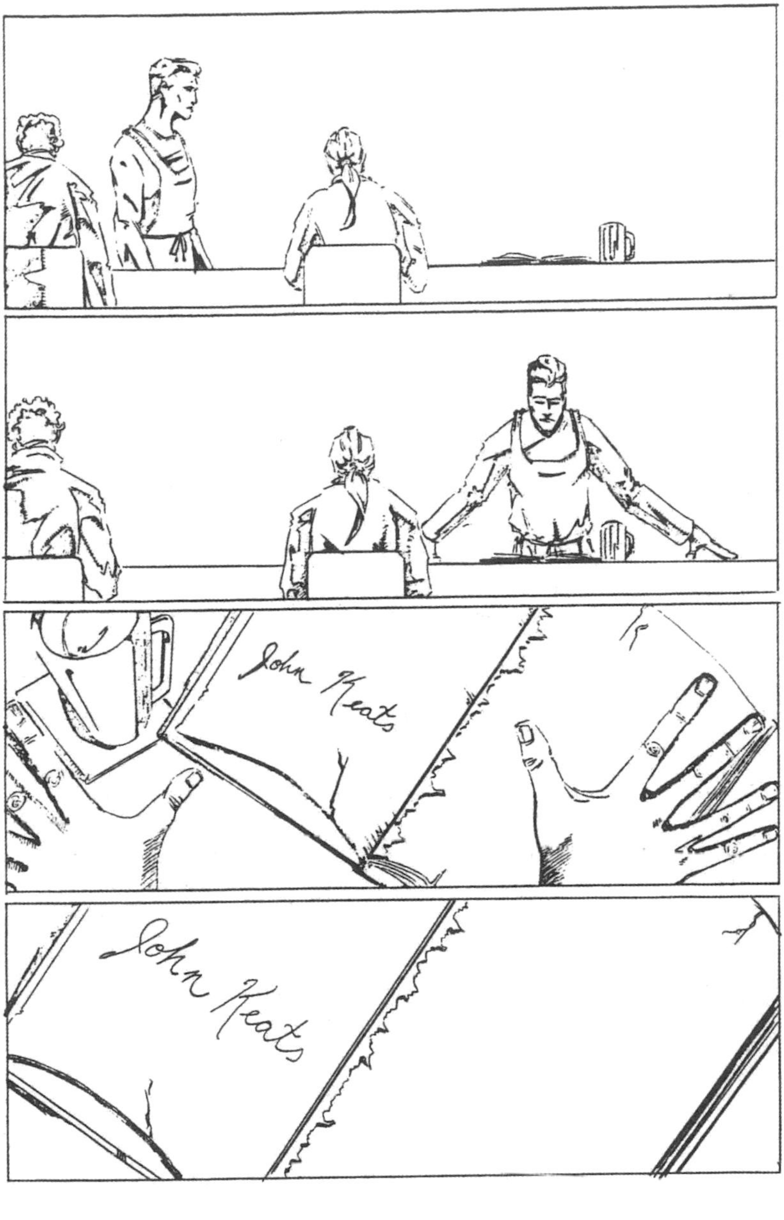
John Keats
John Keats

PAGE SEVEN

PANEL ONE CLOSE UP of ALEC as he smokes a cigarette. He is outside and his posture is now much straighter and self assured. He seems tense but confident. He is on a mission.

1 CAPTION   Existence without mission is the gate to heaven without the key

PANEL TWO UP SHOT of a MUSEUM from just behind ALEC. We can see him looking up at the building once again lost in thought.

2 CAPTION   I can imagine the boy with only the slightest hints of intelligence fantasizing about the tree

PANEL THREE MEDIUM SHOT of a GRECIAN URN. The URN is the center of this panel, a light is shining down directly on the URN and all else is in shadow. No other objects should be visible in this panel.

3 CAPTION   "Of the tree of knowledge you shall not eat, for in the day that you eat of it you shall die"

PANEL FOUR MEDIUM SHOT of ALEC as he approaches the URN from around a corner. In his hand ALEC holds the page which was torn out of the BOOK on PAGE SIX. In the background are various artifacts including a painting and a Greek statue of a javelin thrower (minus the javelin)

4 CAPTION   What is death to an immortal? The grandest gift

PANEL FIVE MEDIUM SHOT from behind. ALEC is standing in front of the URN but not looking at it. Self-doubt is creeping in.

5 CAPTION   No, Adam did not eat the fruit out of naivete

PANEL SIX CLOSE UP of ALEC and the URN. He is staring at the URN intently. He has become angry. He stares in the same way a mother would after discovering a stash of hard-core pornography under her child's bed. He is disgusted.

6 CAPTION   He ate the fruit so he could die.

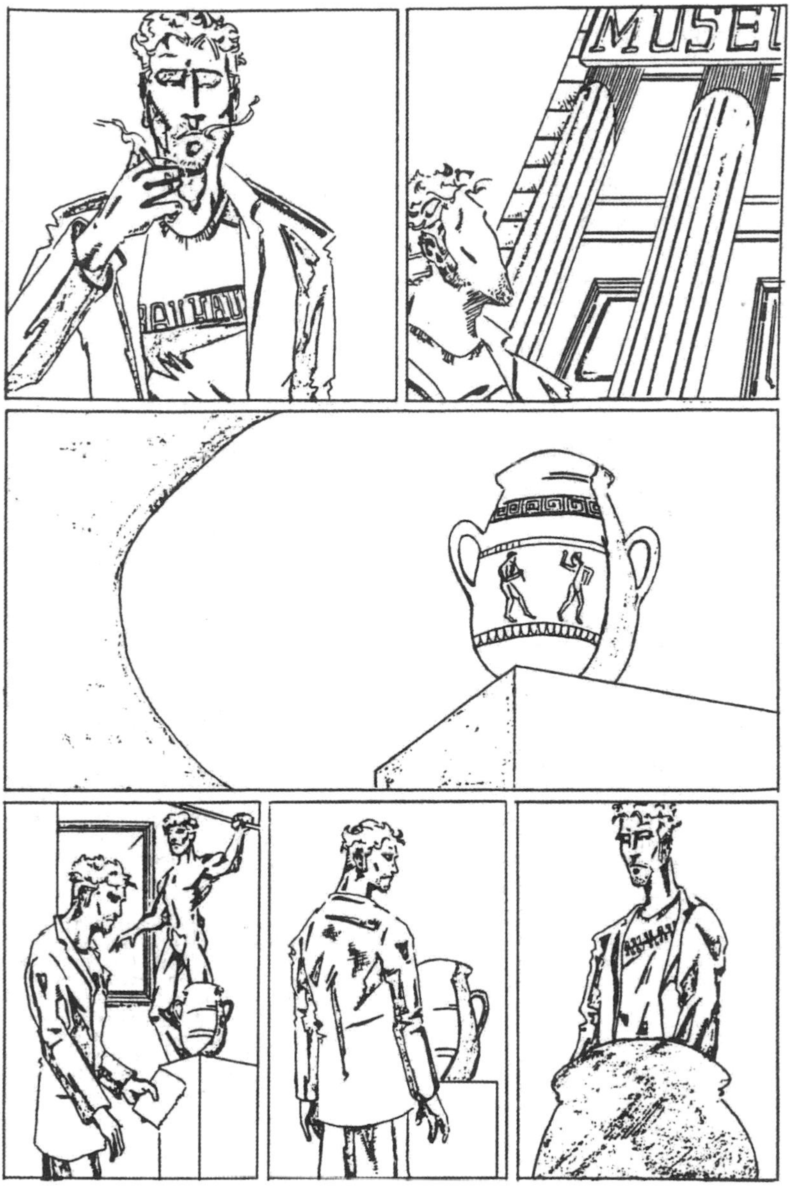
MUSE

PAGE EIGHT/SPLASH

DOWN SHOT on the broken remains of the URN. Large chunks are scattered chaotically around the torn page from the BOOK. Scribbled across the back of the page (which is facing the reader) are the words:

1 CAPTION   NOTHING SHOULD LAST FOREVER

2 CAPTION   Keats' "Ode to a Grecian Urn"

1

Thou still unravished bride of quietness,
  Thou foster-child of Silence and slow Time,
Sylvan historian, who canst thus express
  A flowery tale more sweetly than our rhyme:
What leaf-fringed[1] legend haunts about thy shape

Of deities or mortals, or of both,
  In Tempe[2] or the dales of Arcady?[3]
What men or gods are these? What maidens loth?
What mad pursuit? What struggle to escape?
  What pipes and timbrels? What wild ecstasy?

2

Heard melodies are sweet, but those unheard
  Are sweeter; therefore, ye soft pipes, play on;
Not to the sensual ear, but, more endeared,
  Pipe to the spirit ditties of no tone:
Fair youth, beneath the trees, thou canst not leave
  Thy song, nor ever can those trees be bare;
  Bold Lover, never, never canst thou kiss,
Though winning near the goal — yet, do not grieve;
  She cannot fade, though thou hast not thy bliss,
For ever wilt thou love, and she be fair!

3

Ah, happy, happy boughs! that cannot shed
  Your leaves, nor ever bid the Spring adieu;
And, happy melodist, unwearièd,
  For ever piping songs for ever new;
More happy love! more happy, happy love!
  For ever warm and still to be enjoyed,
  For ever panting, and for ever young;
All breathing human passion far above,
  That leaves a heart high-sorrowful and cloyed,
  A burning forehead, and a parching tongue.

4

Who are these coming to the sacrifice?
  To what green altar, O mysterious priest,
Lead'st thou that heifer lowing at the skies,
  And all her silken flanks with garlands drest?
What little town by river or sea shore,
  Or mountain-built with peaceful citadel,
  Is emptied of this folk, this pious morn?
And, little town, thy streets for evermore
  Will silent be; and not a soul to tell
  Why thou art desolate, can e'er return.

5

O Attic[4] shape! Fair attitude! with brede[5]
Of marble men and maidens overwrought,
With forest branches and the trodden weed;
  Thou, silent form, dost tease us out of thought
As doth eternity: Cold Pastoral!
  When old age shall this generation waste,
  Thou shalt remain, in midst of other woe
Than ours, a friend to man, to whom thou say'st,
  "Beauty is truth, truth beauty," — that is all
  Ye know on earth, and all ye need to know.

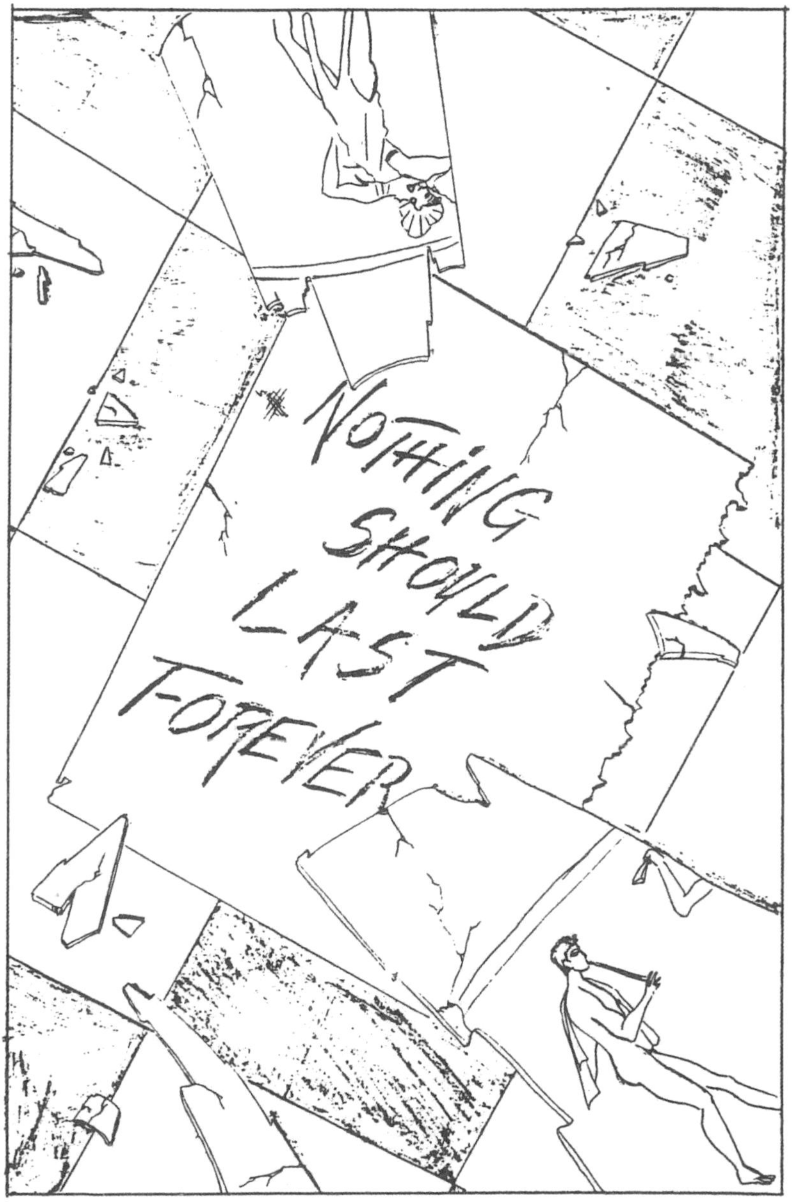
NOTHING SHOULD LAST FOREVER

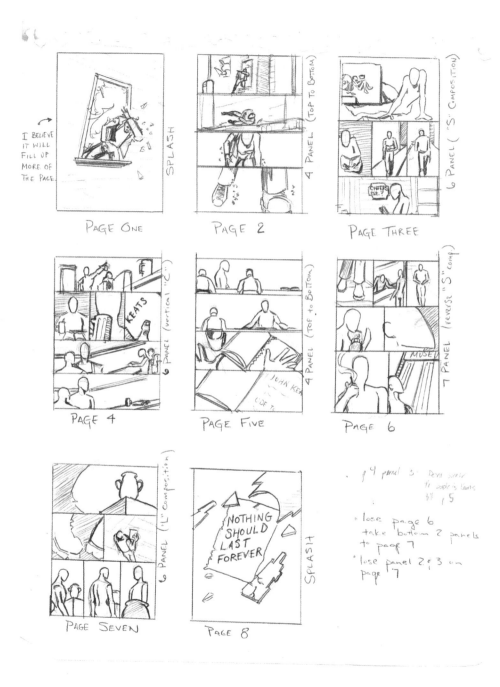

extreme close-up of cigarette
hitting ground. Camera far right.
Slow-mo.

pull back to close-up.
pan rt. and up along body.
pan around figure to front at
waist.

FREQUEN

close-up of hand w/unlit cig.
move up front of figure.

close-up of lighting.
hold camera, figure stops walking

dolly along in front of Alec
walking down street

follow along w/ Alec
background moves

establishment shot

way bird's eye view

light behind and above

lens flare and one light source

1 strong lights source lots of smoke

zoom close to catch mouth exhaling smoke

cut to reaction shot

pull in for conversation

cut to worm's eye view & toss money at the camera

pull back and Brian
stands up

rotate camera to Alec's
POV

cut to a few moments
later, light on Alec
as Brian dances

zoom in for close-up of
Alec

Brian enters frame

cut shot

camera raises slightly
and rotates down

establishment shot
of NYC, Empire State
Building is prominent

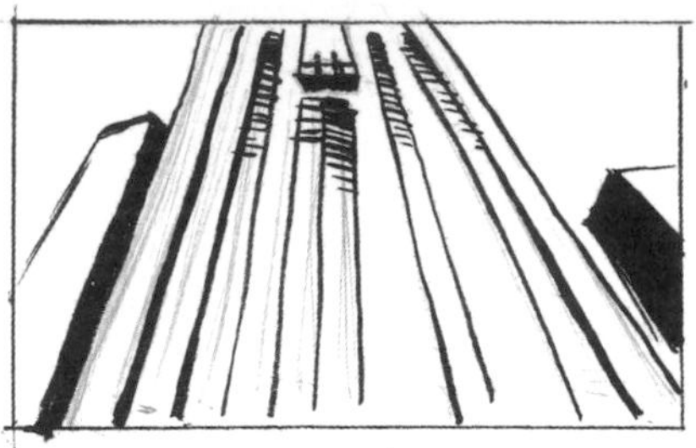

extreme worm's eye view of Empire State Building

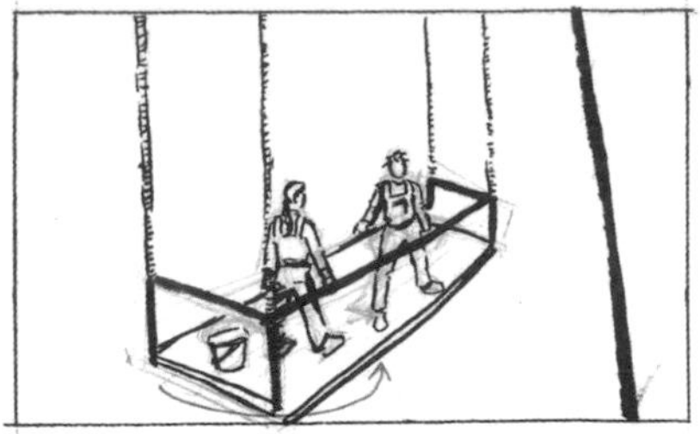

cut to slight eagle view

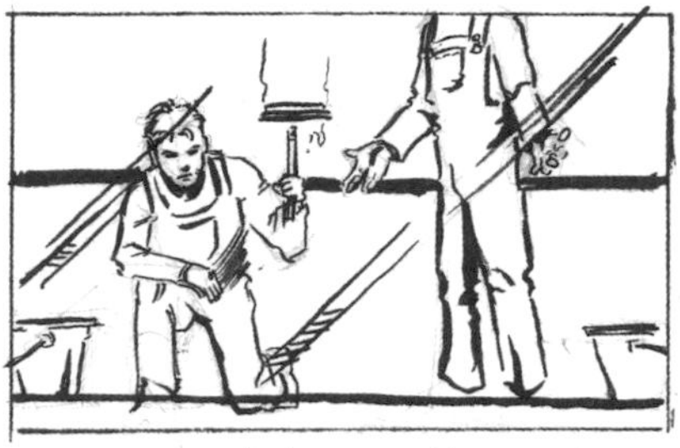

swing into medium shot

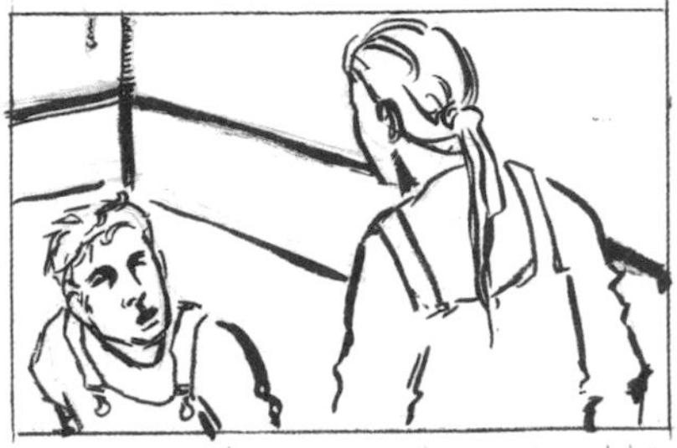

cut to over the shoulder shot

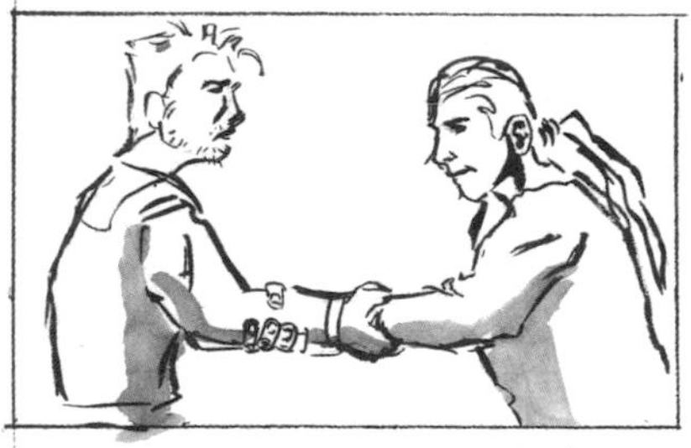

cut to medium shot as they clasp hands in a "mexican handshake"

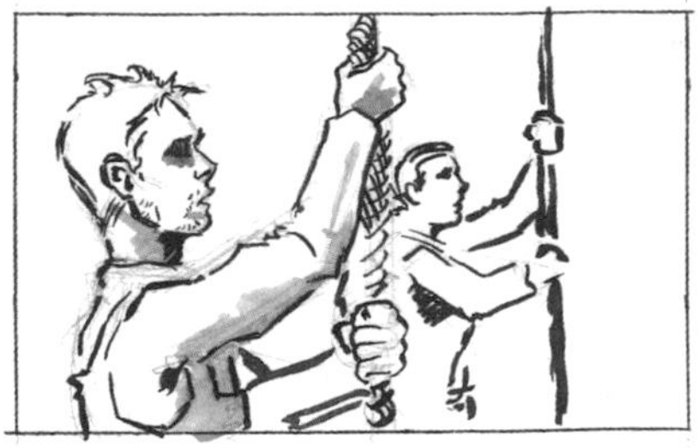

medium shot

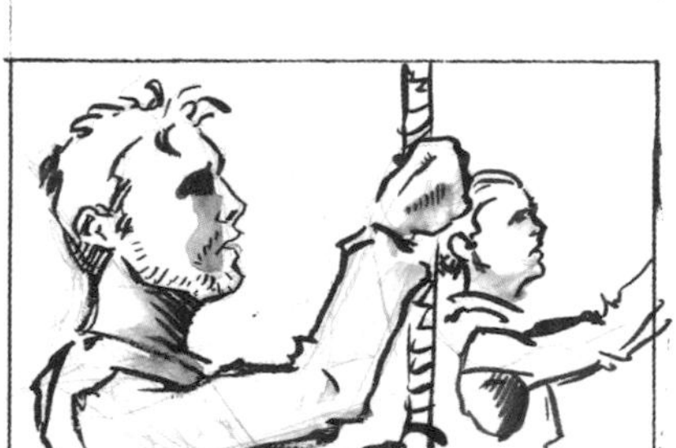

begin zoom

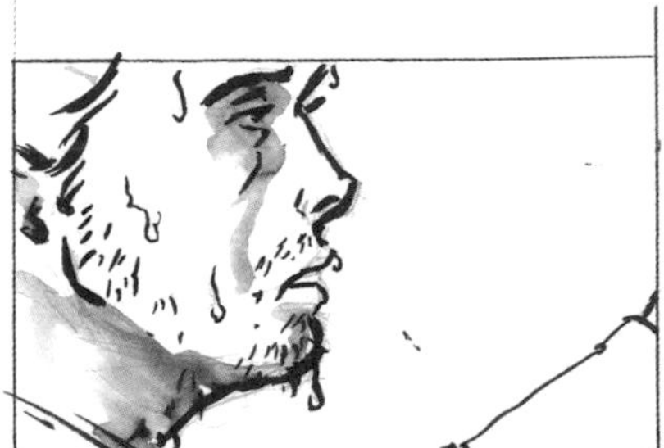

zoom on Alec's face

extreme close-up

pan down in extreme
close-up

medium through window

opposite of previous shot

COVER GALLERY
art by: **Thomas Nachlik**
color by: **Dave McCaig**

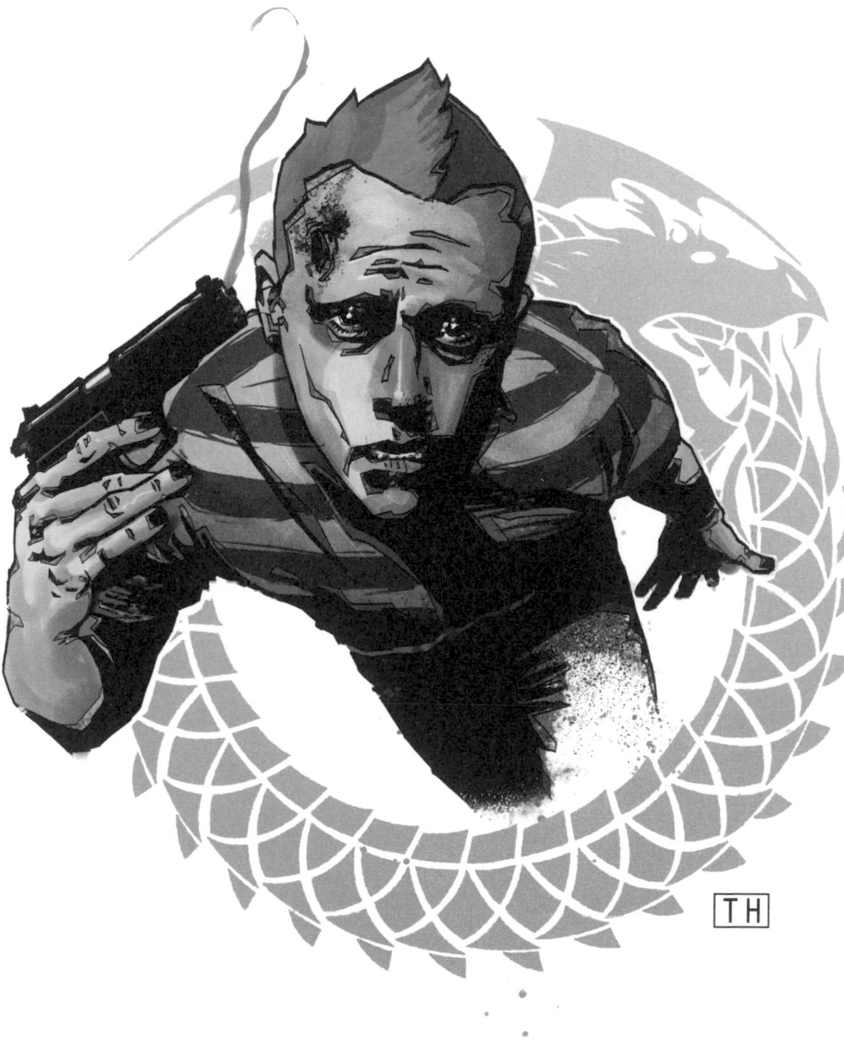
TH

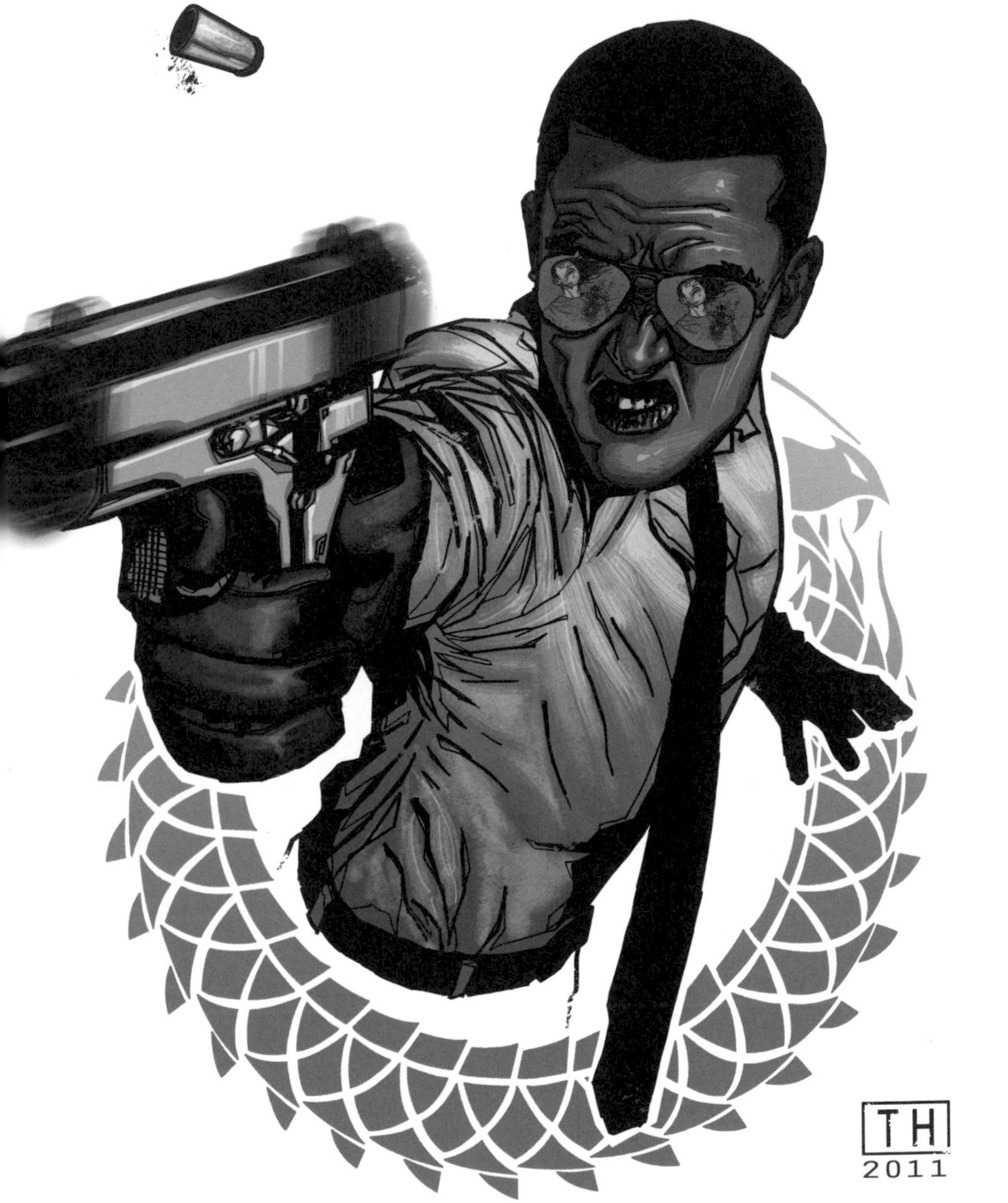
TH
2011

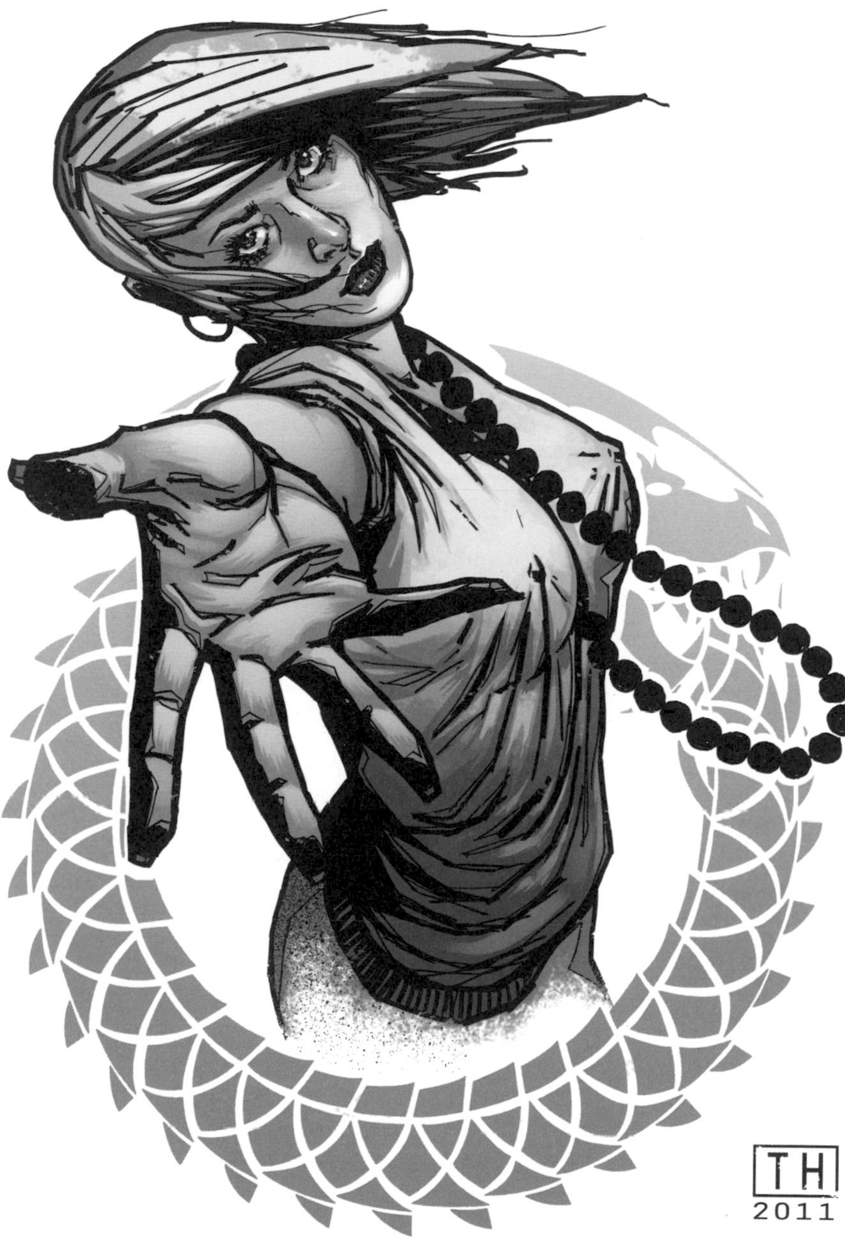
TH
2011

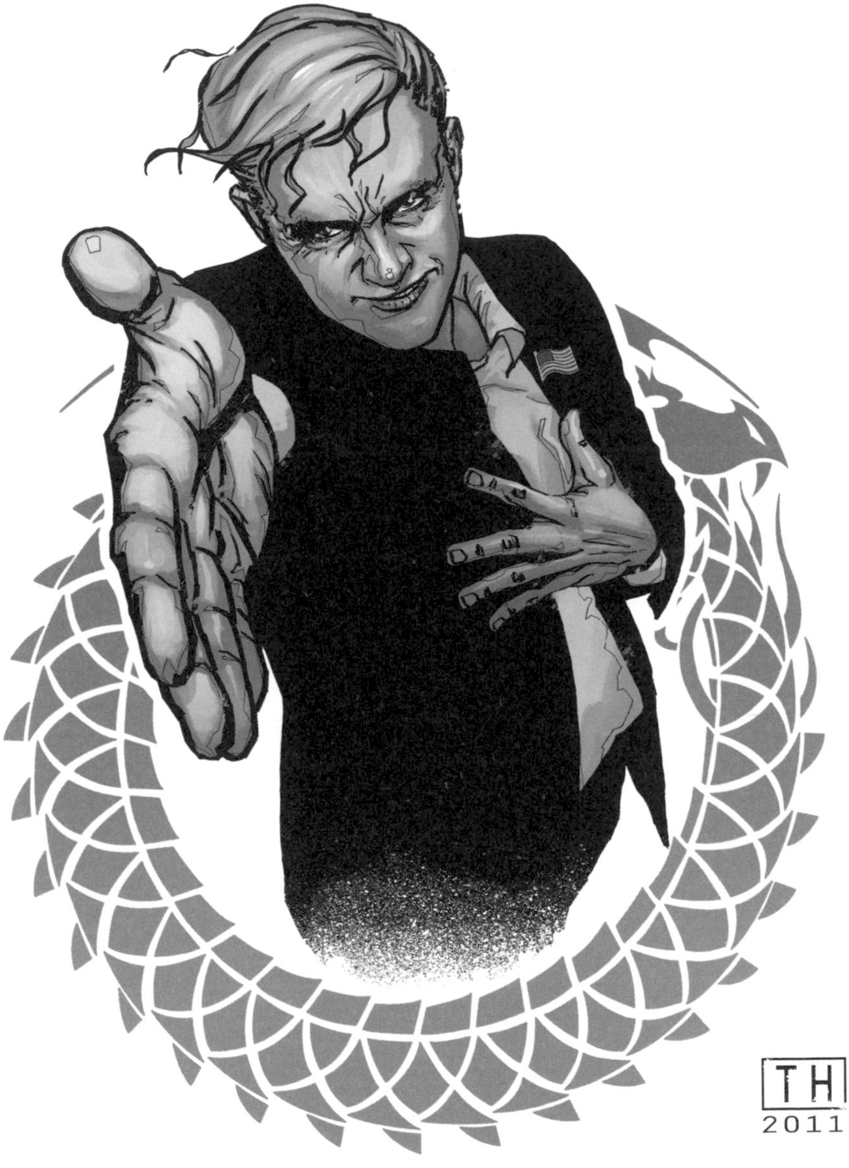
TH
2011

Previews Ad for Last Mortal

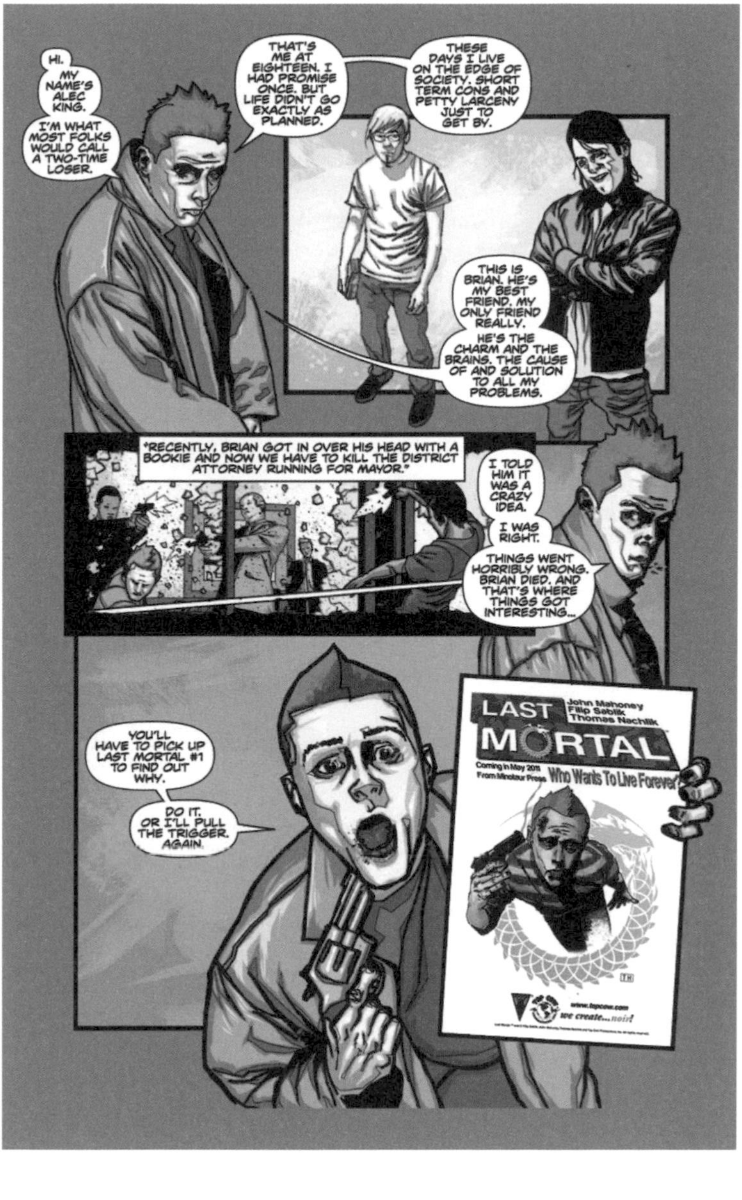

HI. MY NAME'S ALEC KING.
I'M WHAT MOST FOLKS WOULD CALL A TWO-TIME LOSER.
THAT'S ME AT EIGHTEEN. I HAD PROMISE ONCE. BUT LIFE DIDN'T GO EXACTLY AS PLANNED.
THESE DAYS I LIVE ON THE EDGE OF SOCIETY. SHORT TERM CONS AND PETTY LARCENY JUST TO GET BY.
THIS IS BRIAN. HE'S MY BEST FRIEND. MY ONLY FRIEND REALLY.
HE'S THE CHARM AND THE BRAINS. THE CAUSE OF AND SOLUTION TO ALL MY PROBLEMS.
"RECENTLY, BRIAN GOT IN OVER HIS HEAD WITH A BOOKIE AND NOW WE HAVE TO KILL THE DISTRICT ATTORNEY RUNNING FOR MAYOR."
I TOLD HIM IT WAS A CRAZY IDEA.
I WAS RIGHT.
THINGS WENT HORRIBLY WRONG. BRIAN DIED. AND THAT'S WHERE THINGS GOT INTERESTING...
YOU'LL HAVE TO PICK UP LAST MORTAL #1 TO FIND OUT WHY.
DO IT. OR I'LL PULL THE TRIGGER. AGAIN.
LAST MORTAL
John Mahoney
Filip Sablik
Thomas Nachlik
Coming in May 2011
From Minotaur Press
Who Wants To Live Forever?
www.topcow.com
we create...noir!

Afterword by THOMAS NACHLIK

When Filip asked me to write an afterword for the Last Mortal collection I found myself overwhelmed. I didn't even want to write anything at all. So much happened during the production of the series I could write about; things in my personal life that very much influenced the look and mood of the book. For example, I was diagnosed with ADHD (Attention Deficit Hyperactivity Disorder) while working on the third issue, which not only explained why it sometimes took me so long to draw even one panel, but also why my style changed from issue to issue. Even my work technique changed from drawing on paper, to drawing on a tablet, to drawing on an interactive pen display, to drawing on all three while making music, while running on a treadmill. Blame it all and much more on a brain anomaly. But what my afterword is truly about is how thankful I am for Filip and John not just letting me draw the project, but also being so patient with me and giving me so much freedom creating the world and characters of Last Mortal. I also have to thank Matt and Marc for letting us publish the book under the Top Cow banner. This sounds like an Oscar speech, but seriously, publishing a series at Top Cow felt and still does feel like receiving an Oscar to me.

Thomas Nachlik
Munster, Germany
November 2011

Afterword by JOHN MAHONEY & FILIP SABLIK

Our man, Alec King's, story has had quite an exciting journey since it was first published in the back of Top Cow's First Look anthology in July 2010. Since then we have taken Alec on the road, beginning that fall at the Virginia Comicon, through the North Carolina Comicon in November 2011, but his grand debut was on May 21, 2011. On that day Collector's Paradise in Winnetka, CA, hosted a Last Mortal Launch Party that was unique in multiple ways. Not simply because this may have been the first ever signing with 1/3rd of the creative team appearing live via video conference, when our dedicated artist, Thomas Nachlik, sketched and interacted with fans all the way from Germany. But also because Filip had the iconic ouroboros symbol from our covers, tattooed on his back live at the event. Although truth be told, Filip did it simply to not be outdone by Thomas, who had several weeks earlier tattooed our grand ouroboros symbol across his chest. Since then the three of us have shown the book at conventions around the world, from Berlin to the Bay, and in that time we have heard bunches of feedback, most great, some critical, and we would like to answer some of the more off the wall of these comments here:

1) We displayed our lack of knowledge of fine liquor when we showed Alec drinking out of a glass whiskey bottle in issue 2 because everybody knows that whiskey comes in plastic bottles.

As he pounds away on his phone typing these words, John is standing beneath the oddly green fluorescent lights of his local liquor store. He is standing in the whiskey aisle and stares at the bottles of Jack Daniels, Johnny Walker, and Jim Beam. Not one of these bottles is plastic. So, no, gentleman at Heroes Con in Charlotte, NC, John doesn't think we were wrong when we had Alec break a whiskey bottle over the Fixer's head and later had the same Fixer stab Alec in the throat with a glass shard. Maybe the liquor store near you produces special plastic bottles just for you, but where we come from - whiskey comes in glass bottles.

2) Alec listens to really crappy music. Seriously, T-Rex? Nobody listens to that glam rock crap anymore!

Filip appreciates each and every human's right to their very own opinions, but as he sits here this evening watching television, he hears not one, but two separate commercials advertising their wares using T-Rex songs. One of these is trying to associate their product with the unity of all teenagers around the world; the other simply wants you to associate their fast & hard car with some fast & hard music. They both use T-Rex to make these points because they are brilliant marketing geniuses. Filip thinks he has made his point and will say no more to defend the musical tastes of Alec King.

3) When you introduce Victoria in issue 3...well actually, we'll leave that one out because it's completely accurate. We can't believe we missed that one!

On a more serious note, the journey of what eventually became Last Mortal and the first chapter in the tale of Alec King has been one we've been on since before we could drive. Alec has traveled alongside us as we learned to drive, dated, went to college, married and much more. Through good times and not-so-good times, Alec has been a constant companion. The collection you hold in your hands is truly the culmination of a childhood dream and a passion project in the truest sense. We hope the love we hold for these characters, the themes we were trying to express, and all the passion we have to tell more stories is self-evident in the first chapter you've just read. As with anything that took this long to create, there are countless individual we owe thanks and gratitude to. As one final request, we ask you indulge us as we offer up an abbreviated list. We'd like to thank all of the teachers, mentors, and other creators, who offered up priceless advice and molding us as creators. Thank you to the comic store owners and managers who helped nurture our love of this medium as young men and supported Last Mortal by stocking a title on their shelves by three relatively unknown creators. A sincere thank you to Marc Silvestri and Matt Hawkins, who graciously gave us a home to publish Last Mortal and our partner-in-crime Thomas Nachlik, whose vision completed our story. A humble thank you to our wives, who have shown endless patience and support during the creation of this project. And finally, to our parents, our first fans, who encouraged us to create and made us believe that two young kids from Roanoke creating their own comics was worth pursuing.

John Mahoney & Filip Sablik
Durham, NC and Los Angeles, CA
December 2011

The Top Cow essentials checklist:

For more info , ISBN and ordering information on our
latest collections go to:

www.topcow.com

Ask your retailer about our catalogue of our collected
editions, digests and hard covers or check the listings at:

Barnes and Noble,
Amazon.com

and other fine retailers.
To find your nearest comic shop go to:

www.comicshoplocator.com